Praise for David M. Drucker and

In Trump's Shadow

"David Drucker is part of a sadly vanishing breed of political reporters who want to know what the story is, not what they wish it would be. David's analysis is fact-driven, superbly sourced, and fair-minded. His work is an essential tool for understanding the 2024 landscape."

—Chris Stirewalt, author of *Every Man a King*

"Even as the avalanche of books looking backward at the events of the Trump Presidency continues to crush reviewers, David Drucker had the wisdom—to look ahead! The 2024 GOP contest for the right to lead the party in the presidential contest is at least the equal of any modern campaign in suspense, and it's going to take a three-tiered platform to get all the candidates onto the debate stage at the same time. Drucker is the only reporter to at least get the list of possible Republican candidates right as 2021 slides toward 2022. That's because he's a reporter's reporter. Drucker's a weekly guest on my radio show simply because he's always ahead of the curve...and is so again with this book."

—Hugh Hewitt, host of *The Hugh Hewitt Show*

"David Drucker serves up well-reported portraits of a host of Republican and conservative players, neatly capturing their struggles to navigate the strange new world of post-Trump GOP politics. Watching the 2024 hopefuls adapt to the GOP base's hunger for Trumpian performative populism, racial dog whistling, and own-the-libs bluster is almost enough to make you pity them. Almost." —Greg Sargent, columnist, *Washington Post*

"Deeply reported, gracefully written, and eminently readable. Hurray for David Drucker!"

—Brit Hume, senior political analyst, Fox News Channel

"Drucker delivers." —*Kirkus*

"This is a book that tries to answer the question we're all asking: What, exactly, is the future of the post-Trump Republican Party? An essential read for anybody who cares about our politics and the country's political future." —Eliana Johnson, editor-in-chief, *Washington Free Beacon*

"One man may dominate the race, but IN TRUMP'S SHADOW is a comprehensive and indispensable form guide to the wide field of contenders for what may be a tumultuous Republican presidential contest in 2024." —Gerard Baker, editor-at-large, *Wall Street Journal*

"Extensively reported." —*Publishers Weekly*

In Trump's Shadow

The Battle for 2024 and the Future of the GOP

David M. Drucker

TWELVE

NEW YORK   BOSTON

Twelve
Hachette Book Group
1290 Avenue of the Americas, New York, NY 10104
twelvebooks.com
twitter.com/twelvebooks

First published in hardcover and ebook in October 2021
First Trade Paperback Edition: October 2022

Twelve is an imprint of Grand Central Publishing. The Twelve name and logo are trademarks of Hachette Book Group, Inc.

The publisher is not responsible for websites (or their content) that are not owned by the publisher.

The Hachette Speakers Bureau provides a wide range of authors for speaking events. To find out more, go to www.hachettespeakersbureau.com or call (866) 376-6591.

LCCN: 2021942521

ISBNs: 978-1-5387-5403-0 (trade paperback), 978-1-5387-5402-3 (ebook)

Printed in the United States of America

LSC-C

Printing 1, 2022

For my beautiful wife, Jenny,
who has made my life
a wonderful success story

Contents

Author's Note

It's sort of ironic.

Despite Donald Trump's firm grip on the Republican Party, many Republicans have long been planning—actively planning—for the day he fades to black and they are afforded the opportunity to compete for his spot at the helm of the GOP. They couldn't even wait for his reelection campaign to conclude.

That's what occurred to me in the fall of 2019, the first time the light bulb of the idea that would become this book flashed on in my head. My colleagues and competitors had produced some good scoop on Vice President Mike Pence's uniquely independent and robust political operation within the White House, and the speculation that led to. Later, I added my own contribution to Pence watch. But around the same time, I had noticed that Trump's loyal No. 2 wasn't the only Republican who appeared to be planning for the future. It was the winter of 2019. Election Day 2020, and Trump's political fate, were practically two years away, and other prominent Republicans (on good terms with the White House) were busy sketching the architectural drawings of a 2024 presidential bid. In some instances, they had begun assembling the infrastructure of an actual campaign apparatus.

In Trump's Shadow started out like that: an attempt to suss out the unfolding campaign for the Republican presidential nomination in 2024, with all of the secret meetings, sibling rivalries, and political action happening hidden, right in plain sight, even as Trump was gearing up to fight for his political life. The forty-fifth president was a force to be reckoned with, he had proven in 2016. But the rejection Trump suffered in the midterm elections two years later, with Democrats capturing the House of Representatives in a forty-seat swing even as the economy roared like gangbusters, was proof positive he was not Superman. So 2020 was hardly a foregone conclusion, and this was long before the coronavirus pandemic and George Floyd's death would roil the country and upend our politics.

None of that stopped ambitious Republicans from doing what ambitious politicians do. I thought the early planning was unusual. And agree or disagree with that particular assessment, I thought it would make a cool story, in the form of a book. My agents at Javelin, Keith Urbahn and Matthew Latimer, and everybody at Twelve Books, thought so too, and so I set out to tell it.

Now, when gaming out the field of contenders in an upcoming presidential contest, it's natural to focus on who is likely to run; who is likely to raise and/or invest the resources required to mount a vigorous campaign; who is likely to have a good chance of winning his or her party's nomination. I did that. But I had some parameters and constraints to attend to also. First and foremost, the theme of my book necessitated that I include viable candidates who were engaged in early planning. Not every possible Republican 2024 contender, including some that either then or now appear especially competitive for the party's nod, satisfied that metric, and so they were never going to make the cut.

There was also the issue of practicality. I had to limit the number of potential 2024 candidates I would explore, or I would never finish the book. Or at the very least, I wouldn't finish the book before the first votes were cast in the next presidential primary. These criteria shaped the initial list of White House hopefuls I would feature in the book.

All this is to say, you're going to read the book and think to yourself, "You didn't write about him. You didn't write about her. This one can't win. What about this one who can win?" I hear you. I don't disagree, per se. But the point was not to predict the future, an impossible task. It was to report out a story that might provide a glimpse of different, possible futures for the Republican Party after Trump was no longer president and, as ex-presidents usually do, disappeared from the scene.

Along the way, the story I was telling evolved. What started out as a behind-the-scenes look at the Republican knife fight for the 2024 presidential nomination and leadership of the party after Trump turned into a broader examination of Trump's generational impact on the GOP, through the prism of how the 2024 primary might unfold. What sort of candidates were vying to succeed Trump atop the party? How was his presidency, and, as it turns out, his continued presence as a major political figure postpresidency, affecting the Republican Party's present—and its future?

And then Trump refused to concede defeat to President Joe Biden. And then, on January 6, 2021, the former president's grassroots supporters ransacked the US Capitol. What of the implications of all of that? This is that story.

Finally, a word on the mechanics of my reporting. Over the course of several months, I spoke to countless Republican Party activists, campaign strategists, insiders, operatives, politicians, and everyone in between with an interest in the GOP and GOP candidates. I spoke with pro-Trump, Never Trump, maybe Trump, and pragmatic about Trump. I spoke with "used to like Trump" and "used to hate Trump." I spoke with establishment Republicans and movement conservatives. I spoke with neoconservatives, conservative insurgents, Trump populists (and other populists), and Ronald Reagan conservatives.

In order to extract their candid insights and obtain coveted nuggets of information, I granted interviewees the option of talking to me on "deep background": I could report the details they revealed to me but would not disclose them as the source of those details. Most preferred that option and took me up on the offer. Where I quote private comments and conversations, this reporting is based on information relayed to me by various sources who are familiar with what was said.

Anonymous sourcing has rightly come under scrutiny as it has become more accepted in political journalism. I'm sympathetic to complaints about the practice, especially complaints from readers. But I have found over the years that the most experienced, knowledgeable political operatives, the ones who are able to tell me what is really going on, and why, prefer to remain anonymous. They have clients running for office whom they are not permitted to speak for. They have clients running for office whom they would lose if those clients knew what they really thought. They have clients who would suffer politically if the views of their consultants became public. And some, believe it or not, just don't want their name in the proverbial newspaper.

This was a judgment call that I made. Please forward complaints to the management.

In Trump's Shadow

CHAPTER ONE

The End of the Beginning
(But Not the Beginning of the End)

*D*o you miss me yet?" Donald Trump asked.

    As a matter of fact...

The crowd, packed into a Hyatt Regency hotel ballroom in Orlando, Florida—coronavirus pandemic be damned—was roaring. Nearly fourteen hundred rambunctious grassroots Republicans greeted the former president, less than four months shy of his seventy-fifth birthday, with chants of "USA! USA! USA!" as he took the stage at the Conservative Political Action Conference (CPAC). It was a Sunday evening, and Trump was delivering his first public speech since exiting the White House a mere thirty-nine days prior. It was a "#MAGA" campaign rally of sorts. American voters had fired Trump after a single four-year term, the first such ouster of a sitting president of the United States in nearly thirty years, hiring Democrat **Joseph Robinette Biden Jr.**, a former vice president and ex–US senator from tiny Delaware, to replace him.

You never would have guessed it at CPAC. The first formal gathering of conservative activists was a four-day victory parade, despite a disappointing 2020 election cycle that finally ended on January 5, 2021, with the Republican Party losing control of the US Senate after being swept in a pair of runoff elections, in Georgia of all places.

"We love you!" the CPAC audience intermittently shouted back at Trump as he transfixed them with one of his classic, Il Duce–style screeds.

"You won!" They weren't trying to soothe an old man's wounded ego after a bruising political season nor reward him with a grateful, gold-watch send-off into political retirement for all he accomplished as president in just four years. And love Trump or hate Trump (is anyone in between?), underneath all the populist invective, the forty-fourth man* to swear the presidential oath of office had accomplished much, politically and substantively.

No, they were being deadly serious. As far as they were concerned, Trump had not been vanquished by Biden almost seventeen weeks earlier. He simply wasn't the president *right now*. At CPAC, both the conservative activists in attendance and the carefully curated guest list of prominent Republicans and "Make America Great Again" loyalists they showed up to see seemed to be suffering from an acute form of cognitive dissonance, born of anxiety stemming from the collective trauma of an election gone horribly wrong.

The annual conference, around since the early 1970s—the middle of Ronald Reagan's second term as California governor—is typically held in or near Washington, DC. But with a winter surge in COVID-19 cases afflicting the national capital region, the District and adjacent Maryland and Virginia municipalities had tightened the screws on existing, stringent gathering limits and social distancing mandates. CPAC was forced to decamp to Florida, where state and local authorities employed a balanced pandemic regulatory regime that sought to resolve both the health and economic challenges posed by the coronavirus. Face masks were required indoors *and* the bar was open, for drinks and seating. Plus, Florida had sufficient infrastructure to host a convention that attracted thousands of people from across the country who, theoretically, wanted to avoid piling right on top of each other.

The Hyatt Regency Orlando, roughly eleven miles northeast of Disney World, is massive. The thirty-one-story hotel features two towers

---

* Trump is the forty-fifth president because Grover Cleveland, elected to two non-consecutive terms, is considered the twenty-second and twenty-fourth president.

and nearly 1,650 rooms, common areas with high ceilings and wide corridors, ample convention and meeting space, and, perhaps most important, a spacious indoor bar and lounge. CPAC filled it up, transforming a sedate venue decorated in matte color tones into a festive, red, white, and blue Taj Mahal to Trump. There were "Trump Won" baseball caps and of course plenty of the iconic red hats with "Make America Great Again" splashed across the front in white. There were T-shirts emblazoned with "Not Voting for the GOP If It's Not for Trump" and "Biden is Not President." There was the African American man with the T-shirt "Black Guns Matter." There was the Caucasian woman sitting alone at the hotel bar reading *1984*, George Orwell's dystopian 1949 novel warning of a coming totalitarianism that so many Trump supporters feared was upon them. There was the young child wearing a protective face mask that read, "This mask is useless."

Inside private CPAC receptions, intimate gatherings of conference guests and benefactors mingled over drinks and hors d'oeuvres in expansive top-floor suites as they discussed the tragedy of an election stolen, or an election so unfairly and unlawfully manipulated by the Democratic Party that it might as well have been. They were a more refined group: former and aspiring Republican politicians, conservative media personalities and executives, entrepreneurs and business owners, lawyers who had been on the front lines of the dozens and dozens of Trump's ultimately futile legal challenges. Some lawsuits alleged unconstitutional changes to state election law in key battlegrounds; others made charges of ballot fraud on a grand scale. They were all turned away, by conservative and liberal judges alike. The refusal of these men and women to accept the legitimacy of Biden's election as the forty-sixth president, affirmed and reaffirmed with every ballot audit, and recount, of key counties and states, was subtle. There was a cloud of patriotic resignation hanging over them. Another election was less than two years out. They were not constitutional arsonists. But they were no less committed to the party line that the forty-fifth president should still be in the White House. There was the affable middle-aged man I spoke with who made the air quotes sign with his hands while raising the topic of the "quote, riot" at the US Capitol on January 6, 2021, an insurrection by grassroots Trump supporters who intended to deliver him a second term by blocking congressional certification of Biden's victory. There was the engaging elderly couple who created homemade circular lapel pins with an American flag and the words and hashtag "We Are #74MillionStrong," referring to the 74.2 million Americans who backed Trump in the 2020 election. Is Tucker Carlson correct, they asked me, when he argued on his top-rated prime-time Fox News program that the QAnon conspiracy movement, whose ardent followers are heavily invested in Trump as some real-life Gozer the Gozerian, is not actually real?

If the theme of CPAC 2021 was "America Uncanceled," the B-side to that single was that Biden was a fraudulent president. Each day, the main stage of the conference featured a panel of experts detailing for a ballroom audience that didn't need any convincing to begin with how thieving Democrats robbed Trump; how the Democrats stole from them. During an unrelated panel discussion on the final day of CPAC prior to Trump's keynote, conference organizer Matt Schlapp, genial chairman of the American Conservative Union and fierce supporter of the former president, offered gracious comments about George W. Bush, whom he worked for on the campaign and in the White House. Bush is the only Republican president in more than three decades to win reelection—and win the national popular vote. Yet Schlapp felt it necessary to caveat those remarks, aware that the forty-third president has become an apostate to many in his own party.

"And as far as George Bush is concerned, I know there will be different opinions in this room. My view is, you dance with the one who brought you," Schlapp said. "I have great respect for that man. He did a lot of good."

The conservative activists in the seats didn't boo. They didn't cheer, either. Even after Trump, so to speak, the Republican Party, the conservative movement, were thoroughly his.

That development will become abundantly clear as 2024 approaches. For the first time in more than forty years, there will not be a Reagan, or a self-proclaimed Reagan heir, campaigning for the GOP nomination. At least not among the contenders with a chance to win. Every candidate with a chance to win, especially but not exclusively if Trump does not run himself, will be running as the next Trump. Some will be understated, others obvious. Almost all, to the man and woman, will make assurances that the former president is their North Star.

———

Trump did not premeditate the unconventional speech that launched his 2016 presidential campaign and immediately rocketed him to the top of the polls in the Republican primary, a position he would more or less never relinquish.

The embargoed copy of the address issued to the media contained mild elements of the populist bluster that would define Trump's candidacy; his presidency and postpresidency, too. But the memorable lines that distinguished Trump from the rest of the contenders, a crowded pack of Reaganites, the stuff that wowed the Republican base, were an accident of instinct that went underappreciated because of how he built a following in the GOP. Trump had spent the years leading up to this announcement calling in to Fox News and ranting about whatever was on his mind, and fanning conspiracy theories that Barack Obama, the first black president, was ineligible for the Oval Office because he was born in Africa.

And yet the future president didn't write a speech demeaning Mexican immigrants, legal and illegal, as "rapists," drug dealers, and criminals, declaring with racial overtones that Mexico wasn't "sending their best. They're not sending you." Nowhere in there did Trump write that he would force the Mexican government to cover the cost of his planned security barrier along the southern border. Trump's prepared speech did not mock his GOP opponents for ill-planned campaign announcement events.

"They didn't know the air conditioner didn't work; they sweated like dogs. They didn't know the room was too big because they didn't have anybody there. How are they going to beat ISIS?" Trump said, referring to the Islamic State of Iraq and Syria, a jihadist terrorist group.

Less noticed, but no less important—more important, really—Trump delivered an extemporaneous broadside ridiculing his Republican competition for being too caught up in conservative ideology and not in tune with the apolitical topic that concerned GOP voters most of all.

"I hear their speeches, and they don't talk jobs and they don't talk China," he said. "People are saying: 'What's going on? I just want a job. Just get me a job, I don't need the rhetoric. I want a job.'"

The remarks poured out of Trump's head like water poking a widening hole in a failing dam.

"I wrote it very quickly," Trump told me of the original version of that speech, when I met with the former president at Mar-a-Lago, his private social club and winter residence in Palm Beach, Florida, to interview him. "When I was delivering it, I felt it wasn't nearly strong enough." So much of Trump's first campaign was like that: haphazard. It just so happened that it worked.

It's taken for granted, now, that *of course* it worked. That Trump recognized, intuitively, strategically, perhaps both, that voters in Rust Belt battleground states whom Republicans had been losing for decades, in places like Michigan, Pennsylvania, Wisconsin, and elsewhere, were just waiting around for a conservative populist like him to come along. That Trump just knew bashing China would work; that the United States post–Cold War—that the Republican Party, of all parties, post–Cold War—was looking inward and just waiting for a presidential candidate to come along and promise protectionism, quasi isolationism, borders closed to legal and illegal immigrants. Trump would eventually classify this agenda as "America First," a phrase discredited generations ago as nativist, xenophobic, and unbecoming a great power that embraced its role as the leader of the free world. But in the beginning of his first campaign, Trump was unsure that any of his unorthodox notions would attract a significant following. They never had before. The celebrity businessman and reality television star had been squawking about his vision for the country since at least the 1980s. In the middle of a resurgence of American global power and domestic dynamism under Reagan, Trump ran a full-page advertisement in the *New York Times* asserting, in an open letter, that American foreign policy was weak; that Japan, the Asian nation bogeyman of the time, and other nations were "taking advantage" of the United States through unfair trade arrangements.

People thought Trump a crank, in the same way Vermont senator Bernie Sanders was once disregarded as an anachronistic, socialist gadfly. There certainly wasn't an audience for this kind of thing in the Republican Party. It might not have helped Trump's case that Japan ended up saddled with stagflation, mired in a two-decade-plus economic rut, while the United States basked in boom after boom.

By the time of the 2016 campaign, the Great Recession and the Iraq War had created fertile political terrain for a populist message that cut against the grain of traditional Republicanism. But for all of Trump's legendary bravado, he wasn't sure of that. He had no idea if voters would buy what he was selling, any more than they had previously. Undaunted, Trump decided to let it ride, and run his presidential campaign on the same agenda he'd been advocating for thirty years.

"I felt strongly about it—and it wasn't Republican," he made a point of saying. "Basically, it was what I thought."

Throughout our conversation, the former president vacillated over whether his hawkish position on border security, dovish foreign policy, or protectionist position on international trade that aligned, historically, with the Democratic Party was more critical to his victory in the 2016 primary. But Trump kept returning to trade and his promise to levy tariffs on America's trading partners, be it ally or adversary, as the most crucial.

"The biggest thing was trade," he concluded, finally.

Well, trade and *The Apprentice*. The reality television show on NBC put Trump in living rooms across the country for a dozen years before he ran for president, giving him unmatched name recognition and familiarity. The former president, the first ever elected without ties to politics or military service, conceded to me that he's not sure any of it would have mattered without that.

"I think the fame had a big impact," he said.

Trump's subsequent success in the 2016 general election spawned reassessment of some aspects of domestic and foreign policy by the GOP establishment of elected officials, party apparatchiks, and think tank intelligentsia. Some undertook the review begrudgingly, initiating superficial tweaks to the traditional Republicanism they were reared on. Others were enthusiastic, pursuing radical philosophical makeovers that left their colleagues' mouths agape.

Republicans on the 2024 primary ballot will reflect this shift away from the ideologically conservative, free-market internationalism of the Reagan era to the culturally conservative, sovereignty-oriented populism of the Trump era. Whether a candidate reflects this transition is material to winning the presidential nomination of a party the forty-fifth president made more working-class and less college-educated. But talk to almost any Republican strategist with half a brain and real-world campaign experience, and they will tell you attitude is king. When the dwindling community of disaffected Reagan Republicans bemoans conservative principles don't seem to matter anymore to the GOP base and prominent members of the party, versus the premium placed on social media trolling and "owning the libs," they're half right. No Republican who is heretical on gun rights, opposition to abortion, or cracking down on countries that engage in unfair trade practices, to name just a few examples, is going to win the 2024 nomination. But what Republican primary voters really want is, specifically, a "fighter"—a nominee who without exception will stand up to the Democrats, to the media, to cultural curators in Hollywood and Manhattan and so-called squishy Republicans everywhere, regardless of the circumstances. Finding an avatar with that quality is far more important to grassroots Republicans than landing an ideologue who checks all the right boxes on some overrated legislative scorecard compiled by self-important conservative advocacy groups in Washington. They don't want the Republican statesman (or woman) of yore—and they don't want fake. (Simply aping Trump is a recipe for failure, posing difficult challenges for the candidate poised to follow in his wake.)

Distilled to its essence, this is the revolution Trump has wrought inside the GOP. "They have to believe you're a fighter," a veteran Republican operative told me, saying in his own way what I heard from dozens of party insiders in my effort to get a handle on what would matter most to GOP voters in 2024, the first presidential primary of the Trump era.

"And by the way," this operative emphasized, "it's going to be the people who study and try to manufacture it that will lose."

I asked Scott Walker to make sense of this, and with all of its implications for the future of the Republican Party, and the country, how it related to the fact that no matter Trump's follies, there was no diminishing his relationship with the party's base of reliable voters—a base the 45th president expanded. The former two-term Wisconsin governor has a unique perspective. Walker was an accomplished chief executive, with the battle scars from fights with all of the right enemies to prove it. That record didn't save him from joining the long list of temperate, Reagan-era conservatives that Republican voters lost interest in and becoming another notch on Trump's belt. To begin with, Walker said, the former president reeks of authenticity, which bred intense trust with GOP voters.

"Donald Trump looks like your uncle would look like if he won the lottery," Walker, who sought the GOP nomination in 2016, told me when I caught up with him at CPAC.

What about the extreme value placed on fighting?

"Many of those voters are people who felt forgotten." In Trump, he explained, "they felt like they had somebody who was, maybe not out of central casting for president, in terms of how he acted, but who—despite some of those challenges—was looking out for them."

The ability to arouse that feeling, that he is listening, that he gives a shit, explains the intense loyalty to Trump among Republican voters that has so confounded his critics. It has altered what they expect from a presidential nominee. None of it is lost on the forty-fifth president.

Incidentally, Trump's accomplishments in the White House, and commitment to his campaign promises, are an underappreciated facet of the fanatical support he has enjoyed inside the party. Trump overhauled the tax code; began construction of a wall along the southern border; moved the US embassy in Israel from Tel Aviv to Jerusalem; pulled the United States out of the Iran nuclear deal; pulled the United States out of the Paris climate accords; renegotiated the North American Free Trade Agreement with Canada and Mexico; slapped tariffs on China and the European Union; appointed hundreds of conservatives to the federal judiciary; oversaw the negotiation of the Abraham Accords—Israel's first peace treaty with an Arab neighbor since 1994; and implemented Operation Warp Speed, which led to the availability of multiple COVID-19 vaccines less than one year after the onset of the coronavirus pandemic.

But when I asked Trump his opinion of how he changed the Republican Party, he didn't refer to this list of achievements. He didn't mention trade policy or demographic realignment of the political parties, or any other quantifiable metric to make his case. Trump talked about fighting.

"I've given the party spirit, real spirit, which other people haven't been able to do," he said instead. "And I think I've taught the party how to fight. They didn't fight. They still don't fight hard enough."

To make his point relevant, Trump compared his refusal to concede to Biden, and that so many of his Republican allies in Congress would not accept that defeat, to how Mitt Romney handled losing to Barack Obama in 2012.

"He lost; he lost the election. But he just immediately concedes," Trump said, astonished. "There was a lot of crooked stuff going on there in my opinion. But he immediately concedes. I think we taught them about fighting."

———

Marco Rubio likes to describe Trump as the political incarnation of Evel Knievel.

The daredevil motorcyclist made a good living in the 1960s, '70s, and '80s performing death-defying stunts. Literally. Robert "Evel" Knievel managed to stick motorcycle jumps—over buses, cars, trucks, canyons, almost anything he could dream up—that eluded competitors. And no matter how many times he crashed—and he crashed constantly—and no matter how many bones he broke—and he broke most of them more than once—it's like nothing that surely would have killed or permanently maimed anybody else could keep him down. Knievel always got back on his bike for another spectacular jump. (Pulmonary disease finally killed him in 2007, at age sixty-nine.)

That's Trump, Rubio is fond of telling associates. The senior US senator from Florida is himself a casualty of the former president's political rise. Trump has a history of intemperate behavior and vile utterances. He has weathered allegations of sexual assault and extramarital affairs. He was accused of paying an adult film star hush money. He was twice impeached and implicated in an insurrection against the government. Any single one of these scandals would have toppled a normal politician, Democrat or Republican. Not Trump. He wasn't derailed and certainly wasn't chastened. Humbled? Please. Trump came awfully close to winning reelection. Defeated and with looming legal troubles spawned by investigations into his business dealings by the New York attorney general and the Manhattan district attorney, Trump has remained the axis around which the Republican Party spins. So even if the former president skips the next campaign, how are conventional Republicans, bound by the laws of political physics, supposed to compete with the mythical "Evel Knievel" standard set by the forty-fifth president for what it means to be "a fighter"? And, how are they supposed to do it without looking like a bunch of posers?

Several are intent on trying. Pay no attention to talk of the former president freezing the field as he mulls a third White House bid. It's all nonsense. Republican presidential hopefuls have been preparing to mount a 2024 campaign since virtually the day Trump assumed office. Think about that. They didn't bother waiting for his reelection campaign to run its course, as is customary. Where to begin. When I sat down with Trump to pick his brain about the long list of ambitious Republicans vying to succeed him atop the party, I told him I was limiting my questions for practical reasons. There are so many aspirants, I said, that our conversation just on this topic alone could "go on for days." To which the former president responded by repeating it back to me: "Can I be honest; you could go on for days. It's crazy."

In choosing who I asked Trump about, I placed a premium on early planning and viability—and Republicans who offer a glimpse of the possibilities that await the GOP after Trump. In the process of culling the herd, I realized that "after Trump" is not equivalent to "post Trump." But first things first…

The forty-fifth president was uniquely rebuked in 2020. Trump lost. But discounting the disaster in Georgia that delivered Democrats a fifty-seat majority in the US Senate courtesy of the constitutional tiebreaking vote wielded by Vice President **Kamala Harris**, Trump's party was spared. Republicans picked up fourteen seats in the House of Representatives, coming within a handful of recapturing the majority. Further down the ballot, Republicans lost control of absolutely zero statehouses, a crushing blow to the Democratic Party heading into the decennial redistricting process. Or look at it this way. Biden topped Trump by more than two percentage points in Arizona's Maricopa County. But nearly every Republican running for county office swept to victory. The heavily suburban municipality is the state's most populous and encompasses Phoenix. Its traditionally conservative electorate didn't have a problem with the Republican Party; it had a problem with Trump.

"It was a rejection of him," said a veteran Republican strategist who spent the 2020 campaign advising down-ballot candidates across several states. "They embraced his ideas and his policies, which is why we did so well at the local level, and they rejected his tone and his approach to politics."

Those weren't the only bright spots amid an otherwise dishearten-ing, top-of-the-ticket bust. Trump's performance with nonwhite voters improved over his abysmal showing four years earlier. According to CNN exit polls, support for the Republican incumbent jumped from 8 percent to 12 percent among African Americans nationwide, and from 28 percent to 32 percent among Hispanics. And in Texas, where Democrats had been hopeful of pulling the ultimate upset, Trump's numbers skyrocketed in some of the majority-Hispanic counties along the Mexican border. Trump even won Zapata County with 52.5 percent of the vote, a near twenty-point improvement over the drubbing he endured in 2016 in an area that had not voted GOP for president in a century.

And don't forget, Trump, beginning with his first campaign, made the Republican Party incredibly more competitive in midwestern states that the Democrats had dominated for decades. Four years later, Trump's postelection conduct was destructive. He was culpable in fomenting a riot at the Capitol on January 6 that forced his own vice president, Mike Pence, to flee for his life. But this more fulsome perspective of the for-mer president's impact on American politics helps explain why Trump, or at the very least, "Trumpism"—his conservative, populist agenda—is such a hard habit to break for so many of the Republicans who did not lose in 2020. And so many Republicans who will run for president in 2024.

This book tells the story of some of them.

The history of the Trump era is already being written. Since the moment he first announced for president, it's been written, rewritten, updated, and reassessed in countless articles, books, podcasts, and tele-vision packages; it's been painstakingly researched, stunningly reported, eloquently crafted. This tome tackles the future yet to come, and hope-fully provides a guided tour of a Republican Party remodeled by one man and the voters who flocked to him. It may seem crude at times, like the first maps of a new world given the name "America" in honor of an early Italian explorer. But the goal I set was that it be equally enduring.

Let's start with a few words on the contenders who did not make the cut when Trump and I discussed potential successors. Yes, I realize [YOUR FAVORITE CANDIDATE'S NAME HERE] is considering a presidential bid. Some whom I left out did, indeed, fit the parameters I laid out. Some would have a real shot at the nomination. Some, in the spirit of Newt Gingrich, the former Speaker of the House of Representatives who sought the White House in 2012, would enjoy fifteen minutes of fame in the primary before voters moved on to a shinier object—or a candidate they deemed more rational.

In alphabetical order:

Texas governor **Greg Abbott** wants to run for president—at least that's what Republican insiders in Texas who do not work for Greg Abbott keep telling me. If true, Abbott has to check two items off of his to-do list: win a third term in 2022 and figure out how to create some excitement around an "Abbott for president" campaign. Former Texas governor Rick Perry was the bees' knees with grassroots conservatives compared to Abbott, for all the good it did him.

Tucker Carlson keeps insisting he isn't interested in running for president. And for what it's worth, I believe him. But the highly rated Fox News prime-time polemicist is beloved by millions of grassroots conservatives. During the pandemic, Carlson's five-nights-a-week opening monologue played like the soundtrack of the Republican opposition to the government's response to the coronavirus. Ditto Carlson's commentary on race relations in the aftermath of the murder of George Floyd during this same period. Carlson was a purveyor of "America First"–style populism long before Trump co-opted it for his first presidential campaign. Look for the legitimate populists in the Republican coalition refashioned by Trump to recruit him to run for president in 2024 with promises of tens of millions of dollars in super PAC money to support his bid.

On the extreme opposite end of the conservative spectrum, Representative **Liz Cheney** of Wyoming has not ruled out a presidential bid as part of her zealous mission to exorcise Trump from the GOP. First, the daughter of former vice president Dick Cheney, who was deposed as the No.

3–ranking House Republican because she opposes Trump—and wouldn't keep quiet about it—has to win reelection in 2022. That is no easy feat in a state the former president won twice with nearly 70 percent of the vote.

Chris Christie, the former two-term governor of New Jersey, has distinguished himself by declaring that a third Trump candidacy won't scare him from running. And he is among the few Republicans with the stones to call out his old friend, whom he endorsed at a critical juncture in 2016 and has loosely advised ever since, when he thinks the former president is wrong. There is something to be said for all of that.

"What I want to do is try to lead the party in a productive and smart way. For us to continue to argue for populist-type policies but not to be reckless—not to be reckless with our policies, not to be reckless with our language," Christie said in a May 2021 interview with *Ruthless*, an irreverent podcast hosted by a trio of Republican operatives.

Christie, who will be sixty-two in November 2024, ran for president in 2016. He only made it as far as the New Hampshire primary, which is to say he flailed. But with a previous campaign under his belt and an existing political infrastructure left over, Christie is confident that few Republicans could match his ability to act as a bridge between the Trump and not-exactly-Trump wings of the party in a primary. Then again, when is Christie not supremely confident about Christie?

Florida governor **Ron DeSantis** is already running for president, if you ask most Republicans. DeSantis, like Trump, has mastered the art of waging the culture war that so animates grassroots conservatives. And his record as a governor who gets things done is enviable. DeSantis steered his state through the coronavirus pandemic effectively, and a heck of a lot better than a cadre of Democratic governors who enjoyed more favorable press. Step one is winning reelection in 2022. Step two is learning how to keep a team of competent advisers by his side for longer than five minutes. The prickly former congressman's fickle relationships with underlings matter little to voters. But the ability to build a campaign organization and instill loyalty in hires can be the difference between winning and losing in the throes of a multistate presidential campaign, with fire incoming from all directions. Meanwhile, DeSantis might have an even bigger problem to worry about: peaking too soon. The governor was topping hypothetical matchups of Republican primary contenders, some excluding Trump and others including Trump, throughout much of early 2021.

US senator **Josh Hawley** is on everybody's short list of likely candidates. Everybody's, that is, except Hawley's. The freshman Missouri senator has two young children and is more interested in policymaking than politicking. He would accept the vice presidential nod in a heartbeat. His credentials as an authentic, conservative populist (much to the chagrin of Republican insiders who thought they were getting a Reaganite when they recruited him to run for the US Senate) and strong Trump ties would fit perfectly with an older, less fiery GOP nominee.

South Dakota governor **Kristi Noem**, on the other hand, almost certainly is running for president. Americans of both political parties have a timeless love affair with the unlikely small-state governor who would be president: Vermont's Howard Dean; Alaska's Sarah Palin; New Hampshire's (fictional) Jed Bartlett. Noem, advised by Trump loyalist Corey Lewandowski, would have that lane all to herself. She could go further than people expect running as the conservative folk hero who refused, from day one of the pandemic, to close South Dakota businesses or mandate the wearing of protective face masks to combat the deadly coronavirus. Noem, a shoo-in for reelection in 2022, began hitting the hustings in neighboring Iowa within months of Trump leaving office.

Robert C. O'Brien was No. 4 out of four White House national security advisers under Trump. But O'Brien was arguably the most effective. He managed to run a tight ship at the National Security Council and offer sound advice to his mercurial boss—*and* remain in his good graces. The workmanlike O'Brien, an attorney from California, made a big enough impression with enough people to see his name injected into the 2024 conversation as a possible dark horse candidate with the potential to make a mark in western state primaries, where Mormon Republicans like him sometimes exert outsize influence.

Nebraska governor **Pete Ricketts** also runs a state that borders Iowa, on track to continue its tradition of hosting the first nominating contest of the Republican presidential primary. Ricketts, the mild-mannered scion of the wealthy family that founded a major stock brokerage and owns Major League Baseball's Chicago Cubs, would have a pipeline to a deep well of financial resources—and presumably to his brother's Rolodex. Todd Ricketts served as finance chairman of the Republican National Committee during most of Trump's term, retaining the post into the 2022 election cycle. And he did not treat the role like a ceremonial position. He worked it.

Nebraska senator **Ben Sasse** is often mentioned as a potential presidential candidate. And having won reelection in 2020, Sasse could always run without having to make an either/or decision about his political future. But since he voted to convict Trump at trial in the US Senate on an article of impeachment alleging he incited the insurrection at the Capitol on January 6, the market for Sasse in a GOP primary might not extend past his immediate family—and Cheney, if she doesn't run.

Rick Scott, the junior US senator from Florida, deserves more attention than I am giving him here. He has been preparing to run for president for quite some time and has hundreds of millions of dollars at his disposal to fund a credible campaign. And Scott has proven in two races for governor, and one campaign for the Senate, that he is willing to spend it and that he knows how to win a tough general election. But I have a conflict of interest. My wife and her business partner are Scott's top fund-raising consultants.

However, a quick word here. To steal and rearrange a great line from the hilarious 1997 film *As Good as It Gets*, starring Jack Nicholson and co-written by screenwriter Mark Andrus and director James L. Brooks: "When I think of Scott, I think of Trump, and then add reason and accountability."

Scott entered politics every bit the political outsider Trump was, dislodging the preferred candidate of the Republican establishment in the 2010 primary for governor in Florida. He was flush with cash, having earned hundreds of millions of dollars, including as chief executive officer of a hospital chain, with some of his management practices there coming under uncomfortable scrutiny after the company was criminally charged in a federal Medicare fraud case and paid a mammoth $1.7 billion in fines. Yet Scott was, and still is, the opposite of flamboyant showman. He will never whip a crowd into a frenzy like Trump and can present as socially awkward in public settings. Don't be fooled. What the senator lacks in personality he makes up for in focus and tenacious work ethic, born of his upbringing in poverty and a broken home. Scott cultivates relationships—with activists, colleagues, donors, party officials, staff—as well as anybody in politics. Elected chairman of the National Republican Senatorial Committee (the Senate GOP campaign arm) by his peers for the 2022 election cycle, Scott is positioning himself to take a victory lap for helping the party win back the majority in the US Senate just in time to get a 2024 presidential campaign up and running.

There was a time when **Tim Scott** would have snuck up on the field. Not anymore. The charismatic African American US senator from South Carolina nailed his national coming-out party in August 2020 with among the most effective speeches on Trump's behalf of the entire Republican convention. Eight months later, Scott did it again with a stirring rebuttal to Biden's first address to a joint session of Congress. There is some real gravitas to the senator behind the scenes, too. In the aftermath of Floyd's murder, through two administrations, Scott worked with Democrats as the lead Republican negotiator on major legislation to reform police practices. Republicans would love to be able to vote for an African American for president. Combine this intangible with his innate political skill, and Scott could have the makings of an intriguing presidential campaign. His political team has quietly been planting seeds for a presidential run. In 2020, in an effort to beef up Scott's image and name recognition with grassroots conservatives, the consultants running his digital fund-raising effort placed extra emphasis on soliciting Republican voters in Iowa and

New Hampshire, the states that vote first and second, respectively, in the GOP presidential primary, before No. 3 South Carolina.

The senator's major political liability? He is a bachelor and does not have children. Democrat or Republican, winning the nomination without a family to reassure voters of your essential worthiness, and just give them a way to identify with you on a basic human level, is difficult. Democrat James Buchanan of Pennsylvania, the fifteenth president, elected to a single term in 1856, is the only lifelong bachelor elected to the office. Just five presidents have been childless, and not since 1920 with the election of Republican Warren G. Harding of Ohio. Scott has already announced that his 2022 reelection bid will be his last campaign for the US Senate.

Postscript: No, Mitt Romney, the Republican presidential nominee in 2012 and a *célébrité de la résistance* to Trump, is not running. The former governor of Massachusetts is finally happy, right where he is, as a US senator from Utah. Yes, there will assuredly be a few clowns—some elected officials, some not—whom I am purposely ignoring. And of course, there are probably some serious people I'm leaving out and a few more I'm not anticipating.

———

Here's who's in, and already circling one another like prizefighters in a cage match:

Tom Cotton laid the cornerstone of his 2024 campaign back in 2016, when conventional wisdom, such that it was, suggested Trump was a goner. In ways that matter to the GOP electorate, the US senator from Arkansas was Trump before Trump. He is an immigration hawk opposed to unfettered free trade. What he lacks in Trump's panache he makes up for in discipline and strategic planning.

Ted Cruz, runner-up for the Republican nomination in 2016, is absolutely planning to run for president again. The US senator from Texas is still a Reaganite at heart and might seem shamelessly transparent at times. But Cruz understands the psychology of the Republican base better than most. He is all Trump attitude—all fight—all the time, with one crucial caveat: The senator stopped making enemies of GOP insiders and started making friends. Allies, Cruz learned last time, matter.

Nikki Haley—will she or won't she? Members of the former South Carolina governor's inner circle claim she is truly undecided. But if Haley was planning for the presidency, she would be doing everything she has been doing, and long before Trump tapped her to serve as US ambassador to the United Nations. Haley has natural political skill. It will amount to nothing if the ambassador does not reconcile a rather rocky relationship with her old boss.

There is more depth and wiliness to former vice president **Mike Pence** than suggested by his unwavering loyalty to Trump and midwestern, self-deprecating sensibility. The very simple question is whether Republican primary voters will forgive this staunch conservative for placing loyalty to the Constitution above all else when he bucked the forty-fifth president and supported certification of an election that made him a former veep. Trump certainly hasn't.

Mike Pompeo is gruff and guarded. But the former secretary of state might be the best retail politician of the bunch. He has a knack for making the right political connections at precisely the right time, and he spent his four years in the Trump administration accumulating relationships in the business community and a political network of Republican operatives and activists that will come in handy in a presidential campaign.

And finally, the aforementioned **Marco Rubio**. He has not lost the White House bug. The Florida senator has the little matter of his 2022 reelection to deal with first. If Rubio manages that, he will have the chance to find out if his attempt to channel attitudinal Trumpism into a coherent set of populist policies is of interest to Republican voters.

Then, of course, there is the prince of Palm Beach...

Just once in American history has a conquered president achieved redemption by recapturing the White House. In 1888, amid claims of voter fraud that might sound familiar, New York Democrat Grover Cleveland won the popular vote but lost reelection in the Electoral College to Republican Benjamin Harrison, US senator from Indiana. Contra

Trump, the twenty-second president graciously conceded and attended his successor's inauguration. Four years later, Cleveland staked his claim to history when he was elected the twenty-fourth commander in chief. The forty-fifth president won't have the broad goodwill enjoyed by Cleveland to carry him should he make a play to become the forty-seventh. Even some of the initial 2024 polling suggests that, as commanding a lead as Trump begins with, Republican voters' desire for a fresh face to lead the party in 2024 is percolating beneath the surface. If Trump runs and wins the nomination a third time, he can count on the exceptional loyalty of grassroots conservatives to provide him a higher floor of support than a typical politician might count on. Under those conditions, Trump always has a fighting chance (to win the Electoral College, at least).

The infatuation runs in both directions. Trump worships the Republican base like a mother dotes on her only child, to the exclusion of the other key factions of the party's governing coalition. The former president believes they are the fount of his magical political powers. Trump explained it best to a closed-door meeting of about 100 CEOs during a June 2019 conference in Washington hosted by the Business Roundtable, a trade association representing top executives of the biggest corporations in the United States.

The Business Roundtable extends a standing invitation to the president to attend its quarterly meetings and address its member executives. Trump accepted midway through his term, on the heels of suffering a major rebuke in the 2018 midterm elections and within a few months of the Democratic Party taking control of the House of Representatives.

Let's call this crowd Trump-skeptical. They loved the $1.3 trillion tax overhaul that included a steep cut in the corporate tax rate; they hate the tariffs on imported goods. Trump's impolitic style makes them queasy; Democratic policies tend to leave them uneasy. But businesspeople are practical, if nothing else. Trump was the president, so they were going to listen to what he had to say, unpredictable as it might be. And besides, the Republicans had gained two seats in the US Senate. The forty-fifth president was running for reelection and the opposite of a lame duck.

Trump showed up at Business Roundtable headquarters in Washington with an entourage—Treasury Secretary Steven Mnuchin; chief economic adviser Larry Kudlow; press secretary Sarah Huckabee Sanders; and daughter Ivanka Trump, a White House adviser who had attended a previous event hosted by the group.

As they exited the elevator, Trump's aides scattered and he proceeded by himself to a holding room. Once introduced, it was like he'd flipped a switch. The scowl on his face vanished as he walked onstage to applause from the assembled CEOs, arms stretched out and a big grin on his face.

"Wow, look at all of the great people in this room. I must be president or something," Trump said, as his aides gathered to the side.

Craig Menear, CEO of the Home Depot, was conducting the interview. JP Morgan Chase CEO Jamie Dimon was in the front row, and so was Dennis Muilenburg, at that time CEO of Boeing. Jeff Bezos and Larry Fink, CEOs of Amazon and Blackrock, respectively, were in the back, occasionally shaking their heads in disagreement (or disgust, or frustration) as Trump did his thing. The first question for Trump, from one executive in the audience, was pretty standard: What was next on the deregulation front? The president had been aggressive his first couple of years in undoing the thicket of business regulations promulgated by President Barack Obama.

"You definitely want to see me reelected if you want to keep being in business," Trump answered. "You've got this Green New Deal. It's completely crazy. It'll completely shut down American energy. And it's from this failed geek, Alexandria Ocasio-Cortez. They call her AOC."

Trump did not mince words when it came to the socialist environmental agenda championed by Representative Alexandria Ocasio-Cortez, who upset a senior House Democrat in the 2018 primary as a first-time candidate and quickly established herself as a leading progressive with national reach. Trump respected that about his fellow New Yorker and progeny of the outer boroughs—he from Queens, she from the Bronx.

"Let me tell you something about AOC. Let me tell you something about her. I've watched her walk down the halls of Congress, and I see these old men shiver in fear—they shiver in fear whenever they see her," Trump said. "You want to know why? Because AOC has a base, *just like me.*"

There was nervous laughter in the room, as if this high-powered group could not figure out how they were supposed to react, perhaps not realizing that Trump had just revealed to them the most important animating aspect of his political persona and his presidency.

———

When I sat down with Trump at Mar-a-Lago to talk about the future, his and the Republican Party's, I decided to break the ice by showing him that homemade pin I picked up at CPAC a couple of months earlier from the elderly couple who were among his devoted followers. I figured "We Are #74MillionStrong" might disarm the former president and put him in the mood to dish. I reached across the table and handed the pin to Trump, who seemed only mildly amused by it.

"That's great. The spirit is unbelievable. The anger is perhaps even more unbelievable," Trump added, setting the tone for our discussion.

"The anger is absolutely unbelievable," he continued, before winding his way back to the pin. "That's cute; that's really nice."

Trump put the pin down on the table, to his left. I didn't want to be rude, so I made a mental note to scoop it up after our interview. I had planned to give the pin to a relative who is one of those "74 million strong" after I finished showing it to Trump. And then, out of nowhere, in the middle of answering a completely unrelated question about a third of the way through our conversation, Trump looked down and to his left and picked up the pin. "I'm going to put this in my pocket—it's cute—so I don't forget it."

It disappeared into the inside breast pocket of Trump's suit jacket. Maybe it will end up in the Trump presidential library...if the former president is willing to part with it. That's a good way to understand

Trump's spell over the Republican Party. Defeated and out of office, the forty-fifth president is nonetheless showing no indication he is willing to part with command and control of the GOP. There are consequences, both for the party and the men and women who would purport take Trump's place—even if he chooses to sit 2024 out.

CHAPTER TWO

CamelBak

O n a Monday evening in late June 2020, as rioters tried to pull down the bronze statue of Andrew Jackson in Lafayette Square, directly across the street from the White House, President Donald Trump and Senator **Tom Cotton** connected by telephone.

The Arkansas Republican had called the commander in chief in the afternoon to discuss immigration policy. But now, hours later as he sat down to dinner, Cotton was riveted by the news coverage of civil unrest dominating his television screen. Protests sparked by George Floyd's death had been ongoing in cities across the United States for weeks. About a month earlier, Floyd, a black man, died in the custody of the Minneapolis police after a white officer jammed his knee into Floyd's neck, with the full force of his body weight, for more than nine minutes, suffocating him. Other officers at the scene—one white, one Hmong, and one black— stood around as Floyd said he couldn't breathe and begged for his life. In the midst of nationwide lockdowns implemented to arrest the deadly coronavirus pandemic, protests against racial injustice ensued. Some were peaceful, some were violent, some were cannibalized by criminals and anarchists to feed their hunger for mayhem. In Washington, DC, some mixture of all three made targets of the capital city's collection of statues honoring political and military figures from American history—the long forgotten and others, like Jackson, long remembered. In fact, Trump fancied himself a Jacksonian populist. Upon entering the White House in January 2017, the forty-fifth president honored the seventh president with a portrait, prominently placed, in the Oval Office. That made the assault on the statue of Old Hickory tantamount to a personal attack on Trump. "Have you looked out your window to see what they're doing across the street?" Cotton asked Trump. The president had returned the senator's call as the attack on the statue of Jackson in Lafayette Park was unfolding.

"I'm watching it on Fox right now," Trump responded. "It's terrible. These people—I just can't believe it." Trump, typically, was spending his days and nights upbraiding the mob like a bar stool commentator. He vowed to bring "law and order" to the streets, but without any coherent or consistent strategy. Enter Cotton. It wasn't just the statue of Jackson, plainly visible to Trump from the White House, that was disturbingly under attack. All over the country, rioters (and even otherwise peaceful protesters) were subverting the law as they attempted to tear down memorials to revered Americans. Many, though not all of those so recognized, were historically consequential—integral to the development of the United States as a global superpower and multiethnic, pluralistic democracy. Some, like Jackson, were slaveholders or espoused racist views common for the era in which they lived. Cotton put his legislative team to work scouring the federal code for a remedy—and he found one. The senator told Trump about the Veterans Memorial Preservation Act, a law that makes it a crime (with penalties of up to ten years in prison) to deface, desecrate, destroy, or otherwise harm a monument or statue of someone serving in the US military; ditto regarding any memorial that depicted a veteran's military service.

As a former president, Jackson was a political figure. But he also was a celebrated military general. The statue of him in Lafayette Square, placed in 1852, commemorates Jackson's service leading American troops in the legendary, and victorious, Battle of New Orleans during the War of 1812 against Great Britain. Cotton pointed this out to Trump, emphasizing that the memorial renders Jackson on horseback, in military uniform, with his saber drawn, making any effort to bring it down a clear violation of the Veterans Memorial Preservation Act. Intrigued, Trump promised to look into it. The next morning: voilà.

"I have authorized the federal government to arrest anyone who vandalizes or destroys any monument, statue or other such federal property in the US with up to 10 years in prison, per the Veterans Memorial Preservation Act," the president tweeted. "This action is taken effective immediately, but may also be used retroactively for destruction or vandalism already caused. There will be no exceptions!"

It was hardly the first time Cotton had whispered in Trump's ear to lend his often erratic, albeit preternatural instincts for what conservative voters want to hear some sorely needed legal and ideological grounding. And so what might a sophisticated version of Donald Trump have looked like? He might have looked something like Tom Cotton.

Early in Trump's tenure, amid flashes of reassuringly conventional political behavior, the chattering class in Washington pondered whether a *pivot* was afoot. Was the new president, at long last, transitioning from Brioni-clad campaign fusillade into something—anything—resembling a Brooks Brothers statesman? Would Trump govern with a modicum of self-control rather than consumed self-regard? Most of Trump's new Republican allies on Capitol Hill, some who watched his most unusual campaign for the presidency in awe, others who fixated on it like a car crash, were asking the same question. And so was some significant percentage—though by no means all—of the voters that took a flyer on this political apprentice in 2016.

Sometimes this pivot seemed visible after Trump delivered a cogent speech with the aid of a teleprompter. His first address as president to a joint session of Congress early in 2017, a State of the Union by any other name, comes to mind. Sometimes it was after he mediated a bipartisan, bicameral working group of lawmakers at the White House (yeah, they were televised, but fine). During a couple of these sessions, one to discuss immigration reform and another to pursue gun control, a charming Trump appeared so intent on compromising with the Democrats, exasperated Republicans sitting around the table were compelled to rein him in. On camera.

And sometimes it was after the president consoled Americans with words of unifying moral clarity in the emotional wake of a domestic tragedy or overseas atrocity. "So many young, beautiful, innocent people living and enjoying their lives murdered by evil losers in life," Trump said in May 2017 after a jihadist terrorist murdered concertgoers in Manchester, England, with a suicide bomb. "I won't call them monsters because they would like that term. They would think that's a great name. I will call them, from now on, losers, because that's what they are."

In 2018, after seventeen students were gunned down on the campus of Marjory Stoneman Douglas High School in Parkland, Florida, Trump hosted the victims' parents at the White House and listened empathetically as many of them asked the fervently pro–gun rights president to change course and support new federal restrictions on gun ownership.

There are more examples of what I like to call *Meeting Trump*—the courteous, thoughtful, almost soft-spoken Trump who shows up to private meetings or is visible in a variety of public settings. When I interviewed the president in the Oval Office on the afternoon of Halloween 2019 with three of my colleagues from the *Washington Examiner*, just as the inquiry that would lead to his first impeachment was getting under way, he offered a cordial handshake, asked if there was anything I'd like to drink, and repeatedly called me by my first name throughout a ninety-minute conversation in which I was constantly freaking out that his subdued voice would not register on my iPhone audio recorder.

But as numerous as these examples may seem when lumped together, they were the exceptions to the rule. There was no *pivot* from the campaign to the presidency. There was only and ever the campaign. The Trump that is, of his signature, populist revival-style arena campaign rallies. I might have said that it all culminated on January 6, 2021, with his call, during a massive gathering in Washington, to march on the US Capitol and pressure Congress to overturn his loss to President Joe Biden. Except that event turned out not to be the last of Trump's raucous rallies cum MAGA-mania political festivals.

He is and always was what I like to call *Rally Trump*—pugilistic, provocative, divisive. After a while, the whole discussion of a Trump pivot became an inside joke.

But if Trump had pivoted, if the 2016 campaign had simply been a big act to get elected, as some Republican voters suggested to me at the time, he might have ended up like Cotton. "He is a very analytical person," said a Republican insider who has worked closely with him. "He has a fixed ideological approach and is an intellectual ideologue. But tactically, he has the mind of a military strategist. All tactics are up for debate and negotiation."

A Harvard-trained lawyer, McKinsey-trained business consultant, and US Army–trained soldier, the forty-four-year-old Arkansas senator is regimented, scrupulous, efficient. And prepared. No decisions are made without a spreadsheet (more on this in a bit). Decorum matters. Cotton wrote a whole book on it. *Sacred Duty: A Soldier's Tour at Arlington National Cemetery* is the senator's account of his service in the Army unit that conducts military funerals at the veterans' burial ground in Arlington, Virginia, as well as a history of the "Old Guard" and the meticulous protocols that are central to the role it plays in helping the survivors of America's greatest heroes make peace with heartwrenching loss.

You won't hear Cotton suggest contempt for the First Amendment by denigrating the media with the banana republic charge of "enemy of the people." Instead, Cotton submitted an op-ed to the *New York Times* urging Trump to invoke the Insurrection Act to quell the rioting that erupted in some cities after Floyd's death. He could not have predicted the newsroom insurrection and firing of top editors his op-ed led to. But Cotton didn't choose the *Times* by happenstance. The senator calculated that placement there, rather than in a friendly outlet like, say, the *Wall Street Journal*, would position the op-ed to spark maximum outrage on the left. When the top brass at the *Times* regretfully apologized for publishing Cotton's typically dry, matter-of-fact op-ed, the senator couldn't believe his good fortune. Cotton used the row to cast an embarrassing spotlight on a politicized media, in the process raising his profile with the sort of grassroots conservatives who are primarily driven by cultural issues and hold the key to his political ambitions. (They showed their appreciation by sending Cotton millions in small-dollar donations, in what amounted to an unprecedented fund-raising spike for his operation.)

You won't hear Cotton malign illegal immigrants from Mexico as "rapists" or rant that poor nations in Africa and the Caribbean are "shit-hole countries." The senator won't entertain rapturous crowds with an extemporaneous reading of the poem "The Snake," a xenophobic parable about the danger of immigration. You will see Cotton propose carefully crafted legislation that aims to reduce levels of legal immigration into the United States and discuss the proposal with the charisma of a certi-fied public accountant. The emotionally charged culture war Trump has waged on illegal immigration might have more to do with his rise in the Republican Party than any other issue since the day he announced his presidential candidacy in June 2015. But as a matter of concrete policy, Cotton has been there all along. His consistent opposition to easing the way for more legal immigration predates the Trump administration and in fact positions Cotton to the right of a president who has often said he planned to build a border wall with a big, beautiful door for people who want to enter the United States lawfully.

On trade, too, Cotton is no convert to conservative populism, but a progenitor of what we might now think of as Trump Republicanism.

Cotton won't embarrass the United States by declaring, "China is killing us." Nor will he ask, as though caught in a 1980s time-loop, "When did we beat Japan at anything?" Yes, Trump upended decades of Republican Party orthodoxy on the issue of trade with his deep suspicion of international agreements and liberal use of tariffs on imported goods to force foreign countries to make their markets more hospitable to American exports. But it was Cotton who coined the populist insult "Davoisie Elite" back when Obama was president, to mock the so-called "globalist thought leaders" who attend the annual World Economic Forum in Davos, Switzerland, which, ironically, counts Trump among its devotees. Free trade agreements have significantly lowered the cost of household goods at big-box chain retailers like Walmart, headquartered in Bentonville,

Arkansas, saving American consumers trillions of dollars over the years. The senator argues that this collective savings has been squandered by the millions of manufacturing jobs that have moved overseas and domestic wages that have plummeted to keep pace with foreign competition.

Unusually for a Republican, Cotton is even on record in support of increasing the minimum hourly wage, first in Arkansas, and then, a few years later, federally. If you're filling out your populist scorecard at home, this makes Cotton a more interesting figure in a presidential primary than his reputation for being a neoconservative national security hawk would suggest.

"He's been in the Trump position before Trump," said a Republican strategist who has followed Cotton's career. On that: The senator is not an "America First" conservative through and through. He breaks with Trump and the rest of the populist crowd on foreign policy, in that, like the Reaganites who dominated the Republican Party for the latter part of the twentieth century and early on in the twenty-first, Cotton believes in projecting US power abroad and in maintaining a US-led global world order. Though choosy with his words, it was plain to me in our interviews early in Trump's term that Cotton was not a fan of the forty-fifth president's decision to give the puny thug who runs North Korea, Kim Jong-un, his grand photo op. That, and Cotton's vote against criminal justice reform, gives the senator a way to explain his fidelity to Trump as rooted in shared values versus sycophancy. That quality, which would become more apparent in early 2021, might come in handy in 2024.

———

In early December 2012, Cotton was milling about Capitol Hill, participating in meetings for freshman orientation.

If that sounds like college, it is. In the weeks after winning their first election to the House or Senate, incoming members of Congress travel to Washington for seminars, where they study the basics of their new job. They find office space, hire staff, receive committee assignments, learn how to navigate Washington and a legislative process that can be rather arcane—and figure out where the private bathrooms are. Yes, there are "members only" bathrooms. Among the incoming class for the 113th Congress was Cotton, all of thirty-six years old, and even younger looking than that, physically fit, with a military buzz cut. He had captured Arkansas's Fourth Congressional District in a blowout in the November elections that saw President Barack Obama defeat Republican nominee Mitt Romney for a second term. Mitch McConnell wanted to talk to him. Urgently.

The Senate minority leader was coming off of a disappointing campaign. He wasn't up for reelection in Kentucky for another two years. But for the second consecutive general election, McConnell saw a tantalizing opportunity to fulfill a lifelong ambition to become Senate majority leader wasted by a bad batch of Republican candidates. Two years previous, Sharron Angle frittered away an opportunity to oust Senate Majority Leader Harry Reid in Nevada, while Christine O'Donnell, despite insisting that she was not, in fact, a witch, doused another GOP pickup opportunity in Delaware. This time around—in 2012—McConnell's bid for majority leader died on the altar of three seats in red states the Republicans should have won without much trouble: Indiana, where Republican nominee Richard Mourdock gaffed away a guaranteed victory to Democrat Joe Donnelly down the stretch with ill-timed comments on abortion; Missouri, where Republican nominee Todd Akin gaffed, or gifted, the campaign to Senator Claire McCaskill, perhaps the most vulnerable Democratic incumbent of the entire election cycle, with bizarre comments about "legitimate rape"; and North Dakota, where Republican Rick Berg lost to Democrat Heidi Heitkamp, not because of some gaffe, but because he was just that awful.

McConnell was fed up. Within days of the 2012 elections, he was plotting a course for a Republican takeover of the US Senate in 2014, a campaign that would unfold in Obama's second midterm year and on turf hospitable to the GOP—if the party fielded competent candidates. So, McConnell got to work recruiting. To set the table for a Republican pickup in Arkansas, that meant planting a bug in Cotton's ear and grooming him to challenge Democratic incumbent Mark Pryor.

But McConnell was having trouble connecting with Cotton, who was racing from one orientation meeting to another. Impatient, he turned for help to John Boozman, Arkansas's Republican senator. McConnell dispatched Boozman on a frantic mission to track down Cotton. Arkansas's senior senator, quiet and unassuming, does almost nothing frantically. So when Boozman reached Cotton by phone and delivered McConnell's urgent request for an immediate sit-down, it made an impression. Thirty minutes later, the Senate minority leader and the representative-elect were meeting just off of the Senate floor in his ornate suite of offices.

McConnell was blunt: Avoid any actions, commitments, or comments in the months ahead that would create obstacles to a 2014 Senate bid. Don't tell your constituents that you have no interest in higher office; don't accept plum committee assignments from Republican leadership in the majority GOP House that are predicated on promises to run for reelection to Arkansas's Fourth Congressional District. Keep your options open. Cotton took McConnell's advice to heart—and he followed it.

That is the story of how Cotton began laying a foundation to run for US Senate before he ever cast a single vote on the floor of the House of Representatives and rolled his convincing victory over Pryor two years later right into a quiet but aggressive campaign for the Republican presidential nomination—at first with 2020 in mind, but later for 2024.

In November 2019, a full year before Trump asked voters for a second term—smack in the middle of the Democratic Party's contentious primary to pick the president's 2020 opponent, Team Cotton convened its first 2024 strategy session. They met in McLean, Virginia, in a small office that serves as the Washington headquarters for the senator's political operation. Joining Cotton that day was senior adviser Brett O'Donnell, a veteran Republican operative best known for his work as a debate coach to GOP presidential nominees; Brian Colas, an old associate of the senator's from McKinsey & Company who picked up politics as a second career when the senator recruited him to oversee the day-to-day operations of his campaign team; plus the chief of staff in Cotton's Senate office, Doug Coutts; and Aaron MacLean, the senator's legislative director. Among them, they sketched out a blueprint to transform a small-state US senator with minimal access to deep-pocketed Republicans back home (because, per capita, there are fewer of them) into a national fund-raising power-house. They laid plans to transform a politician with minimal name iden-tification outside of Arkansas—and the politics-obsessed everywhere else—into a household name and the top choice of GOP primary voters in Iowa, New Hampshire, South Carolina, and the quadrennial, front-loaded universe of the Super Tuesday states. Team Cotton had even identi-fied a potential campaign manager: seasoned Republican operative Steven Law, a close confidant of McConnell's who runs the majority leader's des-ignated super PAC, the Senate Leadership Fund. Over the course of the following year, Cotton got to work.

He endorsed a Republican Senate candidate in New Hampshire, pro-viding an excuse to spend time and make friends in a crucial early primary state. That was a no-brainer. The Granite State, host of the first primary on the GOP presidential calendar and second nominating contest overall after Iowa, is a revolving door of sorts for Republicans (and Democrats) looking to build political support for a White House bid. Cotton also returned to Iowa in July 2019—yes, *returned*—to deliver a speech on reli-gious liberty. Cotton, at the time looking ahead to 2020, spent the wan-ing days of the 2016 campaign in the Hawkeye State, and kept coming back throughout Trump's term. Social conservatives are king in the Iowa caucuses, which as of this writing is still scheduled to render the first ver-dict of the 2024 Republican primary. To build support among this key bloc, Cotton addressed an audience of locals who gathered for a summit hosted by The Family Leader and paid homage to the group's leader, Bob Vander Plaats, whose endorsement is much sought after by GOP presi-dential candidates. But Cotton's activities were not limited to the early states. He also backed a Republican running for the House in a special election in a northwestern Wisconsin congressional district, turf rich in

Republican primary and general election votes in a state considered key to the GOP's White House fortunes. Late in the 2020 election cycle, Cotton injected himself into a Tennessee Senate primary in what amounted to a last-minute proxy battle against Ted Cruz. Cotton's Texas colleague put his political muscle behind Manny Sethi, a conservative physician who tried to elbow out Bill Hagerty, Trump's handpicked successor to Lamar Alexander, who retired from the Senate at the end of 2020. Cruz offered up his endorsement unprompted and traveled to Tennessee to headline a campaign swing with Sethi across the state. Cotton followed, offering a preview of sorts of the 2024 Republican presidential primary. Cotton spent time in Tennessee down the stretch of the primary campaign stumping for Hagerty, while his affiliated super PAC, aptly named America One, directed by former Cotton legislative aide Jonny Hiler—taking cues from the senator—spent $375,000 (not exactly chump change in a race like this) to air a series of hard-hitting attack ads going after Sethi. Cotton wasn't finished. Five weeks before Election Day 2020, following the death of liberal US Supreme Court justice Ruth Bader Ginsburg, the senator's political operation sprang into action to influence the confirmation battle over her replacement. Cotton moved quickly, before Trump nominated Ginsburg's eventual successor, Amy Coney Barrett, a conservative. Team Cotton established an "emergency" war room, complete with its own website, scotuswarroom.com, to bolster a confirmation process in the US Senate that Republicans were counting on to help deliver Trump a second term and protect their precarious majority. Republicans had in mind the blowup over the confirmation of Supreme Court justice Brett Kavanaugh two years earlier. Cotton's war room volleyed the aggressive Democratic attacks on Coney Barrett and acted as a resource for Republicans, providing useful information and positive messaging to bolster her confirmation. Around the same time, Cotton was active in Georgia, ground zero for control of the US Senate. The senator became close friends with GOP colleague Kelly Loeffler after she was appointed to the US Senate in early January to replace Republican Johnny Isakson, who resigned for health reasons. To boost Loeffler's chances in a November 3 special election and subsequent January 5, 2021, runoff, Cotton traveled to Georgia regularly, beginning in October, to stump for her. Their political teams were in constant contact, conferring on messaging and other aspects of campaign strategy, with Cotton taking it upon himself to launch the particularly vicious attacks against Democrat Raphael Warnock that might have appeared unseemly coming from Loeffler. She would end up defeating the other Republican running in the special election for the right to finish the remainder of the six-year term Isakson won in 2016. But after advancing to the runoff, Loeffler fell short against Warnock, a loss that helped put the Democrats in the majority for the first time in six years.

If Cotton was interested in running for a GOP leadership post in the US Senate, his extracurricular activities might be explained that way. Although, truth be told, aspiring Senate leaders tend to work within the party's leadership hierarchy. And that hierarchy has clearly defined roles for who is in charge of campaigning and messaging to bolster the party's legislative and political interests. Aside from the fact that McConnell controls everything, to the extent that he delegates, political activity tends to be the purview of the National Republican Senatorial Committee chairman, and messaging the province of the Conference chairman. Cotton's decision to act independently of this pecking order is revealing.

———

It is almost impossible to overstate how much Cotton values advance preparation. He leaves nothing to chance and obsesses over seemingly minor details. All of that planning finds its way into a spreadsheet or PowerPoint presentation for him to review and track progress. Most of his contemporaries attempt to deal with or sidestep political obstacles, but Cotton, in Machiavellian fashion, tries to eliminate them altogether.

"He can also take a punch. That's a quality most people don't have in politics," the Republican insider said. "Getting hit just doesn't faze him. He just hits back." It all gets back to his military training and, in particular, lessons learned in Army Ranger School.

Watching the September 11, 2001, terrorist attacks unfold on a television screen in a common area of Harvard Law School, Cotton decided to volunteer for military service, as so many others of his generation did after watching the Twin Towers fall and the Pentagon smoldering—and hearing about the everyday American heroes who took down a hijacked jetliner in a Pennsylvania field. The twenty-four-year-old third-year law student planned to drop out of law school immediately and enlist in the Army. He wanted to see combat. But Cotton was persuaded by a couple of close friends who had worn the uniform to first earn his juris doctorate and work long enough to pay off the pricey tuition. About three and a half years later, he joined up, and would spend about five years leading troops in combat in Iraq and Afghanistan until his honorable discharge from the Army in 2010. If not for the fact that Cotton has exchanged his fatigues and weapons for a suit and tie, it might be impossible to tell Cotton the soldier from Cotton the politician. Credit Army Ranger School. The instructors there taught the senator to top off his canteen with water before heading out on patrol. Not 95 percent full—but to the brim. Was water that important? In the scorching deserts of Iraq and remote mountain regions of Afghanistan, obviously. But soldiers could always share water. Cotton likes to frame his approach to politics by telling this story—about how he was trained to fill up his CamelBak. Otherwise the water would make noise sloshing around in an unfilled canteen and eliminate the advantage of stealth as he hunted or evaded enemy troops.

The anecdote explains, succinctly, how the senator's move to clear a path to a presidential campaign in 2024 began early in 2017, around the time of Trump's inaugural. It was then that Cotton put in motion a strategy to identify and extinguish the most formidable Democrat who might challenge him for reelection to the US Senate in Arkansas in 2020.

Cotton is personable enough, to borrow a phrase. But the senator isn't going to win any popularity contests. He's not going to come in second or third, either. I could tell you he makes up for it with a stirring stage presence or that, privately, he can be quite charming, both pretty good qualities to have in politics. But I'd be lying. Trump, for all of his foibles, has more than enough charisma to fill an arena, and can be rather enchanting behind closed doors. Cotton . . . not so much.

"Even in a room where he's gone and done a very good presentation, people say, 'That guy's smart.' And he is really smart," a veteran Republican insider said. "But you don't hear, 'God, I wish he'd run for president.' They know he wants to. But there's something that he needs to do that causes people to say, 'He's going to be a great candidate.' "

It's a serious vulnerability, leading a GOP consultant for a potential 2024 rival to declare, dismissively, "He's obviously going to run. I mean, somebody's got to get last place."

What Cotton does do well is so much else. His mind is highly organized, his drive to succeed is intense, and his sense of mission is unwavering. Cotton also has another personal attribute that I don't know quite how to characterize other than to say that he just doesn't give a shit. Cotton is wholly unapologetic for his beliefs and completely incapable of feeling remorse for the steadfastness with which he wields every legal and constitutional weapon available to effect policy outcomes in line with those beliefs. He is simply impervious to outrage—at least the political kind he tends to inspire in Democrats and the occasional Republican naysayer. Or, for that matter, from people like me (the dreaded media). In my fifteen-plus years covering Capitol Hill and congressional and presidential campaigns, he is the only politician I've met, other than McConnell, who does not feel the human compunction to at least acknowledge a question, if not outright answer it. If Cotton's not interested in addressing a reporter's question, he'll just walk on by, no ducking through a back stairway or fraudulent cell phone conversation necessary.

With that sort of steely resolve, Cotton in 2017 ordered Colas to identify the twenty most formidable Arkansas Democrats who might challenge his reelection in 2020 and compile dossiers on each. The senator was not content to trust his political future to how reliably ruby red his state has become over the past two decades. Team Cotton investigated their backgrounds, assembling reams of opposition research available to deploy at a moment's notice. The black books included potentially controversial social media posts these Democrats might choose to scrub from the internet if it ever occurred to them to run for the US Senate. As campaigns for the 2018 midterm elections kicked into high gear, Cotton became especially fixated on Clarke Tucker. Tucker was the Democratic nominee running against Republican representative French Hill in Arkansas's somewhat competitive Second Congressional District, and the senator concluded that he was the most dangerous threat to his 2020 campaign. It made sense. Trump's first midterm election was shaping up to be a disaster for the Republican Party—and ultimately would be. And Tucker, a member of the Arkansas House of Representatives, presented a triple threat in any potential US Senate race: As a cancer survivor, he had a compelling personal story, he was the scion of a prominent political family, and he was becoming a draw among Democratic donors across the country.

Cotton knew from experience that Tucker would be Senate Minority Leader Charles Schumer's first call if the Democrat ousted Hill in 2018, just as McConnell quickly spotted him as the GOP's best opportunity to dislodge Democratic incumbent Mark Pryor after he won election to the House of Representatives in 2012. So what did Cotton do? Dust off his Tucker oppo book and lay in wait? No. He jumped right into the 2018 Second District campaign and unloaded, coming at Tucker with advertising on television, digital platforms, and through direct mail. At the time, the senator wasn't so flush with campaign cash that he wanted to burn through it two years early, so he was strategic with his ad placement. In one instance, Republican Majority Fund, Cotton's political action committee, ran a narrowly tailored direct-mail campaign targeting Tucker and the homes of his immediate neighbors with pamphlets charging that Tucker wouldn't do anything about illegal immigration. The senator wanted to rattle the Democrat and make sure he would think twice about running for the US Senate. It worked. In late September 2018, Tucker called a news conference where he held up copies of the Cotton leadership PAC mailers and complained, much to the senator's delight. "These are intended to scare people," the Democrat said. "They're fearmongering. And as you can see from these mail pieces, they're inherently racist." The mailers certainly appeared to do the trick with Tucker. He would lose to Hill less than two months later, falling 52 percent to 46 percent.

With the 2020 election cycle now under way, Cotton prosecuted a two-pronged strategy aimed at easing his path to reelection in a state Trump won with a twenty-seven-point cushion in 2016. But that's Cotton: thorough and taking nothing for granted. Step one: Make abundantly clear to any ambitious Democrats left in Arkansas that Cotton's reelection was inevitable and that daring to challenge him would be exceedingly painful. Step two: Prepare to chop off the head of any Democrat who decided to challenge him nonetheless. Cotton launched an advertising campaign to coincide with the state's uniquely early November filing deadline. In Arkansas, candidates for office must file their intent to run in the November before the election year. Cotton couldn't believe his good fortune when the Democrat who raised his hand for the assignment was Josh Mahony.

Cotton's dossier on Mahony was thick. There were hints of scandal and a questionable employment history. The opposition research was so juicy, in fact, that Team Cotton kept its powder dry, not wanting to scare Mahony off and give Democrats an opportunity to field a better challenger, or at least a less flawed challenger. The senator settled on a plan that called for nuking Mahony the day after Arkansas's filing deadline had passed. At the time, Cotton's main objective was to undercut Mahony's fund-raising and soften up his image for later in the campaign. With the filing deadline in the rearview, the Cotton campaign flooded local reporters with the opposition research on Mahony it had painstakingly collected. Then the Cotton campaign worked with the Arkansas Republican Party to bring a complaint against Mahony with the Federal Election Commission alleging he had misrepresented his finances and employment history in federally mandated disclosure documents. Cotton had more Mahony oppo in the kitty ready to go, and there were plans to hire a heckler to follow him around in public and place billboard ads in his hometown with the headline "What does Josh Mahony do for a living?" But all of that turned out to be unnecessary. The initial dump scared Mahony out of the race altogether, leaving the Democrats without a candidate and the Republican incumbent unopposed on the 2020 ballot except for a token challenge from the Libertarian nominee.

"It's a classic Cotton play, where you don't just fire all of your bullets all the time," the Republican strategist said. "You wait for a moment, you strike, and you win. And, you're done." Cotton could hardly have asked for a better outcome. Unencumbered by his reelection bid, he pivoted to 2024.

Twenty twenty was now about building a political infrastructure that was national in scope and capable of seeding a presidential bid.

———

In Washington, there are "secrets" and there are "open secrets." Cotton eyeing the presidency is neither. It's just known. That fits Cotton's personality. Where others tread cautiously, Cotton leans in.

With no Democratic opponent on the Arkansas ballot in the fall of 2020, he could afford to. But the obvious benefits—being a shoo-in for reelection, to name just one of them—were accompanied by some liabilities. For instance, if you're a Republican donor whose phone is ringing off the hook from the Trump campaign and an array of vulnerable Republican senators with the US Senate majority on the line, why would you write Cotton a check?

Red state, no major opponent, no need for any of your hard-earned cash... The same goes for grassroots conservatives who contribute in small amounts. What sort of urgent email appeal was Cotton supposed to send?

"Dear so-and-so, we're approaching the end of the month and I'm in dire need of resources to make sure my campaign is not overrun by... Oh, wait, I don't have a Democratic challenger."

To compensate, Team Cotton got creative.

Rather than dialing for dollars, Cotton dialed for friends. In political jargon, the phrase is "make the ask." Calls with wealthy political donors are highly choreographed: A fund-raising consultant with a preexisting relationship with a high-dollar contributor makes preliminary contact, sometimes directly, sometimes with a go-between the contributor uses to handle his or her political activity; the consultant gauges a donor's interest in his or her client, whether on issues the donor cares about or simply a desire to accrue political influence; if there's a match, the fund-raising call is scheduled. The really good fund-raising consultants usually know the answers to these questions up front, including how much money the donor might be inclined to contribute, and can quickly assemble a list of contributors most suitable to a particular client. That way, when it comes time for the politician to "make the ask," it's less like an awkward telemarketing call and more like a confirmation of sale.

However, what the really good fund-raising consultants understand is that whether or not a donor is willing to write large checks comes down to relationships—it's as important, if not more so, than their presumed desire to want to exert political influence. And so the smart consultants, and the smart clients, will work on forging personal connections with donors first, before they get around to asking for money.

Which gets us back to Cotton and the fund-raising dilemma created by the fact that his reelection was a fait accompli. Rather than take a break from fund-raising (others might have; politicians despise fund-raising more than many realize), the senator in January 2020 transitioned to friend-raising—forming personal connections with wealthy Republicans who could write big checks when it counts. All the information he gathered—about the ins and outs of their businesses, the issues they care most about, even relevant information about their personal and family lives—ended up stored on an Excel spreadsheet.

The campaign was more aggressive with its small-dollar fund-raising. After first considering putting digital prospecting on hiatus, Cotton fired up the email engine in early 2020. The process provided a low-pressure opportunity to message-test and figure out the baseline support for Cotton as a standalone figure in Republican politics. The results, though modest, were better than his team hoped: $40,000 to $50,000 per month raised online. In June of that year, after Cotton touched off a circular firing squad inside the newsroom of the *New York Times*, his grassroots online fund-raising spiked to $500,000 for the month. In July, Cotton collected another $300,000. Even more than the money—well, maybe just as much as the money—this development is potentially significant because it offers evidence of Cotton growing his email list of grassroots donors. Years ago, a presidential candidate's initial strength rested on the size of their Rolodex of traditional campaign contributors—individuals capable of writing checks up to the legal limit or bundling stacks of such checks from individuals in their list of business and personal contacts. In the digital age, it's hard to be a serious White House contender without an email list of grassroots donors big enough to match such outsized ambitions.

Next, Cotton endeavored to increase his national media profile. If you're a Republican, that goal lends itself to a simple strategy, even if it's not simple to pull off: Get yourself on Fox News (and since the November 2020 election, upstart competitors Newsmax and One America News Network). For Cotton, it was relatively simple in that the set of issues he has immersed himself in—pushing presidential administrations past and present to get tough with Iran, cracking down on China, choking off illegal immigration—are issues Fox News beat reporters tend to chase and issues the network's highly rated prime-time opinion hosts tend to showcase.

The senator never missed an opportunity.

Cotton traveled to Tulsa, Oklahoma, in June 2020 with a coterie of other high-profile Trump supporters for what turned out to be the president's ill-fated attempt to restart his mega rallies despite the dangers posed by the coronavirus pandemic. While the rest of the bunch stayed up late the night before celebrating the forty-fifth president's return to the live stage, Cotton turned in early so that he could appear on *Fox & Friends Weekend* the following morning to discuss the event. Cotton also uses *Breitbart News* as a conduit to reach grassroots conservatives and expand his base of support among potential GOP primary voters. But here's the punch line. Colas is closely tracking the social media mentions generated by Cotton's television and radio appearances, op-eds, and related activities.

And Colas is building a similar database for the range of Cotton's potential White House rivals, with plans to use all the data to develop a comprehensive political strategy that positions the senator to wage a strong campaign for the 2024 nomination. Not to put too fine a point on it, but (as you might have guessed by now) all of the information ends up in a spreadsheet for the senator to review on a regular basis.

Meanwhile, the super PAC America One and an affiliated political nonprofit organization, America One Policies (names eerily analogous to Trump's designated outside groups while he was president, the super PAC America First Action and aligned 501(c)4, America First Policies), were propped up to promote Cotton's political and policy agenda and put under Hiler's supervision. Under federal law, incumbent politicians and candidates for office are not permitted to coordinate or otherwise involve themselves in outside groups formed to boost their political profile or further their policy agenda, although they can engage in some light fundraising activities for such organizations. At Hiler's direction, America One Policies followed Cotton into the Tennessee Senate primary in the summer of 2020. Down the stretch of the 2020 campaign, Hiler deployed the issue-advocacy organization in swing House districts, running digital ads that aimed to put incumbent Democrats on the defensive on China, an issue that takes up a lot of space in Cotton's portfolio.

"The Chinese Communist Party lied about coronavirus; misleading the world, spreading sickness around the globe, killing thousands," the thirty-second spot's ominous voice-over declared, before playing a clip of Dr. Deborah Birx, then a prominent member of Trump's COVID-19 task force, saying "240,000 American lives."

Here's the part that matters—Hiler placed the ads specifically to reach voters in swing House districts in key presidential primary states, districts that Trump won in 2016 but that by the end of the midterm elections in 2018 were represented by a Democrat. What was the point? To make life a little tougher for Democrats running for reelection in those districts, no doubt. But there was another goal. Listen to the conclusion of the America One Policies' China ad:

"Sign up at AmericaOnePolicies.com and join our effort to make China pay. It's time to act."

The group was collecting voter data that might be mined at a later date for contributions or grassroots support for a Cotton presidential bid.

———

On Sunday, January 3, 2021, at 10:09 p.m. Eastern Standard Time, a political hand grenade exploded in my email inbox.

In a carefully crafted 327-word statement, Cotton announced that he would support the certification of President-elect Joe Biden's Electoral College victory when Congress met in joint session on Wednesday, January 6. The senator would vote against any objections. Trump, in an audacious last-ditch attempt to overturn the November 3 election and secure another four years in the White House, had issued a clarion call for Republicans in the House of Representatives and the US Senate to object to state-certified electoral votes from six swing states that had voted narrowly for Biden, delivering him the presidency. In the House of Representatives, the major-ity of Republicans, led by their top two leaders, Minority Leader Kevin McCarthy of California and Minority Whip Steve Scalise of Louisiana—or was it the other way around?—answered Trump's call. They would vote to nullify the will of the voters in Arizona and Pennsylvania, the only two states to ultimately qualify for an objection vote, while signing off on a failed effort to throw out the results from four other states Biden won: Georgia, Michigan, Nevada, and Wisconsin. In the US Senate, the outgo-ing president's pleas for a reprieve were granted by Ted Cruz of Texas and Josh Hawley of Missouri, the former almost certainly a 2024 contender and the latter often mentioned as such. Between the two of them, whip-smart constitutional lawyers both, they had managed to recruit—or was it scare?—about a dozen Senate Republicans into joining their bid to avert Biden's inauguration.

Cotton, stunningly, gave Trump the Heisman. It was not a spur-of-the-moment calculation. For weeks leading up to the January 6 vote, Trump ratcheted up conspiratorial claims that the 2020 election was stolen. Not hyperbole: stolen. It was a fantastical sundae, cooked up by Trump's calamitous legal team and served up by the president to the tens of millions of rank-and-file voters who backed him. The cherry on top was Trump's assertion that Congress, and Vice President Mike Pence, were empowered by the Constitution to sidestep the Electoral College and install the losing candidate as president. In the midst of all this, Cotton, in league with Senate Majority Leader Mitch McConnell of Kentucky, was maneuvering behind the scenes to derail the outgoing president's effort to remain in office past noon on January 20 and marginalize those Republicans who were abetting him.

Cotton had crossed Trump before—on policy.

The senator was openly skeptical of the president's diplomatic gambit with North Korea. Dictator Kim Jong-un and, before him, his father, Kim Jong-il, had enticed Trump's three predecessors to provide crucial humanitarian aid to prop up their failing regime in exchange for what turned out, every time, to be false promises to mothball, if not dismantle, their rogue nuclear weapons program.

"The last three administrations have been Charlie Brown to North Korea's Lucy in that they've granted concessions for the mere act of sitting down to talk," the senator told me in an interview at the time. "It would be deeply foolhardy to do so once again."

Cotton also resisted Trump on criminal justice reform. This was hardly a sideshow for the president. Passing what turned out to be his signature bipartisan legislation was a major part of his political strategy to improve his standing with African American voters and win reelection in 2020. The White House invested a significant amount of political capital into convincing a Republican-controlled Congress to abandon its opposition to the bill. In the US Senate, McConnell and other key Republicans relented, paving the way for passage. Not Cotton, however.

From the inception of Trump the politician, Cotton exhibited a preternatural understanding of the future president's psychological peculiarities and demonstrated an intuitive grasp of the near religious fervor he inspired among a MAGA fan base that was part Republican and part plain Trump.

For the forty-fifth president, all politics was, and still is, intensely personal. More than commitment to the policy agenda that seemed to rev up so many of his loyal voters early on—the border wall, the Muslim ban, trade protectionism—Trump valued deference to himself. Treat Trump "nice," a word he used ubiquitously in tweets and interviews responding to others' views of him, and he was happy with you. Likewise, treat Trump "nice," and his legion of grassroots supporters were happy with you, too. And so from the earliest days of Trump's first campaign, amid the occasional policy disagreement or public admission of reluctance to follow Trump down the road of this or that issue, Cotton assiduously courted Trump *personally* and avoided breaking with him *politically*. In July 2015, roughly one month after Trump entered the race for the GOP presidential nomination, the Arkansas Republican Party invited the upstart outsider candidate to headline its big annual "Reagan-Rockefeller" fund-raising dinner in Hot Springs. (The gala is named for an iconic Republican president, Ronald Reagan, and a Republican governor from an iconic family, Winthrop Rockefeller, who became the first GOP chief executive to lead Arkansas post-Reconstruction when he was elected in 1966.)

As it turns out, Cotton couldn't make it. The senator was scheduled to travel to Europe with Kansas congressman Mike Pompeo. Today, Cotton and Pompeo are budding rivals for the Republican presidential nomination.

But back in July 2015, Cotton and Pompeo were simply close friends who collaborated on foreign policy matters and were headed to the Vienna, Austria, headquarters of the International Atomic Energy Agency to investigate the secret side deals President Barack Obama negotiated with Iran as part of the Joint Comprehensive Plan of Action accord. The "Iran deal" as it is known, was reached in conjunction with China, Russia, and US allies Great Britain, France, Germany, and the European Union. The agreement was intended to freeze Tehran's fledgling nuclear weapons program before it reached full maturity and became an existential threat to Israel and other American allies in the Middle East. Basically, Cotton had more important things to do than glad-hand at a fund-raiser for the state party. But aware that Trump might interpret his absence as a personal snub, Cotton telephoned the insecure reality television star in advance to explain. The senator reassured Trump that his trip abroad was not one of those convenient tricks politicians use to avoid politically uncomfortable situations, nor a silent protest against the Arkansas GOP's decision to tap Trump to keynote the Reagan-Rockefeller dinner. Cotton told the seemingly long-shot presidential contender that he was glad the party asked him to head-line the event and pleased he'd agreed to it. It was their first conversation. Trump, satisfied, talked Cotton's ear off about Iran and immigration. He praised the senator for his hard-line opposition to the Iran deal and made mention, approvingly, of their shared approach to immigration policy. But just in case, to buy a little insurance, Cotton told Trump before hanging up that he was sending his parents to the fund-raising gala as his proxies. From then on, whenever they talked, Trump would ask the senator about his parents.

For the next five and a half years, through scandal and controversy and tweets, Cotton navigated the minefield that is Trump much the same way. He moved deliberately and worked proactively to preserve their rapport—and by extension, preserve his connection to the potent move-ment of voters the forty-fifth president had inspired. It worked...until it simply couldn't.

In the weeks after the November 3, 2020, election, as Trump's aggres-sive multistate legal effort to overturn his defeat foundered in court after court, the outgoing president and his die-hard supporters zeroed in on a new would-be remedy: overturning the Electoral College. To say that Cotton was not swayed by Trump's theory of the case is an understatement. But as is his habit, he wanted to be thorough. In early December, Cotton directed legislative aides on his US Senate staff to research the matter extensively and prepare an exhaustive memorandum. As the senator suspected, it made plain that the Constitution had not, in fact, built in a secret back door for Congress or the vice president to invalidate presidential election results duly certified by the states. In other words, the constitutional argument sold to Trump by his Conspiracy-Theories-Are-Us legal team and a few other populist hangers-on was bogus. In mid-December, after the states had certified their results and the Electoral College had voted, Cotton read in McConnell. Together, they plotted to countermand Trump's bid to overturn the election and neutralize interest in objecting to Biden's victory that was developing in some quarters of the Republican conference.

The majority leader had stubbornly refused to acknowledge Biden's victory, or refer to his former US Senate colleague as president-elect, prior to the December 14 Electoral College vote. McConnell insisted that Trump's legal challenges to the outcome in various states were a normal part of the process and that the results would not be set in stone until then. Once things were official according to that standard, McConnell declared the 2020 election decided and congratulated the president-elect on his victory. It was at this point that McConnell moved aggressively, and very openly, to discourage Republicans from objecting to the electoral count.

Publicly, Cotton remained noncommittal, worried that Republican infighting could tank the party's chances in two January 5 runoff elections in Georgia that would determine the balance of power in the US Senate for the next two years. If Democrats won both, they would control fifty seats and the majority, courtesy of soon-to-be vice president Kamala Harris's tiebreaking vote. McConnell, it goes without saying, shared those concerns. So even as Cotton privately counseled colleagues to follow the majority leader's prompts and ignore Trump's pleadings, he urged that at the very least they all keep their powder dry until Wednesday, January 6, to avoid an intraparty row that might blow up in their faces in Georgia on January 5.

That was Cotton's original strategy—say nothing until Wednesday, ahead of the joint session of Congress to ascertain Biden's 306–232 Electoral College advantage (Trump's exact margin over Democrat Hillary Clinton four years earlier). That morning, in an op-ed the senator planned to publish in the *Arkansas Democrat-Gazette*, he would argue that objections to state-certified electoral votes were unconstitutional and threatened the viability of the Electoral College, and declare his intent to support certification on that basis.

Cotton's strategy was derailed. On December 30, Hawley became the first fly in the ointment. Despite harboring little desire to run for president, the young, intellectual populist is oft-mentioned as a 2024 contender because of his telegenic looks, Ivy League pedigree, and attempts to channel Trumpism into a coherent ideological framework and tangible legislative agenda. One week before certification, Hawley announced that he would object. He singled out Pennsylvania's twenty electoral votes but signaled he might try and throw out votes from several more states.

"Congress should investigate allegations of voter fraud and adopt measures to secure the integrity of our elections. But Congress has so far failed to act," Hawley said as part of a lengthy statement that cited recent Democratic precedent for his objections.

A few days later, on Saturday, January 2, Ted Cruz one-upped Hawley. The Texas Republican, a traditional, Reagan conservative with a combative streak, was runner-up for the GOP presidential nomination in 2016 and is almost assuredly running again in 2024.

Rather than act as a lone gunman, Cruz brought reinforcements, announcing plans to object to Biden's Electoral College victory with the backing of ten Republican colleagues in the US Senate. Rather than target one state's certified results, Cruz and his gang of eleven (including Cruz) would seek to block half a dozen: Pennsylvania, Arizona, Georgia, Michigan, Nevada, and Wisconsin, making the baseless claim that they were not "lawfully given" nor "legally certified." Rather than just object, Cruz and his cohorts were pushing a detailed plan to delay certification while an audit of the results of the 2020 election was conducted by a government-appointed panel that might yet anoint Trump the winner of a second term.

"Congress should immediately appoint an Electoral Commission, with full investigatory and fact-finding authority, to conduct an emergency 10-day audit of the election returns in the disputed states. Once completed,

individual states would evaluate the Commission's findings and could con-vene a special legislative session to certify a change in their vote, if needed," Cruz said in his statement, issued jointly with Senators Mike Braun of Indiana, Marsha Blackburn of Tennessee, Steve Daines of Montana, Ron Johnson of Wisconsin, James Lankford of Oklahoma, and John Kennedy of Louisiana, plus senators-elect poised to be sworn in: Bill Hagerty of Tennessee, Cynthia Lummis of Wyoming, Roger Marshal of Kansas, and Tommy Tuberville of Alabama. With 25 percent of the Senate Republican Conference now on record as planning to object, what started out as a trickle with Hawley threatened to become a flood as members worried how they would explain to their voters in the next GOP primary that they had abandoned Trump in his most desperate hour. The lame duck president had already threatened John Thune, the Republican whip and No. 2–ranking senator in the conference behind McConnell. When reporters started peppering Senate Republicans with questions about whether they would bow to Trump's demands to void the election, Thune, who for four years offered nary a criticism of the president, responded bluntly that there was no basis for Congress to toss Biden's victory and that objection efforts would fail "like a dog."

Trump responded swiftly, vowing on Twitter to back any South Dakota Republican who challenges Thune in the party's 2022 primary. With momentum building behind Cruz, Cotton reevaluated. He hopped on the phone with McConnell and the two mulled strategic options for undercutting what they feared would be a "bandwagon effect" in favor of objecting. After some discussion, McConnell urged Cotton to speed up his timeline for announcing his opposition. The majority leader had been aggressively whipping the issue. But he believed Cotton, with his conservative bona fides and reputation as a Trump loyalist, might be more effective at talking teetering Senate Republicans off the ledge by providing political cover to those who privately wanted to stand behind the certification of Biden's victory but feared the political consequences back home.

Cotton agreed. On Sunday evening, January 3, within hours of the swearing in of the 117th Congress, two days before the Georgia runoffs, and three days before the certification vote, the senator dropped that bombshell of a 327-word statement. It read in part:

> I share the concerns of many Arkansans about irregularities in the presidential election, especially in states that rushed through election-law changes to relax standards for voting-by-mail. I also share their disappointment with the election results... Nevertheless, the Founders entrusted our elections chiefly to the states—not Congress. They entrusted the election of our president to the people, acting through the Electoral College—not Congress... I'm grateful for what the president accomplished over the past four years, which is why I campaigned vigorously for his reelection. But objecting to certified electoral votes won't give him a second term.

The violent siege of the US Capitol, perpetrated by grassroots Trump supporters aiming to overturn the election, ended up changing a few minds. Rather than a dozen Republican objectors, just six voted to throw out Biden's win in Arizona, with the same six, plus a seventh, voting to excise his victory in Pennsylvania. Additionally, while Republicans in the House of Representatives were unmoved by the insurrection and continued with attempts to force a debate over the results from six or more states, Republicans in the Senate declined to join them in that effort, save for Hawley. He insisted on following through with plans to object to Pennsylvania even after the Capitol was ransacked and members of Congress, and Pence, were sent fleeing for their lives. But even before the riot, the number of objectors never snowballed beyond the Cruz eleven; Hawley; Senator Kelly Loeffler, who had been ousted the day before in one of the Georgia runoffs; and Senator Rick Scott of Florida, an aspiring 2024 contender and the incoming chairman of the National Republican Senatorial Committee. Scott, a former governor, revealed in a statement the morning of January 6 that he would support objections to Pennsylvania's electoral votes *only*. Two senior members of McConnell's leadership team, Thune and Senator John Barrasso of Wyoming, No. 3–ranking as conference chairman, emphasized that the whole thing would have gotten completely out of hand if not for the stand taken by Cotton.

"Tom played a very important role, especially as people were starting to waver," Thune told me on Friday, January 8, with the shock of what amounted to an attempted coup, albeit an amateur coup, still fresh in the air. "He took a risk coming out Sunday rather than waiting quietly until Wednesday; he knew it wouldn't be popular with the base."

"His statement was very strong," Barrasso added in a telephone interview from Wyoming the same afternoon. "It came at a critical moment."

———

At the zenith of Trump's power over the Republican Party, when it seemed there would be no exception to the Fifth Avenue rule, some GOP insiders were sure they were spotting the seeds of discontent. The forty-fifth president was stuck in the past. Voters, as they are wont to do, were shifting their gaze to the future. What were the Republicans in charge in Washington, or Republicans like Trump, who claimed to be in charge or vied to be in charge, doing about today's problems versus yesterday's? What were they doing about Biden?

Cotton is no-frills. He doesn't scream larger than life and will never be all things to all people—a helpful skill when running for president that some of his competitors do in fact bring to the table. But he has a knack for fighting the right fight, the fights grassroots Republicans most want their leaders to fight, and does so like a dog with a bone. If there's a market for a "tastes great, less filling" version of Trump, and sales take off, Cotton, or a Republican a lot like him, could hit the jackpot.

CHAPTER THREE

Our Discontent

In a moment of pique, **Heath Mayo** hopped on Twitter and vented:

> Instead of CPAC this year, principled conservatives should huddle at a different hotel during the same days (Mar 1-2) to stand up & reject CPAC's steady abandonment of our principles. Or just grab some drinks and apps somewhere while we air grievances. How many of us are left?

The twenty-nine-year-old financial consultant wasn't being serious. He was just frustrated, like a fair number of Republicans who were trying to make sense of what was happening to their party. What had, in fact, already happened.

Mayo had spent the ensuing months doing what many dismayed Republicans found themselves doing at the outset of the Trump era: ranting, often on social media. Not so much about the president—although, yes, about the president. But even more so, about all of the Republicans in Congress, statehouses, and think tanks that inspired Republicans like Mayo to believe in Reagan-era conservatism—and who rarely failed to scold those who strayed out of bounds. Suddenly, the rule makers jettisoned the rulebook. After decades of excommunicating apostates, the Republican Party's ideological enforcers traded in their pocket Constitutions for *The Art of the Deal* and fell in line behind Trump with barely a whimper. Mayo was furious. About all of it.

On a mid-February day in 2019, it was CPAC that happened to get his dander up. Mayo had knocked on doors for Rubio's presidential campaign in New Hampshire, South Carolina, and Florida, where the White House hopeful's campaign crashed to an ignominious end. In the not-so-distant past, Mayo was among the thousands of eager young conservatives who made a pilgrimage to CPAC to hear from prominent Republicans and steep themselves in the ethos of constitutional conservatism. But Mayo fashioned himself more of a political hobbyist than a political activist. Other than visits to see his girlfriend, trips to Washington were not a part of his usual itinerary. But on this day, at the outset of year three of the Trump presidency, Mayo scanned the guest lineup for the conference and was appalled like only a political activist can be appalled. *Candace Owens?* he thought. *Charlie Kirk?* Even worse: *Sebastian Gorka and Jeanine Pirro?* He was incredulous.

"Be honest. Is this really your idea of a conservative celebration—or even a good time?" Mayo mocked in a tweet so dripping with contempt that even Trump might have appreciated it. "What does the 'C' in CPAC even stand for anymore?"

Mayo pitched sidearm for the baseball team at Brown University in Providence, Rhode Island, and earned a law degree from Yale in New Haven, Connecticut.

But he was raised far from the liberal halls of the Ivy League, in Texas. Not just Texas, but the modest community of Whitehouse in *East Texas*, where fidelity to conservative values is as evergreen as the lush forests of pine, elm, birch, maple, cedar, and dogwood trees that define the landscape. Texas overall has been experiencing a gradual political evolution, as suburban drift toward the Democratic Party and an influx of moderates and liberals lured by the state's low cost of living transform this once deep red bastion of Republicanism into an emerging swing state. But that's to the west, around major population centers Austin, Dallas, Houston, and San Antonio. Out in rural East Texas, a stone's throw from the Louisiana border, where the pickup trucks are often decked out with more frills and are possibly more expensive than the houses they're parked in front of, politics has stood still. In Smith County, home to Mayo's hometown of

Whitehouse, population 8,800, Trump in 2016 won a whopping 69.5 percent of the vote. He trounced his opponents again in 2020, capturing 69 percent. Whitehouse, in other words, is a rather unlikely spawning ground for a committed Never Trump activist.

Blood boiling at the thought of what CPAC, and by extension the conservative movement, had become under Trump, Mayo took to Twitter and fired off his not-really-all-that-serious invitation for like-minded conservative expatriates to join him for drinks. To the extent he was remotely serious, Mayo had no intention of organizing any sort of formal gathering to counter CPAC. He was just looking to see if anyone else wanted to join him to drown their sorrows in their beer in what amounted to a group therapy session to mourn the populist devolution of the Republican Party. Back in Whitehouse, a politically interested Mayo had gravitated toward the GOP as he approached adulthood because he believed it reflected the conservative values that had been instilled in him from an early age: self-sufficiency, fiscal responsibility, dignity. On the issue of abortion rights, Mayo was pro-life. Now, as far as Mayo could tell, Trump had transformed the party into a cult that existed to venerate *him*. The carnival barkers being granted precious time on the main stage at CPAC served as yet another reminder to Mayo of this catastrophe. And that was why he was getting so worked up about a political funfest that most rank-and-file voters might not even be aware existed. As it turned out, Mayo wasn't the only card-carrying conservative who felt this way.

"So this was partly in jest, but it turns out CPAC has turned off more than just a few conservatives—and folks are game! Let's try to make this happen. If you're interested, let us know here," Mayo tweeted after his initial "invitation" received more feedback than he'd anticipated, if he'd even thought that far ahead. With that, a Never Trump activist was born.

———

About the closest the Never Trump movement has come to being the cabal its critics claim is a weekly conference call hosted by Jerry Taylor and the Niskanen Center.

Who? What?

The centrist think tank is named for William A. Niskanen, an economist who advised President Ronald Reagan, and is headquartered in plush offices a few blocks from Capitol Hill. In 2015, Taylor, an energy policy wonk, founded Niskanen after defecting from the Cato Institute, a prominent libertarian think tank in Washington where he was the director of natural resource studies. Taylor wanted to provide safe harbor to center-right political figures and policy analysts who believe climate change is man-made and a threat to the future of the planet. He wanted to give them the intellectual space to develop an agenda that would address an issue generally overlooked, if not outright scoffed at, in traditional Republican policymaking circles. The center has tried to function as a waypoint for the politics of moderation and civility at a time when the nation's capital has grown sharply polarized and combative. With no end in sight. For people like me paid to follow the ins and outs of an evolving Republican Party in the Trump era, Niskanen is better known as Never Trump HQ.

Since the first year of Trump's presidency, Taylor, via the center, has hosted biweekly meetings, aka "the Meeting of the Concerned," for the diverse array of disaffected Republican insiders who comprise a loose-knit coalition of Never Trump activists. In the beginning there were maybe about a dozen or so Republicans, maybe two dozen, who had spent years—decades—working in conservative politics. They would gather around a large conference table at Niskanen to commiserate, network, and share ideas for holding back the crimson tide of Trump that was slowly engulfing all corners of the party. But by the time the 2020 presidential campaign was under way, amid a devastating coronavirus pandemic that halted most in-person activities, Taylor was mediating virtual gatherings with several dozen participants spread across the country who were actively engaged in efforts to oust Trump, and in some instances burn down the Republican majority in the US Senate. The meetings continued after Biden defeated Trump in November 2020.

But a secret, conspiratorial cabal? Hardly. That implies a level of centralized plotting, coordination, subterfuge, and execution that simply never materialized across the Never Trump universe. There was even less consensus inside this resistance about what to do if they actually succeeded. The meetings themselves functioned as a debating society, with Never Trump activist A proposing one strategy for dealing with Enemy No. 1 and Never Trump activist B countering that no, I think my approach is better.

However, in the beginning, when Trump was newly inaugurated and a dozen or so Republicans were showing up at Niskanen to figure out what to do about it, the meeting had a real utility in that many of them didn't know who the others were that were like them. For instance, leading Never Trump operative Sarah Longwell, who partners in several high-profile anti-Trump endeavors with Bill Kristol, had never met the editor of the now defunct *Weekly Standard*,* a conservative political journal, until both showed up at a "Meeting of the Concerned."

"Never Trump" is a misnomer, albeit a convenient one.

The moniker is something of a third cousin, once removed, of "Against Trump," the special issue of *National Review*, organized by Rich Lowry, the editor in chief, that was published on January 22, 2016, as part of a too-little, too-late attempt to block a provocative reality television star's populist takeover of a serious conservative political party. It seemed extraordinary at the time. Here was the conservative intelligentsia that fashioned itself the ideological backbone of the Republican Party coming together under one banner to denounce the party's leading candidate for president of the United States in a collection of scathing op-eds. These were big names: radio talker and founder of the Blaze, Glenn Beck; Cato Institute executive director David Boaz; Media Research Center president L. Brent Bozell III; senior fellow at the Ethics and Public Policy Center, Mona Charen; conservative writer Steven F. Hayward; conservative writer Mark Helprin; *Federalist*

---

* Clarity Media Group, parent company of my employer, the *Washington Examiner*, was owner of the *Weekly Standard* when it shuttered the publication in December 2018.

publisher Ben Domenech; radio talker and publisher of the *Resurgent*, Erick Erickson; editor of the *Weekly Standard* and longtime Fox News fixture Bill Kristol; founding editor of *National Affairs*, Yuval Levin; radio talker and Second Amendment advocate Dana Loesch; conservative legal analyst and *National Review* contributor Andrew C. McCarthy; Club for Growth president and former Indiana congressman David McIntosh; *Townhall* editor and Fox News contributor Katie Pavlich; radio talker Michael Medved; Reagan administration veteran Edwin Meese III; George W. Bush administration veteran Michael B. Mukasey; evangelical activist Russell Moore; *First Things* editor R. R. Reno; celebrated Hoover Institution fellow Thomas Sowell; nationally syndicated conservative columnist Cal Thomas; and John Podhoretz, editor of *Commentary*.

As we would quickly learn, the effort floundered. More important, it was short-lived. Many of these conservative thinkers and media influencers ended up throwing in with Trump, concluding it was worth risking their worst fears of what this unconventional antithesis of conservatism *might* do rather than aiding and abetting that liberal scourge, Hillary Rodham Clinton, and accepting as inevitable their worst fears of what they knew she *would* do. Some would choose studied neutrality, neither drinking the Jonestown cocktail nor cutting ties with the GOP's new management. Only a select few would stick with the resistance and end up embracing the Never Trump label by the time Republicans and conservatives (often the same, but not always) who opposed the president, and the political writers who chronicled them, settled on the slogan as a convenient shorthand.

Never Trump Republicans who emerged as the public and most politically active faces of the movement were never as homogeneous as the phrase implies. Some were "Never Trump" with qualifications: "I won't vote for Trump but I won't support his Democratic opponent" for this or that policy reason. Matt K. Lewis, a conservative columnist for the *Daily Beast*, was sharply critical of Trump throughout his presidency and refused to vote for him in 2016 or 2020. But Lewis, devoutly pro-life on the issue of abortion, made clear the position prevented him from mustering a vote for Trump's pro-choice, Democratic opponent in the general election. Others were "Never Trump" as long as Never Trump did not mean voting for self-described socialist Bernie Sanders.

Perhaps it's not surprising, then, that for some Never Trump Republicans, who did not jettison everything they ever believed in just because their party was co-opted by a man who believed very little of it, that Trump hate had its limits. This was a vital concern for committed Never Trump Republicans in early 2020, when Sanders appeared on the verge of closing out the Democratic primary and permanently retiring Joe Biden to his beach house along the Delaware coast.

"I don't know where the movement goes from here," Jennifer Horn, the former chairman of the New Hampshire GOP, lamented to me in early 2020 as Sanders was surging and Biden was slumping.

Of course, for some, Never Trump meant "never, ever, ever—never." Potted plant for president versus Trump? Potted plant. An aging nudnik and fan of five-year planning who seems to believe money belongs to the state, rather than the people who earn it? Sign me up.

But the most consequential fissures in the Never Trump movement, as new organizations activated and alliances formed to undermine Trump's agenda and limit his presidency to a four-year historical blip, were *tactical*. Some never admitted affiliation with the resistance, nor conceded any hint of sympathy for the cause. They kept their head down and worked within the party structure to mitigate the damage being done as best they could. Some stuck to their normal routine, biding their time for a post-Trump future. Some took the route of saving the Republican Party from itself. Others concluded it was a lost cause, and for all intents and purposes tried to speed along the inevitable—or at least extinguish any vestige of power the GOP might cling to in Washington. Some approached the task of sidelining Trump as a hopeful battle of ideas, in the spirit of the optimistic conservatism that dominated the Republican Party from the 1980s to the early 2010s. They set out to reclaim the party by seeking to cultivate a grassroots rebellion against Trumpism and reestablishing a platform for intellectual conservatism in the center-right political space, if not quite under the GOP umbrella. The bare-knuckle brawlers within the Never Trump camp quietly sneered at such "naiveté."

This collection of pre-Trump-era campaign operatives, with battle scars from a lifetime of trench warfare with the Democrats, were convinced there was one way to take on Trump. To quote Jim Malone, Sean Connery's character from the 1987 film *The Untouchables*, "He pulls a knife, you pull a gun. He sends one of yours to the hospital, you send one of his to the morgue."

Maybe the Republican Party could be resurrected...eventually. First, these Never Trumpers insisted, it had to be fumigated.

Interestingly enough, nobody inside Never Trump seemed to have any idea what they were going to do if they caught the car and the forty-fifth president was toppled on November 3, 2020.

———

The first time **Will Hurd** showed up in Eagle Pass he got a lot of funny looks.

The border community in Maverick County, Texas, is around 90 percent Hispanic and every four years typically delivered a majority of its vote for president to whomever the Democrats fielded as their nominee. So, other than the fact that the community was in the congressional district he represented, the folks down in Eagle Pass wondered what the hell this Republican was doing there. Or maybe they just wondered what a Republican looked like up close and personal. Before Hurd and his staffer jumped into the car for the long drive to this Mexican border town on the banks of the Rio Grande, he received plenty of unsolicited advice. "I mean, I don't know why you're going," he was told, "but if you're going to go, focus on your shared opposition to abortion. They're Catholic, you're pro-life, that will help you bridge the Democrat-Republican chasm." Hurd decided to stake his claim at a *tardeada*—a festive "afternoon party" popular among Americans of Mexican descent that can attract hundreds. As an experiment, the congressman asked his aide to closely track the number of people who approached him.

"Keep count," he told his staffer.

Two hundred twelve of Hurd's constituents came up to talk to him, and all of them asked some version of the same question: "Why are you here?"

The advice Hurd was given, to cough up political-speak about abortion, seemed idiotic to him. They did not know the congressman; they certainly didn't know any Republicans. How was he supposed to establish a rapport with this community of rank-and-file Democratic voters, Hurd reasoned, logically yet unconventionally, if he launched into talking points like some sort of prefabricated political wind-up doll about an issue they might agree on but was not a pressing concern?

So how did Hurd handle the very basic question of why he had driven hundreds of miles to hang out with a bunch of people who, theoretically, would vote for his Democratic challenger every single time?

"Because I want to drink beer and eat cabritos," he told them, referring to roast goat, a Mexican dish that is the equivalent of Texas barbecue down there.

That earned Hurd a chuckle. As a strategy, it also worked. The next time Hurd visited Eagle Pass, his constituents offered a handshake. The third time, they opened up about a problem they were having that, as their congressman, he might be able to solve. After that it was all gravy. Hurd dropped in regularly for more formal constituent services events to help residents deal with a variety of issues. They, in turn, welcomed him with trust and open arms. Over time, support for Hurd in Maverick County climbed from an abysmal 11 percent to a respectable 26 percent. The relationships the congressman forged there sustained him in 2018 as an anti-Trump wave swept Republicans from power in the House of Representatives.

When another Texas Republican, George Herbert Walker Bush, died in late November 2018, the outpouring of appreciation for the man and the politician surpassed anything I can recall during his single term as the forty-first president of the United States and the years that followed. He was just the guy that promised, "Read my lips; no new taxes," and then caved under pressure; the guy who squinted at a supermarket price scanner like a caveman who had stumbled onto an iPhone sent back in time. Even Bush's dutiful eldest son, George Walker Bush, who captured the White House eight years after the Democrat who beat his father was termed out of office, seemed to go out of his way to make it abundantly clear that he was a different sort of Texan than the native Connecticut patrician whom Republicans mocked for his pragmatism and Democrats ridiculed as hopelessly out of touch.

But perhaps so many Republicans' newly discovered reverence for Bush 41—president, vice president, ambassador to China, director of the Central Intelligence Agency, chairman of the Republican National Committee, World War II combat pilot—shouldn't be all that surprising in the eagle-eyed hindsight of history, and not just because the passing of time has magnified his achievements and transformed his faults into achievements. For so many who affiliated with and worked in some capacity or another for the Republican Party in the Reagan era, ideology was important but in some ways subservient to the notion that their country mattered, that therefore the politics of their country mattered, and that, to that end, they had chosen to take up with the party of the good guys to fight the good fight. Maybe the Grand Old Party didn't win every election; maybe it didn't fight absolutely as hard as was conceivably possible on every issue, every time, pulling out every stop. But in its occasionally frustrating restraint, the GOP could claim decency, tolerance, and the principle of putting country over party at moments most critical.

Democrats will no doubt wonder what the hell I'm talking about. But this was how the generation of Republicans reared in the politics of the 1980s and 1990s thought about their party and themselves. It was why they believed so deeply in the work they did, and why they were okay with helping to elect Republicans who did not always share these sacred values. It is why so many are horrified by Trump but have kept quiet about it, unwilling to abandon the hopeful, aspirational, big-tent center-right party they still believe is lurking in there somewhere, if only it is given an opportunity to reemerge. Talk to Republicans at the tip of the Never

Trump spear. They will tell you it is this group of shy Trump haters, the Republicans who stayed—not them—who will emerge with the credibility among Republicans, voters and operatives alike, to engineer a clean break with Trump and lead the party back to the future. If that's even possible. If there's even any interest. That's why a Republican like Hurd matters.

During the last four years of a six-year congressional career that coincided with Trump's first term, Hurd was a favorite go-to for the press every time the president mouthed off (or tweeted off). And that was a lot. Hurd is an African American, the product of a black father and a white mother. He represented a majority Hispanic swing district that ran from the outskirts of San Antonio in the east, along 820 miles of the southern border with Mexico all the way to the edge of El Paso in the west. The seat consists of a decent portion of suburban and exurban San Antonio, modest working-class border towns like Eagle Pass, and lots of rural grassland dotted with mining, ranching, farming, and oil and gas concerns. It is home to lots of immigrants, particularly Mexican immigrants and their descendants. So naturally, a Washington press corps that enjoys Republican-on-Republican violence chased after Hurd every time Trump rang the ringside bell. It was no different outside of Washington, like the time Hurd joined *Real Time with Bill Maher* in February 2019 for a good-natured grilling from the popular HBO television host.

"Isn't the biggest security threat to America the president of the United States?" Maher asked Hurd, during a discussion about Trump's habit of accusing US intelligence agencies of being part of a "deep state" conspiracy to overthrow his administration.

As in many interviews Hurd granted during his tenure in Congress, he did not, under questioning from Maher, shy away from criticizing Trump's actions or policies. But the political satirist was pressing Hurd to unequivocally repudiate Trump personally and sever all ties.

"But I feel like if you were really speaking up, you would speak out against the president and you would break with him," Maher said.

Hurd pointed to a sharply worded op-ed he published after Trump carried water for Russian strongman Vladimir Putin after their summit in Helsinki, Finland, during which, with Putin standing alongside him at a joint news conference, he said he trusted the former Soviet spy chief more than US intelligence.

Maher wanted more. "So, isn't the next thing you say: 'We have to impeach this president? We have to somehow get rid of this president?' Do you honestly think this president puts country first—which is what you did in the CIA."

Hurd wouldn't bite. "I agree when I agree; I disagree when I disagree."

During the first of two impeachment inquiries that came some months later, Hurd, a member of the House Select Committee on Intelligence, asked pointed, process-oriented questions of witnesses, responding periodically with "good copy, good copy," to acknowledge that he understood their answers, a nod to his career as a CIA spy working undercover in hot spots like Afghanistan. Hurd voted against impeaching Trump. He said the president did not break any laws, therefore failing to meet his standard for impeachment. Zero House Republicans joined Democrats in the vote that made Trump just the third president in history to be rebuked with impeachment. It was nonetheless a clarifying moment. On the burning question, for Republicans, of whether they were in or out with a president that prizes loyalty above all else, Hurd was in. And yet.

Behind the scenes, the congressman was maneuvering to chip away at Trumpism and reposition the GOP as a broad and inclusive coalition. There are signs that Republicans began to make headway in that direction in 2020 among nonwhite men, although Trump came nowhere near winning the national popular vote, a task that continues to elude the GOP, much to the chagrin of party elders.

Hurd was troubled by trends that showed either decline or debilitating stasis with suburban voters, women, Hispanics* other than South Florida

---

* Postelection surveys of verified 2020 voters revealed that Republicans ended up making real gains among Hispanic voters across the board, garnering 38 percent of their vote, according to the Pew Research Center.

Cuban Americans, Asians, the college educated, and the young. Basically, any American voter other than a white man older than thirty. He wanted to do something to reverse the rapid decomposition of the party. After his experience as one of two black Republicans in Congress by the time he retired, Hurd concluded that he could have a bigger impact on the party, and therefore the country, if he were freed from the political demands of running for reelection in a swing district every two years. Hurd's consideration of a bid for the Republican presidential nomination in 2024 is not any more complicated than that. It's in character.

Hurd's decision to leave the CIA and run for Congress in the first place was born of a frustrating exchange he had with one lawmaker in Afghanistan while he was in-country running US clandestine operations. During a briefing, it became clear to Hurd that this lawmaker didn't know the difference between a Shia Muslim and a Sunni Muslim despite having spent years as a member of the Permanent Select Committee on Intelligence in the House of Representatives. How can American policymakers make effective policy if they don't know the basics after all these years of the United States waging war in a critical jihadist hot spot?

Hurd ran for Congress to change that. Now he would build a national political operation to tackle a new problem. It began, somewhat quietly, in 2019, with Hurd PAC. Via his political action committee, the congressman began donating to candidates running in Republican primaries for Congress who reflected his vision for the party, candidates who, however subtly, were the unmistakable antithesis of Trump.

In at least one instance, Hurd played in a GOP primary for the sole purpose of ousting Steve King, a member of Congress who, perhaps more than any other Republican, represented the embodiment of Trumpism. Long before Trump, King built a national following as a prominent border hawk. From the homogeneous confines of his rural district in northwestern Iowa, King warned that a tide of illegal immigrants from Mexico threatened to overwhelm American society. But King didn't stop there. He declared too much legal immigration a problem, claiming a flood of new arrivals would dilute American culture, leaving the United States diminished as a beacon of Western civilization. Toward what turned out to be the end of King's career, he was banished from his committees in the House of Representatives for questioning why "white nationalist" and "white supremacist" were offensive terms, suggesting that the Judeo-Christian values upon which the United States is based are a product of white people and majority white Western countries. In what turned out to be King's final GOP primary in Iowa's Fourth Congressional District, Hurd (and ultimately many other Republicans) endorsed challenger Randy Feenstra, who proceeded to retire what had for years been among the most coveted endorsements of the Iowa presidential nominating caucuses.

Meanwhile, through Hurd PAC, the congressman endorsed a slate of nine Republicans: eight House candidates, one Senate contender. Reflecting Hurd's priorities, six of the nine were military veterans. Also like Hurd, most were successful. Seven of the eight House candidates he backed were sworn into office when the 117th Congress convened on January 3, 2021. Six advanced after winning highly competitive general election contests, including incumbent California representative Mike Garcia, who topped his Democratic challenger by a mere 333 votes.

The second piece of Hurd's bid to go national is Future Leaders Fund, the super PAC opened on his behalf by close confidant and Republican political consultant Justin Hollis. The group can accept contributions in unlimited amounts and affords Hurd a crucial political platform that could serve as a forerunner to a presidential bid. Even before Hurd retired from Congress and was permitted to direct the organization's activities, it began playing a significant role in Republican primaries with candidates that fit Hurd's big-tent mold of a party less dependent on the quadrennially shrinking white vote. Future Leaders Fund invested in Wesley Hunt, a black Army combat veteran who ran for Congress in 2020 in Texas's Democratic-trending Seventh Congressional District encompassing suburban Houston; Tony Gonzales, the Hispanic Navy veteran of the Iraq War who ran in Texas's Twenty-Third Congressional District—the seat Hurd vacated; August Pfluger, a white Air Force veteran who flew combat missions and won an open contest for Texas's Eleventh Congressional District in 2020; Stephanie Bice, who defeated Democrat Kendra Horn in Oklahoma's Republican-leaning Fifth Congressional District; and Ashley Hinson, a former journalist who challenged a Democratic incumbent in Iowa's First Congressional District.

———

The Lincoln Project doesn't do subtle.

The smashmouth, Never Trump super PAC, run by a renegade band of Republican strategists, produced some of the most scathing attacks on the forty-fifth president of the last four years. That's not compared to just the other Never Trump political groups. That's compared to *all* groups, of *all* political persuasions. The Lincoln Project spots were acutely personal and had little to do with any policy differences. Much the way Trump mercilessly assaulted his political opponents and other critics, the group's ad makers put Trump's character flaws under a microscope—and flayed him. In one digital ad, the Lincoln Project blamed Trump for deaths caused by the pandemic. "Donald Trump has recovered from COVID-19. But more than 200,000 Americans will never recover from Donald Trump," the group charged in the spot, which was posted online in October 2020 after the president was discharged from Walter Reed National Military Medical Center, where he was treated for the coronavirus.

Because of the money the Lincoln Project raised (more than $85 million in less than two years), the notoriety of its founders, a splashy feature by CBS News's *60 Minutes*, plus the viral videos, the group cast a long shadow over other Never Trump outfits. Indeed, in the eyes of many rank-and-file voters, the Lincoln Project came to embody what they thought of when they thought of a Never Trump Republican. Democratic voters loved their ads. So did Republicans who had totally rejected Trump and weren't going to come around—no matter what.

However, some of the most important players in the Never Trump movement didn't think much of the Lincoln Project's strategy, questioning its effectiveness with coveted, fence-sitting Republican voters who appreciated Trump's policies but were disgusted by his behavior. But on balance, the Never Trump movement gave the Lincoln Project two thumbs up. The founders of the group were so high-profile, some were even public figures in their own right. The Lincoln Project's very existence acted like a gigantic permission slip for lifelong Republican voters who wanted to throw Trump overboard but were unsure whether they could bring themselves to pull the lever for a Democrat for president.

In other words: If Stuart Stevens, the chief strategist for 2012 Republican nominee Mitt Romney's campaign, could do it; if Steve Schmidt, the campaign manager for 2008 Republican nominee John McCain, could do it; if George Conway, veteran Republican lawyer and husband of Kellyanne Conway, deputy campaign manager for Trump's 2016 campaign, could do it... You get the picture.

Some weeks after the 2020 election, as the Lincoln Project took a victory lap, group cofounder Reed Galen acknowledged publicly what by then was painfully obvious: "At this point, we're as much Never Republican as we are anything else," he told *Politico*'s Laura Barron-Lopez and Holly Otterbein.

Trump hadn't been the Lincoln Project's only target. The group distinguished itself from other Never Trump organizations by declaring the entire GOP to be party non grata. Even pragmatic Senate Republicans, like Maine's Susan Collins, had to go, the Lincoln Project claimed, because she was a Trump enabler. So the group waged an ultimately failed effort to exterminate the Republican majority in the US Senate. Yes, Republicans lost control. But credit for the two devastating runoff losses in Georgia that turned the chamber over to the Democrats belongs to Trump.

In any event, there's a word for Never Republican—*Democrat*—and a whole political movement dedicated to the proposition that Republicans should never hold power. It's usually referred to as the Democratic Party. Galen, accidentally or not, had revealed not just what the Lincoln Project was, but where, politically, the group belonged—and it sure as heck wasn't the center-right.

Then again, they may not be accepted anywhere on the spectrum of American politics at this point, if there's anything left of them by the time voters head to the polls again in 2022, never mind 2024.

Before Trump had cleared out of the White House to make way for Biden, the Lincoln Project began to unravel. First, after being exposed in press reports, cofounder John Weaver admitted that he had been using his position to sexually harass young men. Top officials with the Lincoln Project—those who hadn't already headed for the exits—professed ignorance amid allegations that they were fully aware of Weaver's behavior. Next, Federal Election Commission filings revealed the fact that the Lincoln Project had become a cash cow for its most senior founders, with their preexisting businesses—and, presumably, their personal bank accounts—reaping tens of millions of dollars in revenue from advertising and other political services the organization funded from donations. That tawdry revelation begat infighting over who was getting paid what. It was all very messy, all very public, and all very Trump-like. One by one, many of the Lincoln Project's most prominent founders and advisers stepped away, with some calling for the organization to fold. The Lincoln Project, George Conway tweeted March 8, 2021, "should shut down...I know LP's supporters want to continue to fight against Trumpism, and I urge them to do so in some other way."

In retrospect, the hatchet men over at the Lincoln Project were obvious. Media savvy and versed in the dark arts of political combat, this battalion of Never Trump Republicans would almost inevitably take the road most traveled and join forces for a no-apologies campaign operation to cut off Trump's second-term prospects at the neck. And they would inevitably attract the most attention. **Sarah Longwell** was the surprise.

Other than a stint as board chairwoman of the Log Cabin Republicans, a refuge for Washington's small but influential community of politically active gay Republicans, Longwell didn't really do trench warfare politics. Longwell's specialties were policy and public relations, crafts she honed under Washington super-lobbyist and Republican advertising maven Richard Berman. Longwell was a lifelong Republican who overlooked the party's historic opposition to same-sex marriage and latent hostility to gays and lesbians because she believed the GOP was a responsible governing party committed to Reagan-era, reformist conservatism on most of the critical issues that animated her personal politics.

Trump displayed no particular animus toward same-sex marriage, by now declared the law of the land by the US Supreme Court. Trump would even appoint the very capable Richard Grenell, a gay Republican passed over for prominent foreign policy posts over the years because of his sexual orientation, as ambassador to Germany, a key ally of the United States. Trump also made Grenell acting director of national intelligence.

Longwell wasn't interested. Trump was not conservative. He was making a mockery of the Republican Party. Absolutely worst of all, the president threatened to undermine American democracy—*the* fear that fueled the Never Trump movement. Longwell was catalyzed. By the time Biden found himself limping through the early primary states of the Democratic Party's 2020 presidential primary, Longwell had launched and overseen a variety of political organizations that existed solely to oust Trump.

With one group, Longwell tried to turn the Russia investigation into an albatross for Trump. The federal probe into Russia's meddling in the 2016 presidential campaign was led by former FBI director and special counsel Robert Mueller. It didn't work.

Longwell tried to recruit prominent Republican critics of Trump to challenge him in the 2020 Republican presidential primary. Most visibly, Longwell and collaborator Bill Kristol pitched Maryland governor Larry Hogan. Didn't work.

Longwell figured Trump's blatant attempt to hold American military aid to Ukraine hostage in exchange for dirt on Biden and his family to undercut the former vice president's White House bid would finally elicit pushback from Republicans in Congress. She approached the impeachment inquiry in the House of Representatives and subsequent trial on two articles of impeachment in the Senate with a sense of optimism. Didn't work.

Notwithstanding the very real rebuke Trump suffered in the 2018 midterm elections, the forty-fifth president weathered the controversy, emerging with his political standing remarkably stable and within striking distance of reelection. But amid those failures, a few of the projects Longwell pursued bore fruit. She assumed the role of publisher of the *Bulwark,* the online Never Trump publication she cofounded with Kristol and other *Weekly Standard* expats after the indispensable home for neoconservative thought was closed by its owners.

Longwell also got into the focus group business. To escape the Beltway media bubble and figure out what drove support for a politician she could not imagine supporting under any circumstance, Longwell held dozens of sessions with swing-state voters who supported Trump in 2016—particularly women. First it started out as a form of therapy, and an open-ended research project. "What the heck had happened in 2016?" Longwell wanted to know. As she formulated a strategy to impact the 2020 election, the information Longwell collected in those focus groups became the building blocks for a messaging campaign she would use to subvert Trump among the very voters who put him in the White House in the first place.

But first...Biden needed a little help. It was January 2020. Sanders was surging in the Democratic presidential primary and the former vice president was sputtering, holding out hope the South Carolina primary on February 29 would salvage his third White House bid and save him from an embarrassing hat trick. Team Trump was rallying for "Crazy Bernie," trying to give the socialist Vermont senator a boost in a bid to extinguish the one viable, mortal threat to the incumbent's reelection.

In fact, if Democrats were serious about electability, they'd nominate the guy who actually won primary contests and proved he can play David to Goliath in key places four short years ago. Sanders bested Clinton in 22 states in 2016, including battlegrounds such as Michigan, Wisconsin and Minnesota, while earning more than 13 million votes and 1,800 delegates.

—Kellyanne Conway, adviser to President Trump, writing in the *Washington Post* on January 23, 2020, thirty-seven days before the South Carolina Democratic presidential primary

The Crooked DNC is working overtime to take the Democrat Nomination away from Bernie, AGAIN! Watch what happens to the Super Delegates in Round Two. A Rigged Convention!

—Donald Trump, writing on Twitter on February 18, 2020, eleven days before the South Carolina Democratic presidential primary

Their meddling gave Longwell a germ of an idea. If Team Trump could interfere in the Democratic primary, so could she—but on behalf of Biden, who stood a better chance against the president in the general election. Or, to be more precise, stood any chance. Tim Miller, the veteran Republican consultant turned outspoken Never Trump political operative, helped transform Longwell's idea into an executable game plan. Miller, who is gay, spent what seemed like a lifetime in Republican politics in Washington as a pithy, slice-and-dice communications strategist with a sharp eye for narrative: spokesman for the Republican National Committee; spokesman for former Utah governor Jon Huntsman's 2012 presidential campaign; spokesman for former Florida governor Jeb Bush's 2016 presidential campaign; original cofounder of America Rising, a Republican super PAC that concentrates on digging up, and weaponizing, opposition research against the Democrats. After Bush's White House dreams faded, Miller pivoted to Our Principles PAC, possibly the first of the anti-Trump groups, in a bid to block the Republican front-runner from the nomination. Miller, then, was more than a Never Trump gun for hire; he was a true believer.

Skip ahead four years. Miller had left Washington and decamped to the Bay Area of Northern California. With the first votes of the 2020 presidential primaries about to begin, Miller and his like-minded circle of Republican expatriates were talking about what they were going to do. They weren't voting for Trump—obviously. But with a remotely viable GOP challenger failing to emerge to give them another Republican option, what to do? Should they vote in the Democratic primary? Could they? If they wanted to, and if they could, how would that work, logistically?

All of that got Miller thinking that there might be a lot of Republican voters, or independents who regularly participated in Republican primaries in states with open nominating contests, who were like him and his friends: contemplating voting Democrat for the first time in their lives but with no idea how to go about it.

Together, through Center Action Now, a political nonprofit they founded, Longwell and Miller married the ideas of giving Biden a leg up in the Democratic primary by playing in states that allowed non-Democrats to participate, boosting the participation of disaffected Republicans and center-right independents. The plan was to generate votes for Biden by encouraging registered Republicans, conservative independents, and swing voters opposed to Trump to support a so-called moderate alternative to Sanders—and educating them how to do so. Longwell and Miller had a pretty good idea of who these voters might be, too.

Between the approximately three hundred thousand people who had signed up to support Republicans for the Rule of Law, the group Longwell and Kristol started to support the Russia investigation, plus subscribers to the *Bulwark*, she had amassed a decent list of prospective voters, many of them living in the suburbs, who identified as moderates, Republican-leaning independents, and soft Republicans who tended to be unhappy with Trump's leadership and open to supporting his 2020 Democratic challenger. With the purchase of additional voter lists and bolstered by knowledge of the electorate gained through her focus group work,

Longwell and Miller ran a very robust but very under-the-radar digital campaign, text messaging and the like, targeting these voters. It wasn't a persuasion advertising campaign. Center Action Now was not specifically advocating for Biden. It was simple electioneering: show up and vote. Longwell and Miller figured if their target audience participated in the Democratic primary, they were more likely to punch the chad for Biden; former South Bend, Indiana, mayor Pete Buttigieg; or Minnesota senator Amy Klobuchar than they were Sanders (and by extension, überprogressive Massachusetts senator Elizabeth Warren). And that was good enough.

In New Hampshire, where the effort started, Sanders still won. But Buttigieg and Klobuchar finished a close second and third. In South Carolina, where Longwell went next, Biden resurrected his campaign with a resounding victory. There, she focused on turning out voters in suburban Greenville, in the Upstate region. Next, Longwell took her turnout game to suburban Dallas and Houston, in Texas, as well as Virginia. Both Super Tuesday states helped Biden solidify what was then a growing lead in nominating delegates. This effort was the progenitor of Republican Voters Against Trump, the group Longwell and Miller would unveil next to elect Biden, the eventual Democratic nominee who they had a hand in boosting at a critical time.

As much as Longwell and Miller despised Trump, they learned something along the way that some of his detractors, especially the Democrats among them, couldn't come to terms with. He had won in 2016 because so many Republican voters who would never countenance a racist, or an authoritarian, or a crook, didn't think he was any of that. Was Trump the dictionary definition of "moral rectitude"? Obviously not. Personally offensive and taken to hyperbole? Obviously yes. But the country was broken and maybe this pragmatic businessman provocateur could fix it. And that was the thing—in the swing states that matter in presidential elections, a majority of voters didn't see Trump as particularly ideologically threatening. This image, and pure, unadulterated distrust in and distaste for Clinton, helped the 2016 Republican nominee hold on to traditional Republican voters while expanding the GOP tent by adding a bunch of white working-class Democrats and former Democrats. This crucial community of traditional Republican voters was not tiring of Trump because of the record number of conservative judges he appointed to the federal bench, or because he moved the US embassy in Israel from Tel Aviv to Jerusalem, or because he championed a historic $1.3 trillion overhaul of the federal tax code.

No, what gave them pause was his conduct (the frothing, impolitic tweets and public utterances): the chaos in Washington that he fomented, that he thrived on, of which the most troubling aspect was his seeming lack of command over the government response to the coronavirus and his penchant for spraying gasoline on the fire of racial unrest that gripped the country in the aftermath of George Floyd's death. Longwell and Miller figured out how to reach those voters, and where they could make a difference—states like Arizona, North Carolina, Pennsylvania. (Biden won two out of three.) They listened to disappointed Trump voters in focus groups and tested advertising. Mean spots that hit voters smack in the face with the litany of Trump's supposed failures, the stuff the Lincoln Project was peddling, were a turn-off. This is the sort of politics Trump practiced that they were, theoretically, trying to get away from. So instead, they asked Republican voters who pulled the lever for Trump the first time but wouldn't do so again in 2020 to record testimonials and send them in to Republican Voters Against Trump. These became the ads the group ran in major advertising campaigns in key swing states, raising and spending more than $10 million from July to November. The clips commissioned by Longwell and Miller even showed up at the virtual Democratic convention that nominated Biden as a part of the former vice president's strategy to appeal to disaffected Republican voters.

With Trump defeated, Longwell was preoccupied with one question: Now what? Trump was out but Trumpism still lurked. The GOP made gains down ballot; nonwhite support for Trump increased over 2016, and defections among women were fewer than expected, providing Republicans in Washington little motivation, or really, any logical reason, to abandon the forty-fifth president's brand of antagonistic populism.

She was right. When Trump allies filed a specious lawsuit at the Supreme Court to overturn the results of the presidential election, 126 Republicans in the House of Representatives—well over half of them—signed a legal brief in support. House Minority Leader Kevin McCarthy of California and House Minority Whip Steve Scalise of Louisiana, the first- and second-ranking Republicans, respectively, signed on. Some of the signatories quietly disagreed with the effort but were too afraid to cross Trump.

But Longwell was wary of becoming addicted to resistance politics. Burning it all down—meaning the Republican Party—wasn't appealing either. The last time that was tried, by a faction of Tea Party insurgents and allied conservative groups, the GOP, and the country, ended up with Trump.

Longwell preferred to be proactive. She would embrace Republicans she believed showed potential as responsible actors—in the US Senate, Susan Collins, Lisa Murkowski of Alaska, Mitt Romney of Utah, and Ben Sasse of Nebraska. Through Center Action Now and her umbrella of political groups, Longwell would support center-right Republicans and center-left Democrats in competitive primaries, with the goal of elevating pragmatists and kneecapping hyperpartisans on both sides of the aisle. And she would advocate for good-government, "democracy" reforms that might, through federal legislation, hold the worst aspects of Trumpism at bay. Longwell had in mind laws that might prohibit a president from installing his or her children into key, paid roles in the federal government; laws that might prohibit a president from using his or her presidency to enrich his business interests; laws that might codify the custom of major party presidential candidates releasing their tax returns, a custom followed by every major party nominee since Richard Nixon—until Trump.

———

As Election Day 2020 approached, Never Trump grappled with an uncertain future.

The caricature of this motley crew preferred by the Trump Now, Tomorrow, and Forever wing of the Republican Party is that the heretics rejected the forty-fifth president for left-wing fame and fortune. To the extent they believe anything at all, so the caricature goes, these Never Trump dissidents are clinging to some misbegotten dream that if they could just shove the Exalted One out of the way, the GOP would return to "normal." With their benevolent tutelage, of course. The problem with that narrative is that it largely misses the mark. It was about as true as the conspiracy theory, treated as gospel in some quarters of the Democratic Party, that only racist bigots, unconsciously prejudiced or otherwise, could possibly have voted for Trump in the first place—or continued to support him after seeing what they'd seen.

For **Evan McMullin** and **Mindy Finn**, Republicans who you might think of as "OG" Never Trump, two of the original Never Trumpers, the 2020 election didn't settle questions about the fate of the GOP and their place in the party (if they still have one). On the one hand, Trump lost, along the way becoming the first Republican presidential nominee to fall in Arizona and Georgia since the 1990s. On the other hand, he motivated one heck of a turnout for a loser, helping Republicans pick up more than a dozen seats in the House of Representatives, leaving them just a handful shy of the gavel and denying the Democratic Speaker, Nancy Pelosi of California, a governing majority. Although a repudiation of Trump personally—"it's not me; it's you," exhausted voters fed up with the perpetual controversy and political carpet bombing seemed to be saying—the election was hardly a rebuke of Trumpism. The forty-fifth president's populist message of cultural grievance and nationalist pride, intertwined with boilerplate conservative Republicanism, had produced tangible results. But if the election didn't settle matters for McMullin and Finn, who were dismissed by some Never Trump critics as naïve and some Forever Trump critics as narcissistic, the aftermath of the election and events surrounding the Capitol riot on January 6, 2021, might have.

McMullin and Finn were still registered Republicans, a vestige of stubborn hope that the Republican Party they cherished wasn't a complete goner. But they knew better. Never mind that Republican leaders in

Congress were clinging to a defeated president, legitimizing his outlandish claim that the election was stolen as part of a massive conspiracy worthy of the Smoking Man. Most self-identified Republican voters believed Trump, or believed he was on to something. And this was after the horrifying mayhem at the Capitol, not just before. The market for what McMullin and Finn are selling—responsible, conservative governance in the Reagan tradition, preserving small-*d* democratic norms and respecting the outcome of elections—is small by comparison. Maybe 15 percent of the GOP electorate is interested in that kind of an agenda.

But even as McMullin announced in a *New York Times* op-ed that Trump's hold on the Republican Party might force him and Finn, through their group, Stand Up Republic, to lead the formation of a new, political party, they privately conceded the futility of such an effort in our two-party system. Instead, McMullin and Finn were forging ahead with the creation of what can best be described as a reverse Tea Party, beginning in 2022, to field under a separate banner like-minded candidates for Congress in Republican (and Democratic) primaries. After watching Trump use the bully pulpit of the Oval Office to try and overturn a presidential election, they also decided to invest resources to elect candidates for key state and local offices responsible for administering elections who shared their views about the sanctity of the democratic process.

What they had in mind was not quite the Tea Party of the late 2000s and early 2010s, a movement that represented the committed voting base of the Republican Party. But McMullin and Finn figure the 10 to 15 percent of Republican voters not caught up in the Trump rapture are enough to seed a grassroots countermovement that could begin to chip away at Trump mania. And bottom-up, fueled by voters rather than themselves, was the only path they saw to sustained success. Think West Berlin at the height of the Cold War with the old Soviet Union: outnumbered and surrounded on all sides but a symbolic beacon of freedom instrumental in the implosion of the Iron Curtain.

"Soon, we may field and promote our own slate of candidates running on either party's ticket or as independents, but under our ideological banner," McMullin wrote in the *New York Times*. "To advance this vision and support these candidates, we should further develop the infrastructure we've created over the last four years: including data firms, messaging platforms, research capabilities and grass roots networks." Not so naïve after all.

Late in 2016, McMullin and Finn mounted a suicide mission of an independent presidential campaign, helmed by swashbuckling Republican strategist and future Lincoln Project cofounder Rick Wilson. It was a Hail Mary bid to thwart Trump by a couple of earnest, underfunded unknowns, plus a veteran GOP flame-throwing ad maker from Florida.

McMullin and Finn made for an odd coupling. Then forty, McMullin, the presidential nominee, was a nerdy, unmarried Mormon from Utah, a former CIA analyst and ex–legislative aide in the House of Representatives with a rather apolitical résumé. Finn, his vice presidential running mate, thirty-five, was Jewish and a married mother of two (now three) from Houston. Press-shy and quiet, she could be deceiving in her demeanor. The veteran Washington consultant specialized in digital and data strategy at a time when most Republican strategists were still learning what that meant, and until her break with the party over Trump had assembled an enviable résumé working in the upper echelons of Republican politics. (Disclosure: A few years ago, Finn and I sent our children to the same small cooperative Jewish preschool on Capitol Hill.)

The McMullin-Finn ticket dropped anchor in Salt Lake City, operating out of a nondescript, sparse office, campaigning mostly in Utah but also Idaho and a few other western states. Their plan was to siphon votes from skeptical Republican voters who would not support a Democrat, especially Clinton, but might back a ticket of independent conservatives. The goal was to win a couple of red states out west and block Trump from reaching 270 votes in the Electoral College, thereby forcing the race into the House of Representatives, where it would be decided by a vote of state delegations. They would have gladly settled for helping Clinton the same way independent presidential contender Ross Perot had helped her husband defeat George H. W. Bush lo those many years ago.

McMullin and Finn were tilting at windmills. But the Trump campaign was worried enough to dispatch running mate Mike Pence to Salt Lake City to vouch for the nominee, whose personal crudity and vilification of immigrants caused concern among a dominant Mormon population that prefers leaders who are decent and ethical.

"To be quite frank, if someone were to ask me, 'Who did you vote for?' I would be ashamed to tell them that I voted for Trump," a Republican voter in Utah told me while I was on assignment in the state for the *Washington Examiner* that fall.

Trump ultimately won Utah and its six electors by nearly 18 percentage points, although the McMullin-Finn ticket's third-place, 21.3 percent finish succeeded in holding the Republican nominee almost 5 points under 50 percent. For McMullin and Finn, it was disappointing but clarifying.

Within days of Trump's inauguration, roughly ten weeks later, they stood up Stand Up Republic, a political nonprofit organization dedicated to combatting Trump and creating a home for Republicans, both the prominent and the grass roots, who opposed their party's president. Their first action was a television advertisement accusing Trump of kowtowing to Russia's Putin. They aired it on *Morning Joe*, in the Washington, New York, and Palm Beach, Florida, markets, with only one viewer in mind (this predated Trump's falling-out with MSNBC's Joe Scarborough and Mika Brzezinski).

"Is Donald Trump compromised?" the spot's voice-over asked, invigorating a controversy that would animate official Washington for most of the next two years. "How can we trust him if he won't come clean?"

McMullin and Finn were posing rhetorical questions. They didn't think Trump was very capital-*R* Republican, nor lowercase-*r* republican, for that matter—nor very conservative. The authoritarian populist they saw masquerading as a can-do pragmatist, who they were convinced would shred the values and norms of American democracy to get what he wanted, scared the bejesus out of them.

But what to do? McMullin and Finn weren't sure. Was Trump a tumor, and could the Republican Party be cured by his removal? Or was he merely the most visible symptom of the stage four cancer raging out of control across the GOP, with the damage irreversible? It wasn't clear to either of them in the early days of Trump's presidency. That would change over the course of his first year in office. They saw Republicans in Congress cower before the president's vicious tweets, make excuses for questionable actions and provocative rhetoric they publicly condoned while privately pulling their hair out.

Even then, forming a new political party was an option McMullin and Finn considered. They went so far as to brainstorm names on a whiteboard, field-testing a few of them for voter feedback. Gradually, McMullin and Finn concluded that Trump was only the most visible—risible— aspect of this disease of the body politic. Trumpism, they decided, had metastasized, infecting the Republican Party writ large. Removing him wasn't a panacea.

McMullin and Finn decided on a multifaceted approach. Electorally, they hit a few of Trump's staunchest allies in Congress with sharp attack advertising, and ran finely tuned voter turnout operations in select special elections, harnessing Finn's expertise in data analytics and the small but committed grassroots network they built during their 2016 presidential campaign.

Their results were mixed. Roy Moore, the Republican nominee they opposed in a December 2017 special Senate election in Alabama, lost. So did Dana Rohrabacher, a Republican congressman from Orange County, California, who was Russia's biggest cheerleader in Washington when he was ousted in 2018, Trump's first midterm election. But Representative Devin Nunes, from California's Central Valley, was easily reelected. As chairman of the Intelligence Committee in the House of Representatives, Nunes was perhaps the president's highest-profile defender against allegations he colluded with Moscow to win the White House. Republican Steve King also held on, although barely, presaging his defeat in a GOP primary two years later.

In 2020, McMullin and Finn focused on firing Trump. Through

Stand Up Republic's affiliated super PAC, American Values PAC, they sank resources into Arizona and North Carolina, two states where they believed a narrowly targeted persuasion campaign could swing critical votes to Biden from disaffected Republicans and conservative independents who couldn't stomach another four years of Trump. Plans for field operations were sidelined by the coronavirus, so McMullin and Finn shifted to virtual grassroots organizing, deploying paid teams to each state. In Arizona, Stand Up Republic's effort included a quiet strategy to boost Mark Kelly, the Democrat who ousted Republican senator Martha McSally.

Trump won North Carolina with 50.1 percent of the vote. But he came up short in Arizona. Considering Biden's paper-thin 10,457-vote victory there, McMullin and Finn were satisfied with their impact.

Simultaneously, McMullin and Finn began fostering the grassroots counterconservative movement that would take priority post-2020 by focusing on creating a political infrastructure to support it. They went about the task guided by two presuppositions: The movement they hoped to breathe life into would wither if they lorded over it; and whatever they might achieve in the short run would die out in the long run if it depended on Trump hatred to survive.

So McMullin and Finn developed the outline for what is essentially a party platform, borrowing values, ideas, principles, and policies from the pre-Trump GOP that had been thrown in the trash by the party's new, populist management. Free trade, internationalism, fiscal conservatism, and a restrained executive—the ghost of Republican platforms past, with one crucial addition: a call to arms to revive fidelity to small-d democratic norms of behavior that presidents and members of Congress prior to Trump observed despite no compelling laws.

To accomplish their goal of rooting their fledgling movement in grassroots support, McMullin and Finn organized Stand Up Republic affiliates in the states and put them under local management. They made plans for a major grassroots gathering in Charlotte in August 2020, dubbed the Convention on Founding Principles, to coincide with the Republican convention that would renominate Trump. It wasn't clear there would be any interest. Some Never Trump activists were privately contemptuous of the event, deliberately structured like a major-party political convention, sans the nomination of a presidential ticket, although doing so had been fleetingly considered. McMullin and Finn were pleased with the participation: More than 460 "delegates" from all fifty states, Washington, DC, and Puerto Rico took part in the convention, contributing ideas and voting to ratify a document spelling out the principles of conservative anti-Trumpism. In addition, approximately twenty thousand people signed up as attendees. McMullin and Finn were hopeful that from these two categories they had assembled the beginnings of an activist base that would invigorate the "principled Republican" space they imagined when they first moved to oppose Trump and Trumpism.

Another important aspect of the gathering was the speeches. Dozens of prominent anti-Trump Republicans delivered remarks, with slots reserved, strategically, for veteran political activists, former elected officials, aspiring politicians, and previous political appointees, most of them Republicans or former Republicans, in an effort to lend legitimacy and spark further interest among rank-and-file voters. It's from this crowd that McMullin and Finn expect to field candidates for federal office in the 2022 midterm elections and beyond, preferably as Republicans but potentially as independents.

Who were some of the keynote speakers? Former South Carolina congressman Mark Sanford, former Republican National Committee chairman Michael Steele, former Pennsylvania congressman Charlie Dent, former Wisconsin congressman Reid Ribble, and former FBI director James Comey, among others.

———

Remember Heath Mayo?

The self-activated Never Trump activist's activism caught the attention of McMullin and Finn early in Trump's presidency. He shared their philosophy that Never Trump needed to be about more than Trump, and that the movement would never succeed without a vibrant, grassroots foundation. The Tea Party, Mayo decided, was right about one thing, at least: The Republican establishment in Washington, DC, had become too detached from the voters it purported to represent, opening the door to a character like Trump, who understood the mood of the conservative voter—and the problems and anxieties they were confronted with day-to-day.

Mayo knows as well as McMullin and Finn the David-versus-Goliath battle Never Trump is facing in competition with a robust GOP that turned out more than 74 million voters for the former president. But you can't make an impact sitting on your hands. So he would like to work with McMullin and Finn to launch Principles First on college campuses. Through these chapters, Mayo hopes—*hopes* being the operative word— to expose students to his old-school brand of conservatism, win converts, and, at the very least, make them see that the populist fervor offered by Turning Point USA, the college-focused activist group led by Trump acolyte Charlie Kirk, isn't the only game in town. The next Principles First summit, announced within weeks of Biden's inauguration, was scheduled for the fall of 2021, during which Mayo's idea was expected to receive further consideration.

The Democratic and Republican parties had realigned before, sending factions dispirited with change scurrying to the other side. Often they would infuse their new political home with the values they brought with them. It happened that way with some of the early Reaganites, who, like Reagan himself, were former partisan Democrats. It's not that simple for the Never Trump Republicans. The modern Democratic Party is too left-wing for their taste. And besides, grassroots liberals have no interest in making room for a new bunch who opposed abortion rights and revered the Second Amendment. But because they don't want Trump, the Republican Party, where they still feel most at home, doesn't want them. And so there's this faction of Republicans out there on an island, big enough to redirect political currents but not anywhere near big enough to stop them. Just ask Representative Adam Kinzinger. The Illinois Republican, now one of the most recognizable faces of Never Trump, actually voted for the forty-fifth president in November 2020 after refusing to support him four years earlier.

"It wasn't an easy decision in November," Kinzinger told me, when we spoke by telephone a few weeks after January 6. "It came down to: 'Okay, I'll put the policy at this moment right where I need to on this voting thing.' But, man, it was not an easy decision for me. I certainly wouldn't have voted for Biden. But it was not an easy decision."

CHAPTER FOUR

———◆———

Born Again

On the morning of November 9, 2016, **Marco Rubio** picked up the phone and started dialing.

The Florida Republican had just, somewhat unexpectedly, won a second term in the US Senate in convincing fashion. But even more unlikely than that—way, way more unlikely, so it seemed to Democrats and Republicans alike at the time—Donald John Trump, back then a resident of the borough of Manhattan in New York City, was elected president of the United States. No one appeared more surprised than Trump, who, uncharacteristically, was at a loss for words as he delivered a fairly humble victory speech to overjoyed supporters in a cramped hotel ballroom.

The development had a profound impact on Rubio. The senator arrived on Capitol Hill in 2011 a Tea Party darling, the embodiment of the Republican Party's nostalgic return to its Reagan-era small-government, free-market, up-by-your-bootstraps roots. He was hailed the savior of a GOP whose white voting base was shrinking as a percentage of the electorate and, to be blunt, dying out. Rubio was Hispanic, the son of Cuban immigrants who fled dictator Fidel Castro's prison of an island nation. Like Ronald Reagan, he could deliver a damn good speech. And, just like Ronald Reagan did, Rubio was going to make fiscal conservatism in vogue again. Only Rubio was going to do it for a younger, increasingly ethnically diverse American electorate.

"I think you all know that I've always felt the nine most terrifying words in the English language are: 'I'm from the government and I'm here to help,'" President Reagan said during a news conference in August 1986. Rubio could say it in fluent Spanish.

By now, there's a good chance you've heard the story of Rubio's humble working-class roots. But, as the kids say, ICYMI (in case you missed it): His mother was a maid, his father a bartender. But somehow, by the grace of God and the American Dream, they cobbled together a middle-class upbringing for Rubio and his siblings. Bought a house, sent their kids to good public schools, took the occasional vacation—the quintessential twentieth-century American immigrant success story.

If this brief retrospective sounds curt, it's not meant to. It's an appreciation of the familiar. My own family's American story rings similar, although a generation removed. Instead of running from Fulgencio Batista (and staying away because of Castro), my forebears fled the Russian Cossacks, who I suppose did us the favor of chasing us out of Europe before the Nazis could murder us. "Only in America...," my father, a first-generation American and child of the Great Depression, used to tell my sister and me, emphasizing the endless possibilities available to us just by virtue of the fact that we happened to have been born in the United States. There is a point I'm trying to make here: This lived experience of a hopeful, upwardly mobile America that was already plenty great, made possible by free markets, free trade, and investments in the blood of US troops and the treasure of taxpayer dollars overseas—cementing our status as the globe's reigning superpower—acted like a centrifugal force on Rubio's personal politics. It shaped the public policy he championed, first as Speaker of the Florida House of Representatives, then as a US senator, and ultimately as a leading Republican candidate for president in 2016. Trump's triumph, leavened by what Rubio learned traveling the United States during a yearlong presidential campaign that ended with a blowout loss to Trump in his home-state primary, changed all of that. There was a reason so many voters were drawn to an aging, dour baby boomer (two, really, if you count Bernie Sanders's penetration in the Democratic primary) who ran on a message of a down-and-out America that needed to be made great *again* over the chipper Generation X'er promising a "New American Century." Blue-collar voters in the heartland didn't think the old American century had worked out so great for them. For happy warrior Rubio, it was quite a culture shock.

And so as the freshly reelected senator dialed up aides the morning of November 9, 2016, he was in a hurry. He wanted to immediately get to work charting a policy agenda that reflected the country that had revealed itself the day before; the country that, in retrospect, he realized had been revealing itself all along as he campaigned for president. By extension, Rubio was staking his claim to this realigning Republican Party and altering course to carve a path to the GOP presidential nomination in 2024. Some will quibble with Rubio's assessment of Trump's seismic victory, and for all sorts of reasons, competing theories of the case are viable. At the very least, Rubio concluded that the Republican primary voter imagined by conservative Washington think tanks and political insurgency groups who claimed to speak for the conservative grass roots was just that: imaginary.

Rubio walked away from his year as a supporting character in the Trump show with another epiphany, one with critical implications for the 2024 primary campaign to come. There is a Seven Mile Bridge–wide disconnect between the wealthy, culturally liberal free-marketeers who funded his campaign and the culturally conservative, middle- and working-class GOP primary voters whom he used their money to appeal to. Rubio wanted to bridge the divide. Quickly. But it wasn't like he could just adopt Trump's playbook. Because there was none. Other than promising to build a wall and rip up trade deals, Trump was all political id and cultural zeitgeist. Rubio, at heart, was always grounded in policy.

Well, Rubio, at heart, was always a normal politician. He wanted white papers; he wanted guiding principles; he wanted legislation; he wanted...to govern. Rubio decided to fill in the blanks. The shift elicited scorn in some corners of the party. There he goes again, chasing the latest shiny object, some of Rubio's Republican critics told me—repeatedly and unprompted.

"You have Marco, who is a butterfly," a GOP strategist mocked. "Marco goes to every brightly colored flower and sticks his nose right in the middle of it and takes a little bit of honey and stands in front of it to see if anyone's looking at the flower."

That's their retrospective view of the senator's foray into the political minefield of comprehensive immigration reform in 2013. Immigration reform was a hot topic in the Republican Party back then. Mitt Romney had just been defeated by President Barack Obama, and many GOP insiders blamed the outcome on their nominee's hostile relationship with Hispanic voters (just 27 percent of this growing segment of the electorate supported the future US senator from Utah). I heard more of the same in the spring of 2020, after Rubio played a leading role in the crafting of Republican legislation to reform policing in the aftermath of George Floyd's death. This was despite the fact that racial equality had been front and center on his public policy agenda since his days in the Florida Legislature.

"He's out there bouncing all over the board, and he almost sounds like a joke now," a graybeard Republican strategist told me.

But Rubio's surprising, Trump-induced pushing of the boundaries of what it means to be a conservative Republican appears to be so much more than a passing fancy. Four years later, Trump is no longer president and Rubio is still at it. For now, at least.

———

Rubio's second term in the US Senate unfolded much differently than had his first. In an about-face from his first six years on Capitol Hill, Rubio sidelined his political operation almost completely and focused on policymaking. Many of Rubio's supporters scratched their heads in disbelief. It's not that he would prioritize lawmaking that mystified them, especially in a Republican-run Congress with a Republican in the White House, so much as his apparent choice to allow relationships he worked so hard to build in 2016 to atrophy.

The entirety of the senator's first term was an exercise in laying tracks to run for president—and then actually running. From Rubio's perspective, it was just as well. Barack Obama was president, and for the first four of those six years, Republicans in the US Senate were under the yoke of Nevada's Harry Reid, the wily Democratic majority leader. There was nothing much else to do but politick.

Not that Rubio didn't try to make himself useful. During a brief interlude following the 2012 presidential election, Republicans decided an electoral strategy that revolved around white voters needed some updating. The Republican National Committee commissioned a so-called autopsy, the predictably dubbed Growth and Opportunity Report, that called for the party to diversify its governing coalition. Back then, even Trump thought Republicans were screwing themselves with Hispanic voters, complaining in late 2012 that Romney had alienated this key voting bloc with harsh rhetoric and insensitive immigration policies. Encouraged by GOP insiders, among them Mitch McConnell of Kentucky, the Senate minority leader, Rubio did his part for the cause by joining high-level bipartisan negotiations in the US Senate to craft a sweeping overhaul of American immigration law. The package was to include a path to legal status for the approximately 12 million illegal immigrants living and working in the United States. Not only did Rubio answer the call of duty, but his participation in the group of four Democratic senators and four Republican senators that became known as the "Gang of Eight" was considered the linchpin to the whole effort. Rubio was supposed to give the legislation the imprimatur of Tea Party approval and reassure suspicious grassroots conservatives and hostile right-wing media personalities that the bill's border security provisions were real and substantial.

The legislation died an anticlimactic death. Rubio's presidential aspirations did not, however. The countdown to the launch of his 2016 White House campaign continued apace. Building an email file of small grassroots donors; establishing relationships with wealthy Republican donors who could write six- and seven-figure checks and bundle millions from their lucrative networks of business associates and personal contacts; lining up top Republican operatives and super volunteers to staff the campaign in the key early primary states of Iowa, New Hampshire, South Carolina, and Nevada. Publicly, Team Rubio was downplaying everything, reticent of appearing to be doing exactly what they were doing. That was then.

In his second term, there hasn't been much to downplay. After Rubio won reelection, his political operation went into hibernation. The plan was to stand up a campaign in time to mount a viable 2022 reelection bid, which Rubio did in the spring of 2021. Unlike the indecision that clouded Rubio's Senate plans in 2016, a third go-round was greenlit from the outset. Rubio bristles at the griping about his political operation and disputes that outreach to supporters went dark after his presidential campaign ended.

"I don't know what they base that on," Rubio told me. "Generally speaking, I remain in touch and engaged with a bunch of people from all over the country, on a regular basis, that we met and worked with during that campaign."

But in interview after interview, many Republican operatives and insiders in Washington and around the country who raised and bundled money for his 2016 White House bid grumbled to me that the senator went radio silent. He doesn't call; he doesn't write. For instance, simple thank-you notes for all their hard work. What a waste of a national political network, which, incidentally, Rubio created from scratch and those involved were proud to affiliate with. That's no way to set the table for a 2024 presidential bid, they lamented with a mixture of resignation and disappointment. An exasperated 2016 Rubio bundler recalled admiringly the senator's enthusiastic community of campaign contributors. Many were rookie political donors in their thirties and forties, inspired to participate by the young Florida senator. Some did more than write checks; they hosted fund-raisers and joined the ranks of his bundlers.

Four years later?

"They have never heard from him since," this individual told me. "He spent zero energy maintaining that donor base—at all. Like, nothing. All those people now have gone through a whole other life cycle and forgot about him to a large degree. He just does not endear a lot of loyalty."

These are the sorts of criticisms that paint the picture of a politician who didn't much enjoy running for president and isn't in a hurry to get back in the game. But Rubio hasn't lost the bug. He wants to run again. And in 2024, one major challenge from last time will no longer be pertinent for this married father of four. When Rubio 2016 launched in the spring of 2015, his children were ages fourteen, twelve, nine, and seven. Being away on the campaign trail for weeks at a time created enormous pressure on this family man and proved to be a major distraction. In 2023, when his next White House bid would start rolling, most of his kids will be grown, turning twenty-three, twenty-one, eighteen, and sixteen before November of that year. As Rubio looks ahead to a second White House bid, he has simply decided to do it his way. He spent 2009 and 2010 running for the US Senate, nearly six years running for president, with the tail end of that period consumed by his running for reelection to the Senate. After eight years of nonstop campaigning, Rubio wanted to get back to policymaking.

Regarding that: Some Republicans familiar with Rubio since he was a wunderkind speaker of the house in Tallahassee will insist to you that the senator has always been a not-so-secret populist. In 2008, he endorsed Mike Huckabee in the Republican presidential primary and was the state chairman of the Arkansas governor's Florida campaign. It's hard to remember this far along, but Huckabee was doing the white-working-class schtick before Trump popularized it in GOP circles. Or before the forty-fifth president made it acceptable, at least. Huckabee had picked up on the fact that the Republican base was full of blue-collar voters who supported GOP presidential candidates because they were culturally conservative. They were fervently pro-life on the issue of abortion rights and fiercely protective of their Second Amendment right to own firearms. They weren't necessarily fiscally conservative in the classically Republican sense, and perhaps thought to themselves: It might be nice, for a change, if somebody from the federal government showed up in *my* community and said, "I'm here to help."

Huckabee didn't have to give Rubio the hard sell. The state legislator and future US senator walked into a hotel suite in South Florida where the dark horse GOP presidential candidate was holding meetings and quickly offered his support. "I'm not going to make you chase me," Rubio said. "I'm in." The senator himself is less inclined to lean on the crutch of "This is who I've been all along." What Rubio experienced on the stump throughout a yearlong presidential campaign, validated by Trump's success, persuaded him to try and reimagine a Republican portfolio of issues that had not been seriously updated since Reagan. Step one was to adapt Trump's guttural pseudo-policy utterings into a new, coherent conservatism the senator believed would better serve the new constituency he had just recently discovered.

"When you're not evolving, you're not changing—not your principles, but your views on things—then what's the point of learning?" Rubio said. "What's the point of acquiring information if you're not going to put it to use?"

———

In a significant move, Rubio sought out **Henry Olsen**.

Olsen is a senior fellow at the low-key Ethics and Public Policy Center, a Washington think tank, and a columnist for the *Washington Post*. For more than a decade, Olsen has studied the ins and outs of the American electorate, examining voter attitudes and behavior in midterm and presidential elections. Perhaps no academic analyst inside the Beltway bubble understands the demographic and societal forces driving the ongoing realignment of the Democratic and Republican parties as well as Olsen.

The political phenomenon that in 2016 produced a President Donald Trump? Olsen picked up on the stirrings of white working-class voters in heartland communities in states like Michigan, Pennsylvania, and Wisconsin, as well as Iowa, Ohio, and others, much earlier. In 2010, Republicans reclaimed control of the House of Representatives after just four years out of power with a record gain of sixty-three seats fueled by candidates, and voters, who identified in some fashion or another as "Tea Party" conservatives (in the modern lexicon, *Tea* being short for "Taxed Enough Already"). The Republican wave in that election was in large part a political revolt against Obamacare, which Democrats called by its formal name: the Affordable Care Act. President Barack Obama's massive overhaul of American health care was pushed through Congress by big Democratic majorities in the House of Representatives and the US Senate. The law, intending to eliminate the ranks of the uninsured, forced Americans to purchase health coverage or pay a fine and retrofitted the nation's private health care system with a series of federal mandates dictating what sorts of policies were available for purchase. On the right, the rejection of Obamacare was mythologized. Republican political consultants, party officials, and elected politicians, among them the Tea Party insurgents at odds with the GOP establishment, saw in the uprising a conservative rebellion against big government, excessive spending, higher taxes, and the creeping hand of socialism. Conservative and mainstream journalists tended to share that view. The political backlash sparked by Obamacare was, in actuality, a whole heck of a lot more complicated. It had little or nothing to do with achieving the minimalist federal government of libertarian daydreams or reforming entitlement programs like Medicare, Medicaid, and Social Security—high-minded goals on the GOP front burner in the immediate pre-Trump era.

Olsen saw this. He accurately diagnosed the social convulsions of cultural and economic disruption and understood that Republican electoral advances in 2010 (and 2014 with the party's takeover of the US Senate fueled by a nine-seat flip) had been driven by an electoral voting base that wanted, that *craved*, intervention and protection from the government against the forces and efficiencies of untrammeled free markets, international trade, and abundant immigration. It's no wonder that Obama was reelected in 2012 over a Republican challenger running as the embodiment of conservative Republican orthodoxy as promulgated by the so-called Chamber of Commerce wing of the GOP and doctrinaire think tanks in Washington. No Republican running for national office bothered to tap into the ideology and policy preferences animating the Republican coalition, as it had evolved, until Trump. And while there are plenty of fortuitous circumstances that can explain his victory over Hillary Clinton, there are few, in retrospect, that explain away his success in the Republican primary and the uncommon loyalty of the party's voting base.

Olsen got it. He wasn't the only political intellectual Rubio talked to for counsel after the election as he reconsidered conservative dogma and actualized an agenda. Rubio met with Oren Cass, the executive director of American Compass, a group that describes its mission as one to "restore an economic orthodoxy that emphasizes the importance of family, community and industry to the nation's liberty and prosperity."

And he talked to J. D. Vance, a polemicist and venture capitalist who moved back to his native Ohio and, in 2021, announced a 2022 US Senate bid. Vance's best-selling memoir, *Hillbilly Elegy*, made into a motion picture by Netflix, tells the story of a societal and familial breakdown in the kind of heartland communities that for so long have felt ignored by so-called elites in Washington, and who flocked to Trump in 2016 because he was the only Republican (or Democrat) running who they felt understood them, who cared about them.

But of all whom Rubio sought out for intellectual guidance, Olsen was pivotal—in more ways than one. In Rubio, Olsen saw a fellow traveler of sorts. Olsen had spent years diving into voter data to figure out what motivated American voters for an ongoing project called "the Voter Study Group" and poured much of what he learned into a book he published in June 2017, *The Working Class Republican: Ronald Reagan and the Return of Blue-Collar Conservatism*. Rubio picked all of this up the old-fashioned way—by campaigning. He entered the race for the Republican nomination in 2016 a conservative product of Miami's liberal, urban culture and the Cuban diaspora's unfettered faith in American pull-yourself-up-by-your-bootstraps free markets and freedom from government. He emerged from the campaign having seen a completely different side of the United States, one that arguably had been trampled by free markets, or at least left behind by its benefits, one that desperately wanted to pull itself up by its bootstraps but first needed some help to come by a pair of boots. Through conversations and email exchanges that went on for months, Olsen helped

Rubio translate what he learned into a philosophical framework that could serve as the basis for a conservative legislative agenda. The other role Olsen played in Rubio's evolution was equally consequential: that of headhunter.

———

In January 2018, Rubio was in the market for a new chief of staff after he was forced to fire longtime aide Clint Reed because of misconduct allegations involving his interaction with subordinates (the specific nature of the complaints was never made public). At the same time, Rubio's one-time nemesis, Michael Needham, was looking to exit Heritage Action for America, the combative political arm of the blueblood conservative Washington think tank the Heritage Foundation, where he was nearing his ten-year anniversary as chief executive officer. As Rubio went about making sense of Trump, Needham was similarly digesting the results of the 2016 election while beginning to ponder a career move. When Needham became CEO of Heritage Action for America in 2010, Arthur C. Brooks, then president of the American Enterprise Institute, urged the young professional activist to cap his tenure at ten years to avoid outliving his ability to be effective and innovative. Needham figured Brooks would carve out an exception for himself. When Brooks took his own advice, it really made an impression.

Needham got to know Olsen because of his work as an adviser to the Voter Study Group, and became something of a devotee. As such, Needham was not exactly taken aback by Trump's conquest of the Republican Party. He had argued for years that Republican insiders in Washington needed to start taking seriously the grievances of their party's most committed voters and stop telling them, essentially, what was good for them.

So many Republicans, not just Never Trump Republicans, were flabbergasted that the party of Reagan could countenance Trump's big-spending, debt-ridden management of the federal balance sheet. Needham believed the incredulity would be fair if the party of Reagan was instead the party of Barry Goldwater, the US senator from Arizona and Republican nominee for president in 1964, who planted the seeds of the Reagan revolution that would unfold sixteen years later. Over the years, Needham argues, Republicans have misremembered the Reagan presidency and confused the iconic conservative with Goldwater libertarianism, timeless and unchanging regardless of circumstance. And as remembered, Reagan's agenda of ambitious tax cuts, shrinking the size and scope of government, and projecting American military power abroad became dogma from which GOP presidential candidates would not depart.

Hence the shock waves sent by Trump, who threw it all overboard. Yet Needham saw key similarities between Reagan and Trump, not in guiding principles or a governing agenda, of which Trump offered little, but in the forty-fifth president's ability to pinpoint the problems voters were facing in the moment, rather than forty years ago, and his ideological adroitness, enabling him to consider solutions fit for the times even if they ran afoul of conservative orthodoxy. And if, like Needham, you remember Reagan as something of a refined, principled populist who cared less about the *size* of government than its bureaucratic stranglehold on American life, then Trump's disruption of Washington, and the Republican Party, begins to look a lot more familiar—and so does Rubio's post-2016 pivot.

If Rubio seemed an unlikely Republican to carry the mantle of Trump populism after Trump, Needham would seem all the more unlikely to help him do it. Ten years Rubio's junior, Needham was reared in wealth and raised in affluent Upper East Side society in New York City. He enjoyed top-notch private schooling in Manhattan and graduated from Williams College in Massachusetts and the Stanford Graduate School of Business on the doorstep of California's Silicon Valley. That's hardly the stuff of *Hillbilly Elegy* and a cut above Rubio's résumé any way you slice it. (After moving around a bit, the future senator earned a bachelor's degree from the University of Florida and a law degree from Miami University. Not chump change, but a far cry from Needham's highbrow education.)

Despite his elite pedigree, Needham seemed to grasp the sensibilities of blue-collar populists and the conservative middle class. Five years before Trump's presidential candidacy would ripple like a rolling earth-quake across the Republican Party's established order, Needham launched Heritage Action for America on behalf of the Heritage Foundation, as the think tank sought to do more than just arm Republicans in Congress with ideas—but bring the pressure of grassroots conservative voters to bear to force them to adopt those ideas. In retrospect, some of the fights Needham picked with Republicans in the House of Representatives and the Senate were quaint in how rooted in principled, conservative ideology they were. Needham wanted Republicans to extract concessions from Barack Obama for agreeing to provide their votes to what for years had been noncontroversial legislation to periodically raise the federal debt ceiling—legislation that made it legal for the US Treasury to borrow more money to pay the government's outstanding bills.

Needham wanted Republicans to kill the Export-Import Bank, a little-known federal agency that lends some of the biggest corporations in America money so they can afford to compete with overseas competitors that are subsidized by foreign governments. He said it smacked of crony-ism and that the government shouldn't be in the business of helping big business stay afloat—even, presumably, if American jobs were at stake.

Needham opposed a mundane farm bill, a legislative package that also covers the food stamp program for needy Americans. At the time, the House of Representatives was the only base of power for Republicans in a Washington where Democrats controlled the US Senate and the White House, and House GOP leaders thought they did a pretty good job of negotiating a farm bill with significant conservative reforms. Needham disagreed, apparently, and helped instigate a conservative rebellion in the House to kill the legislation.

Needham also was a driving force behind a quixotic attempt to block the implementation of Obamacare.

In the fall of 2013, a few months after Heritage Action for America helped kill off comprehensive immigration reform, the mischievous conservative advocacy group trained its sights on Obamacare. Texas senator Ted Cruz and Utah senator Mike Lee had come up with an impossible-to-pull-off plan, by which congressional Republicans would force the federal government to shut down unless Obama agreed to halt the implementation of the Affordable Care Act. The law was the forty-fourth president's signature domestic achievement—the Holy Grail of liberal policy that Democrats had tried and failed to pass for more than half a century. Three years earlier, the legislation had cost them more than sixty House seats and seven Senate seats (some of those, but not many, were recovered in 2012). Needham's group got behind the strategy, despite the impossible odds. Heritage Action sponsored forums around the country where Cruz, the primary public face of the strategy, whipped grassroots conservatives into a frenzy, believing Obama would go along with this despite all his party had sacrificed and considering how much of a priority the legislation was for the party for much of its modern existence. The effort would eventually unravel as voters admonished the GOP for the scheme and enough Republicans who supported the Hail Mary relented.

Not exactly a banner moment for Needham the political strategist. But hidden in failure, Needham had correctly identified the mindset of the Republican base. He never took on the Republican Party's pre-Trump, consensus support of free trade and an interventionist foreign policy. He wasn't (and isn't) a culture warrior with a chip on his shoulder like a particular bridge-and-tunneler from Queens. Yet Needham comprehended that at its core, the Republican base was working-class—furious with Washington generally and with the Republican Party specifically. He understood that they felt lied to, if not ignored altogether, and they fumed at the unfairness of a system that the well-connected and well-heeled (like him) navigated just fine but that did nothing to address the problems nagging at their daily lives.

Enter Olsen.

In separate, private conversations that were proceeding simultaneously, Olsen sensed that Needham and Rubio might be a perfect fit at just the right time. He made the introduction and let the two principals handle the rest. Intrigued by the prospect of helping Rubio revive what he viewed as Reagan's true legacy, rather than just complaining from the cheap seats, Needham pitched the senator on taking over as his next chief of staff over dinner in Washington and a series of email exchanges. After a courtship of about four months, Rubio in April 2018 tapped Needham as chief of staff.

The hire raised quite a few eyebrows in Washington. Here was the conservative traditionalist many Republican insiders had recently counted on to save the reigning party establishment putting his US Senate office in the hands of a populist operative who had spent the last decade trying to tear the whole thing down.

Needham, who just a few years earlier had helped sink Rubio's daring effort to reform US immigration law. Needham, who, through the megaphone of Heritage Action for America, fomented a revolt against Rubio on the right, charging that his legislation would provide a blanket amnesty to illegal border crossers and do for immigration what Obamacare did for health care.

But Needham was a perfect match for the Rubio that emerged from the 2016 campaign and the direction he hoped to lead the GOP in the Trump era. Needham quickly became the most influential political adviser in Rubio's orbit, too. In fact, to the extent that the senator's admirers are bullish on his prospects as a presidential candidate in 2024, Needham is the reason they claim confidence in the senator's ability to avoid the myriad mistakes they believe plagued his 2016 campaign.

———

Sometime in early 2019, Needham gave Rubio a homework assignment.

Rubio was working on the scintillating issue of stock buybacks, not usually a topic that caught the attention of Republicans in Washington. Under the practice, companies invest profits not in more obvious economic drivers like hiring, equipment, expansion, or innovation, but to purchase shares of their own stock trading on the exchange. The expenditures are one way for corporations to guard against being undervalued by the market and provide a financial return to shareholders. But Rubio, like most of his Democratic colleagues, saw the flurry of stock buybacks as a clear case of corporate gluttony, especially coming on the heels of the big corporate tax cut he had supported in a party-line vote. The senator also saw the transactions as the consequence of a US fiscal policy that prioritized the wealth of the investor class over the welfare of workers and the well-being of the national economy.

Then chairman of the typically little-noticed US Senate Committee on Small Business and Entrepreneurship, Rubio sought to curb stock buybacks, proposing legislation to discourage the purchases by eliminating their preferential treatment under US tax law and making them less desirable to shareholders. Opponents of the plan labeled it a tax hike, about the worst insult you can possibly hurl at a Republican proposal.

Needham, dissatisfied with how the debate over the bill was unfolding, wanted Rubio to go on the offensive and take control of the narrative. So one evening, Needham emailed his boss a rather lengthy, technical article on the topic, with instructions to read it before returning to the office the next morning. Needham's plan was to use the information in the piece as the basis for a series of tweets making an affirmative case for Rubio's legislation, which the two of them would formulate together. The senator was way ahead of his chief of staff. He had digested the piece on stock buybacks and early the next morning emailed Needham a written draft of what would turn into a nine-post Twitter thread with a short note. "Did I get anything wrong?"

The senator's heterodox enlistment of the tax code to deter stock buybacks was among the policy seedlings that Rubio would nurture into a political philosophy that embraces the use of government power to coerce economic behavior. The senator called it "common good capitalism," and he detailed what amounted to a clean break with doctrinaire Republican policy.

The government, Rubio concluded, had to act to reinject fairness into the compact between employer and employee. The senator almost sounded like he was delivering a socialist manifesto. It was startling.

"What is common good capitalism?" Rubio said. "It's a system of free enterprise in which workers fulfill their obligation to work and they enjoy the benefits of their work and where businesses enjoy their right to make a profit and reinvest enough of those profits to create dignified work for the workers and for America. And our current government policies today get this wrong. We actually reward and incentivize certain business practices that promote economic growth but it's growth that often solely benefits shareholders at the expense of jobs and better pay."

Over the course of Trump's first term, Rubio would become an evangelist for government intervention in the economy. In speeches and essays, the senator urged Republicans and the business community to reevaluate fidelity to free markets, productivity, and profits, and embrace a version of the approach of the Obama administration once ridiculed by elite conservatives and Tea Party activists: picking winners (and therefore losers). Rubio wants Washington to advantage, through legislation and regulation, industries and occupations that inject money and social vitality into languishing blue-collar communities. Rubio believes it would lead to more Americans achieving financial stability and independence, improving familial and communal cohesion.

A year later, Trump would be ousted by Biden and join the ranks of the millions of elderly Florida transplants whom Rubio counts among his constituents. The senator was still at it. This time, in March 2021, he caused a stir by endorsing organized labor's attempt to unionize employees at an Amazon warehouse in Alabama. In an op-ed in *USA Today*, Rubio declared reflexive Republican opposition to Big Labor null and void, even in conservative, so-called right-to-work states like Alabama.

The senator was careful. He opposed Democratic legislation pushed by Biden to undo right-to-work regulations championed by Republicans for a generation and said his position was motivated in part by the cultural liberalism that so many major corporations adopted during the Trump era, even as they continued to lean on conservatives like Rubio for protection from excessive government regulations.

For instance, Amazon had recently announced that it would no longer sell a tome by a respected conservative thinker that questioned the impact of the acceptance of transgenderism. But even suspicious liberals were hard-pressed to dismiss Rubio's support for the campaign in Bessemer, Alabama, to form the very first union of Amazon employees—anywhere.

"One of my earliest political memories was marching with my dad in a Culinary Workers Union strike when he worked as a hotel bartender, and the lesson I took from it—all workers deserve respect—has stuck with me all throughout my career," Rubio wrote in his op-ed.

However else the senator was trying to thread a needle between Democratic and Republican labor policies, he was laying down a marker that the principle of using the power of organized labor to extract better pay and working conditions from corporate employers was wholly legitimate.

———

In the hypercompetitive, cynical world of American politics, especially presidential politics, Rubio's ideological two-step was bound to attract uncomfortable scrutiny and fuel charges of opportunism.

"He's the most talented politician I've ever seen," so many Rubio critics told me unprompted, over and over again. His problem, they would all go on to say in conversation, is that he can't decide who he is. The senator had run for president in 2016 as one kind of Republican—the Reagan kind. As Rubio careened toward an embarrassing, nearly 20-percentage-point drubbing at the hands of Trump in a Florida presidential primary decided by Republican voters who presumably knew the senator best, he warned of unmitigated disaster—for his party and the country—should his populist rival win the nomination, as he eventually would.

"This is a political candidate, in Donald Trump, who has identified that there are some really angry people in America," Rubio said during a news conference in Florida, days before his presidential campaign ended. "That is what he's feeding into. That is not leadership."

The Rubio on display since that day has operated, conspicuously, as a different kind of Republican—not quite the Trump kind, but on matters domestic and cultural, the definitively populist kind. It can all seem rather convenient. And yet Rubio in the Trump years, now the Biden years, has been Rubio at his most content and, in at least one way, his most authentic. Dating back to his tenure in the Florida Legislature in the 2000s when he was a boyish up-and-comer in his thirties, Rubio has always been most comfortable tackling a panoply of issues. Obscure, prominent—it doesn't really matter to the senator as long as he believes it's important.

In 2013, that meant wading into the political quicksand of comprehensive immigration reform.

In 2015, that meant showing up at a mismanaged public housing complex in Jacksonville, Florida—incidentally, in an overwhelmingly African American, Democratic voting precinct. First, Rubio listened to resident complaints about the substandard living conditions, then he stuck around to coordinate a multi-agency government overhaul of the project and used his influence as a senator to place it under new management.

In 2020, that meant sponsoring crucial components of the police reform package proposed by Senator Tim Scott, the African American Republican from South Carolina, and possibly a 2024 rival, amid the social unrest roiling American cities in the aftermath of George Floyd's death.

As chairman of the US Senate Committee on Small Business and Entrepreneurship, Rubio was buried in pandemic recovery work. As acting chairman of the US Senate Select Committee on Intelligence, Rubio was buried in foreign policy and national security matters. But he did not let that stop him from diving into the biggest domestic phenomenon of the moment and using his perch as a US senator to say something about it, to do something about it.

Meanwhile, beginning around 2017, addressing the accelerating US competition with China, the fledgling superpower intent on supplanting American global dominance, became *the* priority around which much of Rubio's legislative agenda has revolved.

In a political culture that deemphasizes mundane but vital governing, and exalts outrageous, celebrity-style trolling, Rubio's immersion in the former has turned him into something of a man out of time.

That's not to say he hasn't tried his hand at playing the provocateur. In 2016, Rubio infamously mocked the size of Trump's johnson. In 2020, while speaking at a Trump rally in Florida, the senator celebrated that an automobile caravan of grassroots Republicans had run a Biden-Harris campaign bus off the road in Texas. Those are just a couple of Rubio's now-and-again MAGA moments. There's a method to it. Republican voters may or may not care about the this-or-that reform proposal that a GOP candidate or incumbent is selling in the heat of a campaign. In the Trump era, they always care if you're willing to fight: fight Democrats, fight the media, fight China, fight so-called big tech—the list goes on. And trolling, particularly the social media kind, has become the primary form of valid identification the Republican base will accept as proof that a politician is willing to fight the fight.

Yet in between these moments, Rubio is consumed with governing, never fully comfortable with the actions he's compelled to take on the campaign trail to preserve the platform nor the notoriety that affords his ability to do so.

"It's a difficult time to be in public service because of that balancing act," Rubio told me during a telephone conversation we had in the late summer of 2020, less than two months before Election Day, with the country still engulfed in a raging pandemic. "There's a price to pay for the decision to deliberately pit people against each other, and often that price comes as the ability to govern at a critical moment."

Rubio elaborated: "What I always remind people of is if 9/11 happened again, now, God forbid, would we as a nation react the same way we did in 2001? I think there's no one that could tell you we would. I think, almost immediately, it would become: 'Whose fault is it?'"

The tightrope Rubio feels as though he is walking, and whether Republican voters have any interest in a leader who would rather govern than provoke, is weighing heavily on his 2024 plans.

Do voters want what he's selling? They didn't last time.

That is the burning question Rubio needs to answer for himself, more so than getting comfortable with mounting a second national campaign on the heels of a two-year campaign to get reelected in Florida, not a certainty but certainly a prerequisite.

"It's not just that if you try really hard and you're the best candidate, you win," Rubio said. "I'm not a surfer, but I equate it a little bit to surfing: You can have the best surfboard in the world; you could be the best surfer in the world. If there's not waves, or if you don't time the waves, you're not going to surf. You don't control that part of it."

The Ronald Reagan Presidential Foundation and Institute is carved into a mountainside in Simi Valley, in the arid hills of Southern California north of Los Angeles.

This mecca to a Republican icon of yesteryear played host to the second presidential debate of the 2016 GOP primary campaign, a September 2015 event made memorable by Carly Fiorina's one shining moment as the only female contender in a sea of men, and to a lesser degree, Scott Walker's one shining one-liner. The Wisconsin governor told "Mister Trump" that "we don't need an apprentice in the White House."

Then Walker faded into obscurity, onstage, for the rest of the evening, and dropped out of the race the next morning. His was the first in a collection of Republican scalps taken by the upstart New York real estate developer and reality television star on his march to the presidency. Five years and two months later, after a single term in the White House, Trump was gone, ousted by Democrat Joe Biden, the seventy-seven-year-old former vice president—and Maryland governor **Larry Hogan** showed up at the Washington offshoot of the Reagan library, a short drive from Annapolis, to dance on his political grave. Where Rubio reacted to Trump by rethinking Reaganism and doing his best to "surf" the waves of change roiling the GOP, Hogan spent the better part of four years stubbornly refusing to throw in with Trump. The governor never voted for the leader of his party and insisted to anyone who would listen that it was a mistake to trade in the timeless, classically conservative virtues of Reagan Republicanism that served the party so well for a generation for the transactional sugar high of Trump's bellicose, culturally polarizing populism. Such talk, sacrilegious in a party where fidelity to Trump became the highest virtue, turned Hogan into a Republican pariah.

But not here, at the Ronald Reagan Presidential Foundation and Institute. The library's DC branch sits in the shadow of the fortieth president's old haunt, occupying space in the gleaming downtown Washington office building on Sixteenth Street Northwest that, appropriately, houses the Motion Picture Association of America, the powerful lobbying arm of the movie industry that employed Reagan before politics.

Here, Hogan was at home. In prepared remarks and a subsequent question-and-answer session, he tore into Trump, accusing the outgoing president of being an abject failure who led the country into a ditch, making a mess of the Republican Party in the process. Subtly, the governor compared Trump to President Jimmy Carter, about the worst insult a Reagan Republican could come up with to slime another politician.

What would Hogan do? The governor said the answer, as forty years ago, lies with Reagan, a Republican president who "went on to truly make America great again." Hogan needled Trump to an audience that nodded approvingly. "Ronald Reagan won two landslide elections and created a movement that endured for a generation because he understood the simple truth that successful politics is about addition and multiplication, not subtraction and division."

Hogan's wide-ranging takedown of Trump's brand of us-versus-them nationalism and the partisan gridlock fomented by both Democrats and Republicans in Washington sounded very much like the kickoff of his 2024 presidential campaign.

After this divisive election, we find ourselves, again, at a crossroads for our party, and at a critical time for our nation. As we search for a way forward, we should look back at how Ronald Reagan transformed our party and restored the greatness of America. Americans believe in civility and pragmatism. They think straight talk is more valuable than empty rhetoric. These are the things that my party is going to have to focus on if we want to win national elections again.

Hogan isn't some crackpot who's never been on the ballot. In 2014, deep blue Maryland boasted the highest per capita percentage of Democrats in the nation. Hogan, a commercial real estate executive and first time candidate for statewide office, won anyway, capturing the governor's mansion with 51 percent of the vote. Four years later, running for reelection, Hogan crushed his Democratic challenger by 12 percentage points, garnering 55.4 percent of the vote.

The governor did it by governing effectively and politicking smartly. Hogan held the line against Maryland's majority Democratic General Assembly where possible and compromised where necessary. Sometimes his vetoes were overridden. He communicated with voters in every community, in every corner of the state, assembling a broad, bipartisan, and multiethnic coalition that carried him to reelection. Impressed, Never Trump Republicans spent the next year wooing Hogan, trying to convince him to run against Trump in 2020 in the GOP presidential primary. The governor was happy to bask in the attention he attracted as a prominent, Republican Trump critic, putting on one heck of a show in interviews with his sharp tongue and quick wit. But in multiple conversations I had with the governor during that period, he assured me he had zero interest in launching a futile "kamikaze mission" against Trump. Which was why Hogan opted to stand pat, determining there wasn't a market for what he was selling, not among Republican voters, in any event.

Which brings us back to that Monday at the Ronald Reagan Presidential Foundation and Institute in Washington two weeks after Trump fell to Biden: Hogan was speaking to a room that was two-thirds empty. Now, *of course*, the governor was speaking in the middle of the deadly coronavirus pandemic, inside an office building, before the availability of the vaccine. The government of the District of Columbia was strictly limiting the size of indoor gatherings, and, no doubt, people chose to attend virtually and watched Hogan via the internet livestream rather than risk contracting COVID-19 by being there in person. But the scene symbolized perfectly the challenge Hogan faces in mounting a 2024 presidential campaign created in the image of Reagan's legacy. It's not clear there would be any takers. Trump indelibly transformed the Republican Party, re-creating it in his image. This remarkable achievement by a man in his early seventies who had never sought public office of any kind and was only nominally associated with the GOP is often compared to a hostile corporate takeover.

As if: Trump was welcomed with open arms by millions of rank-and-file Republicans, and millions more American voters who joined the party because of him. Because he threw conservative orthodoxy overboard. Because of the belligerent tweets. Even in losing, Trump attracted more votes than any Republican presidential nominee in history. Those 74.2 million votes, while well short of Biden's 81.3 million, preserved GOP control of key state legislatures and helped Republicans in the House of Representatives flip more than a dozen seats held by Democrats, leaving them just a handful short of the majority after the smartest political handicappers in the business predicted massive losses. Republican voters didn't walk away from the 2020 elections with buyer's remorse; they walked with regret, bordering on despair, that they missed out on four more years. So much so that when Trump claimed the election was stolen in a massive, coordinated, fantastical conspiracy, a majority of Republican voters believed him.

Hogan, now sixty-five, is a serious politician. He is only the second Republican in Maryland history to win reelection to the governor's mansion. He was chairman of the bipartisan National Governors Association through the worst of the pandemic and in that role ran point on coordination between the White House and the states, balancing his criticism of Trump on the one hand with his close working relationship with Vice President Mike Pence on the other. He has a firm grasp of policy and sharp political instincts, and he is surrounded by experienced advisers. Five weeks after Biden evicted Trump from the Oval Office, Team Hogan produced a slick campaign-style video with clips from his speech at the Reagan library, set to music and dramatic visuals.

"As Reagan said, we are once again at a time for choosing. Are we going to be a party that can't win national elections, or are we willing to do the hard work of building a durable coalition that can shape our nation's destiny?"

But it begs the question: Is anybody watching?

———

About a month after Biden was inaugurated, I met with Hogan in his office in the Maryland Capitol to ask him about that. Annapolis is thirty miles and a thirty-minute drive east of Washington; it feels a world away. Hogan takes great pride in the fact that he goes to work every day in the oldest functioning state capitol in continuous use in the United States, a 250-year-old building where the Continental Congress once met. Maybe it was because the emotional embers of January 6, now six weeks (to the day) past, still hung in the air, but Hogan ventured to guess that Trump's grip on the Republican Party had loosened a bit.

"I was on this life raft, and everybody else was on this ship going by. Well, now, everybody's jumping off the sinking ship, and we need a bigger boat, basically," he said. He would use this analogy later in the conversation, when I asked him point-blank if he was running and if he thought he could be competitive.

Hogan is not that different from the legion of Republican politicians who were molded by Reagan's legacy, except that he is old enough and has been active in GOP politics long enough that, to him, Reagan is more than a nostalgic icon; he is a living, breathing presence. The governor gave me a guided tour of the photographs and other memorabilia adorning his expansive office. Hogan pointed to a picture of himself and his father in 1968, when he was twelve years old and his father was running for Congress. Representative Larry Hogan of Maryland, who served on the House Judiciary Committee that opened an impeachment inquiry into Richard Nixon over the Watergate scandal, would become the first Republican to break ranks and call for the thirty-seventh president to be impeached. The other picture Hogan pointed to was one of himself and Reagan from the early 1980s. The governor was chairman of a youth-for-Reagan organization and was a delegate at both the 1980 and 1984 nominating conventions. Hogan likes to tell the story, as he did in his memoir, *Still Standing*, about serving as an alternate Maryland delegate to the 1976 Republican convention in Kansas City. His father was leader of the faction of Maryland Republicans who wanted to nominate President Gerald Ford. But after hearing Reagan speak from the convention floor, Hogan donned a Reagan hat, grabbed a Reagan sign, and marched in a demonstration supporting the nomination of the former California governor.

So when presented with the argument that the Republican Party has moved past Reagan, Hogan rejects the premise. It's like arguing that vaccines don't work to an American who watched in his or her lifetime as polio, measles, and smallpox were eradicated. The Republican Party was in trouble once before, after Nixon. Reagan was the antidote then, and Hogan simply does not accept that his example, and the political and philosophical principles by which he governed, is not the antidote for that which ails the party after Trump.

And what is that, according to the governor? After all, Trump lost, sure, and Republicans are now the minority in a 50–50 US Senate. But 2020 saw them flip fourteen Democratic House seats, nearly win the majority back after a two-year absence, and register some significant improvements in support from nonwhite voters. Not exactly a party in its death throes, as it appeared after Nixon resigned and the bloodbath of the 1974 midterm elections.

Hogan is worried the GOP is becoming a balkanized party that cannot win national elections. A Republican presidential nominee has not won in anything resembling a landslide since 1988, when George H. W. Bush captured forty states and 426 electoral votes. Since then, in eight presidential elections, a Republican presidential nominee—Bush's son, George W. Bush—has won the national popular vote just once, in 2004. That year, the younger Bush won reelection in a squeaker that rested on 16 electoral votes and 2.1 percent of the vote in Ohio. The first quarter of 2021, with Trump still exerting enormous influence over the Republican Party, saw fewer voters overall identifying as Republicans. Per Gallup, just 25 percent, plus another 15 percent who described themselves as independents who lean Republican, and trending downward. That's compared to 30 percent who view themselves as Democrats and another 19 percent of independents who lean left, creating the biggest advantage in partisan identification the Democratic Party has enjoyed over the Republicans since Barack Obama was reelected in 2012.

And that is what preoccupies Hogan.

"I want to return to a more Reaganesque, big-tent party," he said.

"It was his positive vision for the future," the governor added, that "had a massive appeal to a wider audience" and "won almost every state in the country."

That makes Hogan an unapologetic throwback. Practically every single viable Republican presidential candidate in 2024 is going to position themselves as the heir to Trump and promise to continue his legacy. All of the polling data suggests this is the only viable path to the nomination. Hogan isn't convinced; he sees an opening.

"There are ten or fifteen guys fighting to be the next Trump—men and women. There's no one in this lane that speaks to . . . about 30 percent to 40 percent of the people who actually are now admitting that they feel the way I have."

He corrected himself: "Not no one; there are some folks."

And he's right, there are some—Representative Liz Cheney of Wyoming; Representative Adam Kinzinger of Illinois; Romney. There is a list. But few Republicans with his profile, who are likely to run for presi-dent, have been waging this fight from inside the party as consistently, as doggedly, as Hogan.

"So, I mentioned earlier at the start, the boat, the cruise liner was roll-ing by, and I'm on this little life raft," Hogan said, returning finally to the analogy he used at the beginning of our conversation. "Well, now, there's a lot of people starting to jump off the boat."

CHAPTER FIVE

Born to Run

After being booed off the stage at the 2016 Republican National Convention in Cleveland, **Ted Cruz** retreated to Park City, Utah, to lick his wounds and ponder his political future. Specifically: Did the Texas senator have one? Cruz's quest to succeed Trump as the GOP standard-bearer in 2024 begins here.

Internally, Cruz's political team was torn over how the beaten candidate should handle the convention speech—or, really, whether he should give one at all. At the end of the primary campaign, when Cruz was the last Republican standing between Trump and the nomination, the president's campaign attacked Cruz's wife, Heidi—calling her ugly—and essentially challenged the senator's testosterone count. It was brutal.

On top of that, there was little indication at the time that Trump would turn out to govern as conservatively as he did. That was a bigger problem for Cruz—that Trump would turn out to be the dealmaker he claimed to be but never was and forge common ground with Democrats on all sorts of issues, while nominating judges to the federal bench that were, at best, unreliable conservatives. Given how the primary campaign had concluded, Jason Johnson, Cruz's alter ego and consigliere, wasn't a fan of Cruz speaking at the convention. He advised Cruz against doing so if he was not prepared to give Trump a full-throated endorsement. Jeff Roe, Cruz's campaign manager and chief strategist, believed both the speech and an endorsement of Trump were critical if Cruz was to have a shot at another presidential campaign, or any political future. And to the very end, just before Cruz took the stage, Roe in tandem with Trump campaign manager Paul Manafort was still trying to convince Cruz to insert endorsement language into a deliberate, carefully written speech that would urge convention delegates to vote their conscience—and was already loaded into the teleprompter. The Trump campaign even sent in Texas lieutenant governor Dan Patrick to make the pitch.

But Cruz had modeled the address after speeches by Ronald Reagan and Ted Kennedy, delivered at the 1976 Republican convention and 1980 Democratic convention, respectively, in which neither offered explicit endorsements but the presidential nominees chose to accept their remarks as such anyway in order to unify their parties.

That's not how Trump plays. After Cruz finished, his convention security detail was yanked and the senator and his wife had to push their way through crowds of angry delegates spewing all kinds of vitriol to make their standing invitation to join casino magnate and Republican mega-donor Sheldon Adelson at his suite in the arena. When they finally arrived, Adelson told Cruz and his wife to get lost.

The best way to understand Cruz might be to think of Alex P. Keaton, the rabidly conservative youngster played by actor Michael J. Fox in the classic 1980s NBC sitcom *Family Ties*—minus the aghast liberal, ex-hippie parents. I was raised in liberal Malibu, California, and attended Santa Monica High School, years before Stephen Miller of Trump administration fame—but it was liberal even back then. I didn't know many, or should I say *any*, kids my age who shared my affinity for President Ronald Reagan. I wondered if Alex P. Keaton could represent someone real. He almost seemed like some Frankenstein combination of a comedic nod to Baby Boomer parents with rebellious children and the producers of the show throwing a bone to a country that had so thoroughly embraced Reagan they elected him in two landslides and kept his vice president around for an extra four years to boot. But figuring we were out there, since I was out there: Who in grade school could be that conservative and that interested in politics?

The answer is Cruz. As a teenager in Texas, the future presidential contender donned a suit and tie and traveled all over the state under the auspices of the Free Enterprise Institute, a conservative think tank in Houston, speaking to groups about the US Constitution. Cruz would recite the founding document from memory and then field questions from audiences about its relevance and modern context. At Princeton University, Cruz would write his senior thesis—one hundred pages—on the obscure Ninth and Tenth Amendments in the Bill of Rights. Much of Cruz's initial interest in what would come to be defined as conservative politics had to do with his tutelage. Cruz grew up in Houston, and one of his earliest memories is sitting at his father's feet listening to stories of revolution. Rafael Cruz fled the Cuba of strongman Fulgencio Batista after being imprisoned and tortured for opposing his authoritarian regime, immigrating to a United States he saw as a beacon of freedom in an era when the world was divided between Western democracy and repressive Soviet communism. Cruz also enjoyed similar stories told by an aunt, who fled to the United States from Cuba after being imprisoned and tortured by the dictatorship of Fidel Castro, a thug who replaced Batista's autocracy with his own. And so, the same way so many young boys grow up idolizing their fathers and wanting to emulate them, the young Cruz grew up wanting to be a political revolutionary who fights for freedom. In a typical household of the late twentieth century, interest in politics was about reading the newspaper, watching *60 Minutes*, and voting. Although Cruz is the product of a Cuban father and a white, Irish Catholic mother from Wilmington, Delaware (making her a part of the Joe Biden diaspora, I suppose), politics in the Cruz household took on the urgency of a Cuban household. Politics was not just something you discussed or participated in passively. Politics was a vocation; it was something you were actively involved in. And the politics of the day, especially for an immigrant whose ancestral homeland was a communist police state, was the existential struggle for freedom, with the United States on one side and the Union of Soviet Socialist Republics on the other.

Cruz's other hero, besides his father, was Ronald Reagan. Cruz turned ten years old about six weeks after Reagan was elected the fortieth president. For the following eight years—Cruz's most formative years—he saw in practice, in his eyes, what a modern political revolutionary elected to national office in the United States looked like...

"Here's my strategy on the Cold War: We win, they lose."

"Mr. Gorbachev, tear down this wall."

Cruz was hooked.

Much has been written about what drives Cruz. The senator matriculated through the highest levels of Republican establishment politics; the 2000 campaign and later the administration of President George W. Bush; solicitor general of the state of Texas. That blue-blooded pedigree has led Cruz's critics, and even some admirers, to wonder if all of this rabble-rousing is simply an act of convenience. "CalculaTED," mocked Rubio's 2016 presidential campaign, a take on Cruz's slogan "TrusTED." When Trump gave Cruz the nickname "Lyin' Ted" during that campaign, it stuck—a major problem in an era when voters so crave authenticity, verbal gaffes can actually be a plus.

Cruz's relationships with his colleagues in the Senate were not any better, save for his close friendship with Senator Mike Lee, a Republican from Utah. After Cruz helped bring about some of the Republican Party's lowest favorability ratings on record with his drive to defund Obamacare by shutting down the federal government, and, oh, called Republican leader Mitch McConnell a liar on the Senate floor, senator Lindsey Graham of South Carolina famously joked, "If you killed Ted Cruz on the floor of the Senate and the trial was in the Senate, nobody would convict you."

Cruz's grassroots supporters saw a political outsider willing to disrupt an entrenched political system. So did much of the professional conservative intelligentsia in Washington—the likes of Michael Needham, now Florida senator Marco Rubio's chief of staff, who as leader of Heritage Action for America was a thorn in the side of the Republican establishment. That's certainly how Cruz sees himself. He feels most comfortable playing the role of outsider because he has always felt like an outsider. Growing up, his family life was tumultuous. His parents separated, reconciled, and ultimately divorced in 1997. When he was fifteen, the oil industry business his parents owned went under, forcing them to declare bankruptcy. Cruz emerged a dreaded elitist, in résumé if not in fact. But in the beginning, it was a world he didn't know, one that was intimidating. During his undergraduate studies at Princeton, some of his deepest political discussions were not with classmates, but over the phone with Bill Laffer back in Texas. Laffer, the libertarian son of the celebrity conservative economist Art Laffer, who had worked for Reagan, was about twenty years Cruz's senior and more mentor than friend. Cruz was even made to feel like an outsider by his post-Reagan political idol at the time, his home-state, Democrat-turned-Republican US senator, Phil Gramm. Cruz was so impressed with Gramm's aggressive "over my cold, dead body" opposition to President Bill Clinton's proposal to overhaul the health care industry, he sent a letter to the senator's 1996 presidential campaign offering his services as a volunteer. The letter he received back was cordial enough. It was addressed to some guy with the last name Crews (C-R-E-W-S).

———

If a wake is your idea of a great vacation, then you really should have spent a week with Cruz in Park City in the summer of 2016. He fled to the mountain resort community about thirty-three miles east of Salt Lake City, popular with the jet-set crowd (and Mitt Romney), to reassess the state of his suddenly stalled-out political career after delivering a speech at the Republican convention that landed with a thud.

Losing a presidential election when you actually have a chance to win, versus the prize being a lucrative contract to be a cable television news analyst, is like a dagger to the heart, a punch to the gut, and having a hole drilled in your head—all at once. To clear his head, a depressed Cruz headed to a vacation home owned by Willie T. Langston II, a hedge fund manager in Houston and something of a mentor to the senator, who served as his campaign's finance chairman. Cruz was joined by his wife and two daughters, plus close adviser Jason Johnson and his wife and kids, as he wallowed in despair and uncertainty.

Cruz was not just absorbing the loss of a presidential campaign, which was bad enough. He was having an existential crisis. Though critical of the Republican establishment—well, let's be frank, he tried to take it apart piece by piece until Trump showed up with a blowtorch and incinerated it. But he still thought of the Republican Party as his party. And grassroots Republicans? The voters who were cheering him on as he tried to dismantle the GOP establishment? Cruz had been their hero. After his "vote your conscience" speech at Trump's coronation in Cleveland, the senator was excommunicated by both. Mulling the future in Park City, Cruz candidly confessed to Johnson that he wasn't even sure he could win reelection to the Senate in 2018, an insecurity that proved prescient.

Yes, Cruz was reelected. But he nearly wasn't, defeating Democrat Beto O'Rourke by 2.6 percentage points. And Cruz had to recast himself as a pragmatic legislator, focused on, as the old trope goes, "getting things done," to buy himself that extra 2.6 percent. The break with the old, uncompromising Cruz was stark. In early July 2017, I covered the senator for the *Washington Examiner* as he met with constituents during a town hall meeting in McKinney, an exurban community of approximately two hundred thousand people about thirty-five miles north of Dallas. The amount of time Cruz spent detailing his proposal to repeal and replace Obamacare, and the emphasis he placed on his willingness to compromise with colleagues to pass legislation in the Senate, sounded, stylistically, nothing like the Cruz I had covered up close for nearly five years running.

Meanwhile, in Park City, Cruz was stumped by Trump, unsure what his presidency would look like on the off chance he actually won. Each day that week, Cruz and Johnson went back and forth speculating about what path the GOP's 2016 nominee might take if he beat Clinton, with the underlying theme of their conversations an attempt to figure out what path Cruz should take.

"Is Trump as bad as we think he is? How might he govern?"

They discussed pros and cons. As the week wore on and Cruz's anguish began to subside, the focus shifted to how Cruz was going to claw out a political future in the Republican Party and, therefore, how he was going to find a way to unequivocally endorse Trump for president. The truth is, he loved every minute of the 2016 campaign, except the part where he lost. Rallying voters, a dozen at a time, in intimate, small-town settings? Check. Delivering the big speech to an energetic, standing-room-only crowd? Check. Working a hotel ballroom full of well-heeled donors to raise money? Check. Diving into the campaign strategy sessions with a room full of his top advisers? Check. Drafting a policy agenda? Check. Cruz had every intention of doing it again, has every intention of doing it again. As he would tell me about four and a half years later in an interview for the *Washington Examiner*, "The campaign was the most fun I've ever had in my life."

But first he had to make amends with Trump, because he had to make amends with the grassroots Republicans who had rejected him—who "hate me"—for rejecting a presidential nominee that they were absolutely smitten with. Between Cruz and Johnson, they both agreed that framing an endorsement around the critically important issue of the balance of power on the Supreme Court was the best course of action. After Associate Justice Antonin Scalia died in February 2016, Senate Majority Leader Mitch McConnell refused to give any Obama nominee a hearing, saying it was an election year and that voters should decide which presidential candidate they preferred to have control of the appointment. With millions of Republican voters weighing the same decision, it seemed a plausible way for Cruz to explain his change of heart that also happened to be authentic.

Johnson offered Cruz one crucial piece of advice: If Cruz was going to back Trump, he had to be willing to go all the way, no fancy language or rhetorical contraptions about the endorsement being about anything other than what it was about—supporting Trump 110 percent—or Cruz would never recover.

For all of Trump's faults, and they are legion and legendary, he ended up governing far more conservatively than even many of his biggest supporters ever imagined: hundreds of rock-ribbed conservative judges appointed across the federal judiciary, moving the US embassy in Israel from Tel Aviv to Jerusalem, pulling out of both the Paris climate accords and the deal Obama struck with Iran that was intended to slow the terrorist state's development of nuclear weapons, passing a $1.3 trillion overhaul of the federal tax code that slashed the corporate tax, cracking down on illegal immigration, and negotiating peace agreements between Israel and three Arab nations without making concessions to the Palestinians. It's hard to tell if the Republican base appreciates Trump for these accomplishments or because he is in a constant war against the media and the Democrats. Either way, lucky for Cruz and his political ambitions, he posted this on Facebook on September 23, 2016:

> Our country is in crisis. Hillary Clinton is manifestly unfit to be president, and her policies would harm millions of Americans. And Donald Trump is the only thing standing in her way...If you don't want to see a Hillary Clinton presidency, I encourage you to vote for him.

Cruz and Trump would proceed to have a rather cordial and productive relationship. They talked on the phone often, and Cruz now and again convinced Trump to make this or that policy decision. In 2018, when Cruz was in dire straits versus O'Rourke, Trump even traveled to Houston and put on one of his signature campaign rallies to boost the senator's reelection prospects. (The rally might not have actually done Cruz any good, but it's the thought that counts.) Of course, when Trump ran for reelection two years later and put on a pandemic-altered convention that featured televised coverage of dozens of prominent Republicans speaking on his behalf, Cruz wasn't invited.

"Relatable."

Talk to anyone in the Cruz orbit and they will tell you that the senator's biggest political liability heading into 2024 is that voters cannot relate to him. Away from the campaign trail, the television cameras, and the Senate floor, Cruz can actually come off like a normal dude. He's a father and a husband. He likes good wine, preferably red; he's a movie buff and a Houston sports fan. Have a few drinks with him and he'll talk about that stuff, the normal stuff normal people talk about in a way that sounds...normal and not at all contrived. People who have worked for Cruz will tell you that. I'll tell you that. Catch him at the Capital Grille, a prototypical steakhouse—wood paneling, red booths, great martinis—a short hop from Capitol Hill, and you might wonder: Who is that guy? But when Cruz is working; when he's on, he can remind people of the "Great Moments with Mr. Lincoln" stage show at Disneyland. The figure onstage looks like Abraham Lincoln, the first Republican president. It sounds like Lincoln (as far as we know). But it's nothing more than a robot that, naturally, has been programmed to deliver all of Lincoln's most memorable lines and passages from his historically impactful speeches at precisely the preprogrammed time. Part of this is an accident of Cruz's training, first as a competitive debater and then a litigator. To succeed at both, arguments must be crisp, disciplined, exceedingly prepared, bolstered by expert opinion and precedent. None of that lends itself to connecting with voters on a gut level, on nonideological terms, to being relatable. Cruz and his team recognized this shortcoming. It was probably the biggest realization to emerge from their extensive after-action review of the senator's 2016 presidential campaign.

"The lock that was never really picked," one Cruz booster told me.

Over the past five years, Cruz and his team have gone to great lengths to pick the lock. The challenge for Cruz was not merely a matter of letting voters see the man behind the curtain, although that was part of it. Cruz needed to override years of communication muscle memory and form new habits. He needed a forum to communicate with voters as *Senator* Cruz, but that would give him an opportunity to work on his delivery and practice talking more like *Ted* Cruz.

So Cruz launched a podcast. He didn't skimp, either.

The aptly titled *Verdict* is produced by a team that produces podcasts for the *Daily Wire*, the conservative news and opinion website founded by Ben Shapiro that airs some of the most listened-to podcasts in the country. Michael J. Knowles, a columnist for the *Daily Wire*, hosts *Verdict*, which basically means he introduces the show and closes the show, and in between asks Cruz questions about news of the day, or whatever topic the senator wants to discuss, and then just lets him riff. Several months in the works, the podcast debuted January 16, 2020, on the opening day of Trump's trial in the Senate, which considered two articles of impeachment approved by the House of Representatives. Team Cruz conceived of the show as a daily conversation and review of events at the trial. Each evening after proceedings in the US Senate concluded, Cruz would head to the studio, no matter how late (or early the following morning), and record an episode of *Verdict*.

At one point, the show was the No. 1–rated podcast in the world. Cruz enjoys telling the story about how his daughter, then eleven years old, refused to believe that *Verdict* was getting more downloads than podcaster extraordinaire Joe Rogan, host of *The Joe Rogan Experience*.

Toward the end of 2020, with fifty-nine episodes released, *Verdict* had been downloaded more than 21.3 million times when combining podcast downloads and YouTube views, for an average per-episode download of 216,677. Other fun facts related to *Verdict*: The visual version of the podcast had amassed more than 1.4 million hours of audience watch time from more than 8.5 million views, with a YouTube subscriber base of 167,570.

After the US Senate acquitted Trump on all charges and impeachment No. 1 went away, *Verdict* continued as a vehicle for Cruz to continue work on his relatability, focused on whatever topics strike him. Aside from the whole point of the podcast, Cruz was enjoying the unscripted, long-form format of the medium. He found it freeing from the construct of the five-minute segment on cable television news. There's something else Cruz values about *Verdict* that suggested to me that production was likely to roll right into the spring 2023 launch of the 2024 primary—and keep on going: It's a political security blanket. The way Trump dominated earned media during the 2016 primary campaign, receiving the equivalent of $2 billion in coverage, scarred Cruz. He is determined not to chance it happening again, even without Trump in the 2024 primary. The podcast is Cruz's way of controlling both his message and a platform to disseminate it, just in case the networks pick a favorite or find a contender who can generate huge ratings by airing their campaign rallies uninterrupted.

"Earned media" is coverage by news organizations that candidates "earn" by force of personality, prominence, some legislative proposal, a speech, that sort of thing. It can take the shape of a newspaper story, a brief appearance on a cable news network, an interview on a late-night television talk show—the options are endless. Garnering positive earned media can be the most important factor in a successful candidacy. From the time Trump announced his presidential campaign in mid-June 2015, he so monopolized "earned media" with his traveling road show of tent-revival style rallies and "can you believe he actually said that" rhetoric, it was nearly impossible for his Republican competitors to break through and command the debate or dictate the story line.

At the time, a veteran Republican media maven advising one of the seventeen Republican primary candidates described it to me this way: His candidate would get booked by Fox News for a five-minute segment, ostensibly to talk issues of the day as it related to his presidential bid. The host would spend 4:30 asking his candidate to comment on what Trump did and what Trump said, and then with thirty seconds left in the segment, close with something along the lines of "We have thirty seconds left before we go to a commercial break, so what about *you*?" Cruz experienced this acutely, and the podcast is his work-around.

———

Cruz was sitting on an email fund-raising list of grassroots donors that numbered approximately 4 million at the beginning of the 2022 election cycle. Nearly 25 percent of them were active contributors, and the senator's political team planned to grow that list to 1 million-plus active donors over the course of the following two years. These lists have become essential to the financial viability of a presidential campaign—almost more so than a Rolodex of deep-pocketed donors—and Cruz's collection of grassroots contributors who give in small amounts through digital platforms could provide him a crucial advantage over competitors when the 2024 campaign gets under way in earnest.

If all goes according to plan, Team Cruz will invest $14 million to raise $22 million in 2021 and 2022, which would leave his campaign with about $10 million in cash on hand at the beginning of his second White House campaign. Not bad, but not enough. If Cruz is going to get over the hump this time, he's going to need more influential friends. It's a sensitive topic with the senator.

Primary voters may hate the so-called political establishment, but presidential politics is a team sport. At least if you want to win. I remember interviewing Senator Mike Lee in an otherwise empty, oversized anteroom at the Republican convention in Cleveland in July 2016. The Utah Republican was one of the few good friends Cruz had made in Washington. Lee wasn't ready to endorse the nominee, so much so that he joined with rebellious delegates on the convention floor who were engaged in a last-ditch effort to block Trump's nomination. Lee had concerns, about policy, about judicial appointments, about temperament. Unflappable and stubbornly grounded in principle, Lee is about as opposite of Trump as one can be. But Lee's other big complaint about Trump was the way he had treated his good friend Ted Cruz. He had said so a few weeks earlier in an interview with Newsmax.

"Hey look, Steve, I get it. You want me to endorse Trump," Lee told host Steve Malzberg during an interview in late June, explaining why he was a holdout. "We can get into that if you want. We can get into the fact that he accused my best friend's father of conspiring to kill" President John F. Kennedy.

These are the kinds of allies who might have made a difference for Cruz when he and Trump were the last two candidates standing in the 2016 primary. These are the kind of allies he needs in 2024, but lots of them. There was nobody to go to bat for Cruz because, to put it bluntly, most Republican insiders decided after four years of his antics in the US Senate that he was an asshole.

Cruz has taken steps to rectify the problem, starting with subtle changes in how he interacts with his Republican colleagues. His critics have taken notice, crediting the senator for playing a constructive role in trying to reach consensus on big-ticket GOP legislation, from the twice-failed effort to repeal and replace Obamacare to the successful passage of the party's $1.3 trillion tax overhaul. Cruz explains the apparent shift as the difference between opposing compromise on Obama's terms, as was the case in his first four years in the Senate, and supporting compromise on Trump's terms, as was the case in the last four years. Bottom line: Even amid occasional spirited disagreement, inevitable in the Senate, Cruz's Republican colleagues no longer feel like the senator is treating them like the Democratic opposition. But being merely tolerated isn't enough.

If "the party decides," an old cliché that tends to be true more often than not, then you have to treat it with care, not contempt; you have to be a party builder, not a bulldozer. Even Trump got the hang of it after a rough start as president, when he seemed more interested attacking Republicans in Congress than Democrats. It took McConnell to set Trump straight—to explain that not only did he need their votes, but he was in fact mostly getting their votes, so maybe he should back off and sic his Twitter account on the party that was voting against him in Congress. (Trump listened, although he drew a line in the sand against forgiving and forgetting particularly vocal Republican critics. See: former senators Jeff Flake and Bob Corker.)

So, at Roe's direction, Cruz in July 2020 unveiled "Twenty for Twenty," a program to help Republicans win back the majority in the House of Representatives by raising money for, and providing strategic campaign assistance to, twenty Republican candidates.

It was an undertaking. Cruz personally vetted the candidates. A dozen had endorsed his 2016 presidential bid, among them two vulnerable incumbents, Representative Ann Wagner of Missouri and Representative Chip Roy of Texas. Rewarding loyalty and friendship is the epitome of so-called swampy Washington politics.

Guess what? It's also effective. It's how you build the relationships and establish the trust that makes it possible to convince colleagues in the House of Representatives and the US Senate to take politically risky votes and turn an ambitious legislative agenda into law. Broadly, Cruz selected each candidate because they were running in winnable congressional districts, demonstrated the ability to run strong campaigns, and generally shared his conservative politics. Cruz was so taken with the project that he ultimately included twenty-five candidates in the program. Participants enjoyed access to his robust network of 4 to 5 million small-dollar grassroots donors that he has maintained assiduously since his first presidential campaign. And they benefited from hands-on support from Cruz and his political operation, led by Roe, the senator's 2016 campaign manager, and his top political adviser ever since.

Over the summer of 2020, Cruz hosted a donor retreat in tony Aspen, Colorado, at the posh St. Regis Aspen Resort, for the joint fundraising committee he established for the candidates participating in the Twenty for Twenty program. Around forty to fifty wealthy Republican financiers mingled with nearly two dozen candidates. There were activities: ax throwing, target shooting, plus a dinner put on at a nearby home owned by one of Cruz's wealthy political benefactors. Amid all that fun, Roe, Johnson, and Cruz pollster Chris Wilson held a political briefing for attendees to provide an overview of the political environment and the contests Twenty for Twenty was raising money for. The participating moneyed contributors, culled from a group that has been loyal and generous to Cruz's political campaigns and causes over the years, were permitted to write checks to the program for a federally capped maximum of $161,200. Their support, combined with the online giving from Cruz's grassroots list, helped Twenty for Twenty pull in more than $3.3 million, or an average of $132,000 per candidate, hardly chump change when you're talking

House races. It was more than half a million dollars over the goal of $2.5 million Cruz set out to raise when he launched the program. The money was no doubt a critical aspect of the effort and naturally made headlines about the joint fund-raising committee when it was announced.

But for Cruz, this was about so much more. This was about being a team player and cultivating political allies he can count on in 2024 in what could be a crowded presidential primary that, among others, may include a former commander in chief. With thirteen of the twenty-five House candidates Cruz supported through Twenty for Twenty winning on November 3, 2020, Cruz has assembled the beginnings of a support group inside the GOP establishment, the sort that has proven time and again to be a valuable commodity for Republican presidential contenders—sometimes as validators, sometimes as gatekeepers to crucial constituencies in their states and districts, sometimes as interlocutors to their own loyal collection of influential grassroots activists. For good measure, Cruz spent the final five days of the 2020 campaign crisscrossing the country to campaign for vulnerable Republican Senate incumbents whose reelections were crucial to the party's effort to hang on to the majority. Cruz made trips to Arizona, Iowa, Montana, and North Carolina, jetted to California to headline a fund-raiser for the National Republican Senatorial Committee, the Senate GOP campaign arm, and then returned to Texas to stump with Senator John Cornyn on the eve of the election.

To quote Alan Greenspan, the former chairman of the Federal Reserve, let's not engage in "irrational exuberance" about Kumbaya Cruz. He can still be a pain in the a——.

In 2020, in the Republican primary for the US Senate in Tennessee, Cruz let loose some of his bottled-up insurgent proclivities. Unprompted, he reached out to the underdog conservative in the race, Manny Sethi, and offered his services. The physician was running against the party favorite, Bill Hagerty, to fill the seat being vacated by Republican Lamar Alexander, who was retiring. Cruz wanted to help Sethi pull off an improbable upset. Hagerty is an accomplished and congenial establishment Republican in the Tennessee tradition of Alexander, Bob Corker, and Bill Frist; he is a wealthy businessman, a veteran Republican donor, and a former ambassador. Trump had appointed Hagerty to represent the United States in Japan at the beginning of his term, and along with McConnell, enthusiastically backed his Senate bid. The Hagerty-Sethi primary was the perfect opportunity for an otherwise more circumspect Cruz to exert some independence from the GOP hierarchy, Trump included. He took it, endorsing Sethi and barnstorming Tennessee on his behalf in the homestretch of the campaign. (Hagerty easily defeated Sethi and waltzed to victory in the general election. Among the prominent Republicans present at his victory party on Primary Night that August was Arkansas senator Tom Cotton, a Cruz rival for the 2024 nomination who lent considerable support to the winning side.)

Five months later, Cruz was at it again. On January 6, 2021, Congress would meet in a joint session to certify President-elect Joe Biden's Electoral College victory, a critical albeit usually perfunctory step in the quadrennial constitutional process to install the winner of the presidential election. McConnell, in a private conference call with Senate Republicans, pleaded with them to avoid lodging fruitless objections and join him in voting to support certification. Cruz spurned the request. Although this time, in crossing one leader of the Republican establishment, the Senate majority leader, the Texan planted his feet firmly in the camp of another leader of the Republican establishment, Trump, through a series of moves that would have long-lasting implications for his 2024 ambitions.

The story Cruz tells about his journey to objection to the 2020 election results is at once familiar and fascinating. Familiar because, of course, the instigator of the Obamacare shutdown bucked McConnell and satisfied a Republican base demanding that he (and every other Republican in Congress) object to Biden's convincing Electoral College victory. Fascinating because this time, Cruz wasn't the instigator. He was a politically circumspect follower—of Missouri Republican Josh Hawley, the more populist version of Cruz 1.0 elected to the US Senate in 2018. It was Hawley who broke ranks first, announcing one week before the January 6 certification that he would object to the electoral votes from Pennsylvania. Cruz recognized the Pandora's shipping container Republicans were opening by using Congress to annul a legitimate presidential election. Rather than plunge recklessly into a straight-up objection of the vote, he sought to build some consensus around a constitutionally sound middle ground, proposing the formation of a special fifteen-member commission to examine Trump's claims of voter fraud—not proof, but *claims*—that succeeded in convincing so many of his supporters that November 3 was a sham.

Or…Cruz was just playing crass, presidential politics, ensuring Hawley wouldn't outflank him in a primary.

"We were going to have to vote on the objection. If we voted no—if we voted against the objection, that vote would be heard by tens of millions of Americans as saying, 'You don't believe voter fraud is real, you don't believe it's serious, you don't believe it's significant,'" he said. "That's certainly not true for me."

Take your pick. For one longtime Cruz devotee, the senator's scheme smacked of the latter. Veteran Republican operative Chad Sweet is chief executive officer of the Chertoff Group, a Washington firm specializing in security consulting and investing that he cofounded with Michael Chertoff, former homeland security secretary under George W. Bush. During the 2016 presidential campaign, Sweet put his professional life on hold for two years, moving to Houston to serve as chairman of the Cruz campaign. In all likelihood he would have done so again in 2024 had the senator asked. Like the senator, Sweet is a movement conservative in the Reagan mold, and he believed deeply that Cruz had the fortitude to lead a Republican Party, and a country, being rocked by crisis and transformation from within and without. But when Cruz detailed his objection plans to Sweet in private conversations prior to January 6, Sweet recoiled.

As the former chief of staff to Chertoff at the Department of Homeland Security who years earlier worked in the CIA's clandestine service, Sweet worried that congressional objections to the state-certified electoral votes could undermine American democracy for years to come. Accordingly, Sweet told Cruz their political alliance was kaput if the senator insisted on going through with it. On January 8, two days after Cruz followed through with his plans, the media-shy Sweet quietly posted a public statement to his LinkedIn account disavowing his political support for Cruz and explaining his concerns about the damaging future implications of the objection votes cast by congressional Republicans two days earlier.

"Donald Trump and those who aided and abetted him in his relentless undermining of our Democracy—including Senators Josh Hawley and Ted Cruz—must be denounced," Sweet wrote. "In particular, I made it clear to Senator Cruz, whom I have known for years, before the Joint Session of Congress, that if he proceeded to object to the Electoral count of the legitimate slates of delegates certified by the States, I could no longer support him."

On New Year's Day, two days after Hawley guaranteed the US Senate would hold at least one vote to object to the results from a state Biden won, Cruz boarded a Southwest Airlines flight in Houston and headed back to Washington for a rare holiday session. The chamber was convening that Friday to override Trump's veto of the National Defense Authorization Act, a vote that had to be disposed of before noon on Sunday, January 3, when the 116th Congress would expire along with any open pieces of legislation. Predictably, Trump tried to blow up the last bipartisan piece of legislation in Washington, the annual bill that authorizes the Defense Department to spend taxpayer dollars appropriated to it by Congress, because he was angry at Facebook and Twitter and wanted lawmakers to overhaul the federal regulation that protects social media companies from being sued into oblivion based on the information posted on their platforms. The US Senate joined the House of Representatives in voting overwhelmingly to override Trump's veto. Cruz, Hawley, and Cotton were among the seven Republicans to break ranks to side with the president.

But before Cruz would cast that vote, he was sitting thirty thousand feet in the air on his way to the capital banging out what amounted to a two-page statement on his laptop that explained his plan to object to the tally of the presidential election—an election that saw Republicans dominate down ballot in state and federal contests. As Cruz tells it, he believed he had concocted a strategy for objecting that would shield him from accusations that he was seeking to overturn the election. It also happens that Cruz's strategy would one-up Hawley. Rather than simply object to Pennsylvania, which, on its own, was not enough to hand the election to Trump, Cruz planned to oppose certification of electoral votes from "disputed states" generally understood, per Trump's myriad failed legal challenges, to include Arizona, Georgia, Michigan, Nevada, and Wisconsin, *as well as* Pennsylvania. Taken together, the seventy-nine electoral votes they were worth could reverse the outcome of the race.

So how did Cruz sell this as not that? The commission. It was modeled on the solution Congress came up with to adjudicate an actual disputed presidential election, the 1876 campaign between Republican Rutherford B. Hayes and Democrat Samuel Tilden. Under Cruz's plan, the panel would report back its findings before Inauguration Day. If Biden won, so be it. Cruz was about to rush headlong into releasing his statement when he thought better of it. The senator decided there was strength in numbers, and so he started quizzing some of his Republican colleagues to see what they were thinking—in general, and then about his approach: objecting, but with a caveat. He sent around a draft of the statement he had written. After a series of lengthy conversations, in person and on the telephone, Cruz rounded up ten cohorts, and together, on Saturday, January 2, the eleven of them signed onto his statement and issued it as a group. The effort never took flight.

Cruz and the other objectors were barely getting started January 6 when interrupted by the insurrection and forced to flee the chamber. Shaken by events and motivated by a strong desire to send a message to the MAGA rioters that their revolt had failed, most of the members of Cruz's group chose to drop their objections, and his effort crumbled.

Cruz has since been critical of Trump in relation to the riot at the

Capitol. He has called the forty-fifth president reckless and irresponsible for claiming without proof that he defeated Biden in a landslide and had the election stolen from him.

"You've never heard me use language like that," Cruz said on *Verdict*. "What I've said is, voter fraud is real and we need to examine the evidence."

The senator's critics might not be aware, but it probably wouldn't matter in any event. He was already under fire for choosing to object to Biden's victory in the first place, and that criticism only sharpened in the wake of the ransacking of the Capitol. Some Democrats in Congress said Cruz was as guilty as Trump for fomenting the rebellion and ought to be expelled from the US Senate.

But some weeks after the failed coup, Cruz's political team was conducting one of their periodic checks on the senator's political standing with the public (because he has run for president before, his name identification is extremely high). Lo and behold, his image with Republican voters was…way *up*. Prior to January 6, 2021, Cruz's favorability rating with Republicans was north of 50 percent but hardly worth bragging about. Afterward, he rocketed above 70 percent among "somewhat conservative" voters and was 10 percentage points better than that among "conservatives." And in a hypothetical Republican primary contest, matched up against some of the leading contenders (not including Trump), Cruz led the field, followed by Pence, then Cotton and Haley, who were tied, and then Rubio and Florida governor Ron DeSantis after them. Cruz was also the reigning second choice among them. These numbers amounted to a vast improvement for Cruz, compared, for instance, to how he stacked up against Pence before the ides of January.

There was more. Polling from a not inconsequential midwestern battleground state post-January 2021 showed that Cruz's favorability rating had surpassed 70 percent. Only two Republicans in the 2024 mix scored higher: Pence and…Trump. Apparently, throughout the entirety of the tumultuous postelection period, Cruz committed just one faux pas as far as Republican primary voters were concerned; he showed up in person on the west front of the Capitol to celebrate Biden's inauguration. I know what you're thinking: Weren't Cruz's 2024 prospects derailed in the slightest after his run for the (Mexican) border to escape a major ice storm and the statewide electricity outage? Not really. Yes, it was embarrassing, and kind of stupid, especially for Cruz, who is smart enough to know better. But he, smartly, didn't let his mistake linger too long. And pretty soon, Republican voters in Texas and elsewhere were more annoyed by what they perceived as a so-called mainstream media pile-on than Cruz's abrogation of his duties as a US senator to help his constituents survive a life-threatening crisis.

CHAPTER SIX

◆

Pomp & Circumstance

Sometime in the fall of 2019, roughly a year before Biden would oust Trump, one of the most trusted members of the president's cabinet, Secretary of State **Mike Pompeo**, met in Washington with a small cadre of close advisers to discuss a run for the White House in 2024 and game out a possible campaign.

The meeting was casual. There weren't reams of spreadsheets and data, but gathered at Ulrich Brechbuhl's apartment, Pompeo and his kitchen cabinet examined a potential presidential campaign from the thirty-thousand-foot level: the timeline for getting under way; and what the secretary should be doing between now and then to prepare without running afoul of the Hatch Act, a federal law that prohibits administration officials from overt politicking, so that he could mount a strong campaign should he decide to run.

Joining the meeting were Brechbuhl, Pompeo's counselor at the State Department and longtime friend, business partner, and classmate at West Point—and Brian Bulatao, another close friend and West Point classmate who Pompeo brought with him to the Trump administration. After Pompeo was appointed director of the Central Intelligence Agency, he installed Bulatao as the spy agency's chief operating officer. When Pompeo succeeded Rex Tillerson as the president's top diplomat, Bulatao became under secretary for management at the State Department.

Also at Brechbuhl's apartment to weigh in on Pompeo 2024 was Republican communications strategist and debate coach extraordinaire Brett O'Donnell. Pompeo tapped O'Donnell as an informal adviser for domestic political communications on the basis of a recommendation from his good friend Tom Cotton, whom he collaborated with on national security matters when both served in the House of Representatives.

Finally, the small group was rounded out by Pompeo's adult son, Nick Pompeo, and the secretary's wife, Susan Pompeo, who is without a doubt the most influential adviser in Pompeo's orbit. Nick made a public debut of sorts as a Pompeo surrogate when he introduced his father to grassroots Republicans at the Conservative Political Action Conference (CPAC), hailing the elder Pompeo as "America's first 'America First' secretary of state." Mrs. Pompeo is a regular fixture by her husband's side, and a force behind the scenes. She had her own desk in her husband's congressional office in Washington when he represented Kansas's Fourth Congressional District. She has helped guide Pompeo's effort to cultivate relationships with key political and business figures that might be useful in a 2024 context and essentially functioned as the nation's first lady of diplomacy as her husband traveled the globe for meetings with world leaders, counterpart diplomats, and their spouses.

Not present at Brechbuhl's apartment for this powwow but ever present in Pompeo World is Ambassador Bob Kimmitt. A West Point graduate and a retired Army major general, Kimmitt is a consummate Washington insider, a veteran of the George H. W. Bush and George W. Bush administrations. As Pompeo's longtime friend, mentor, and informal adviser, Kimmitt would likely sit at the head of the secretary's kitchen cabinet in the event of a campaign.

Unbeknownst to most in Washington at the time, but as would become clearer the following year, Pompeo was rather busy using his post as secretary of state to lay a firm foundation for a 2024 presidential bid— and innovatively so. One Republican insider in Washington, a veteran of multiple GOP presidential campaigns, told me in the spring of 2019 that Pompeo's effort was "the most interesting campaign" for the nomination of any of the major Republican figures considered as potential heirs to the Trump throne.

———

Pompeo is a product of the Orange County, California, of the late 1960s and 1970s.

He was raised during a period of intense social and political tumult across the country but was insulated from it by an orange curtain* sewn from lily-white, family-friendly Republican suburbs that formed the bedrock of what was then a reliably red California in presidential elections. ("Orange County is where the good Republicans go before they die," President Ronald Reagan, governor of California from 1967 to 1975, quipped in November 1988.)

Pompeo was born in 1963. The following year the state would support President Lyndon Baines Johnson over Republican Barry Goldwater. Four years later, in 1968, when Pompeo was five years old, California swung right, backing Richard Nixon. The Golden State would stay that way for more than two decades, until Arkansas governor Bill Clinton captured its mammoth haul of Electoral College votes in 1992. As a Southern California native seven years Pompeo's junior, I remember electing ahead-of-his-time progressive Democrat Jerry Brown governor somewhere in there as well. But I also recall approving Proposition 13 soon after, a taxpayer revolt that led to perhaps the most severe restraint on government taxing power in the United States. The measure capped the tax on property at 1 percent of value, and limited increases to no more than 2 percent annually. Which is to say, this era of conservative, anti-tax governance in California, with the exuberant support it enjoyed in Orange County, might have rubbed off on Pompeo.

He headed to West Point in the early 1980s after excelling in public schools both academically and athletically, inclined toward Reagan-era conservatism that defines his public service to this day. Pompeo partisans will tell you the secretary is a pro at retail politics, that is, personal, one-on-one interaction with voters. Gregarious, warm. That's not the terse, impassive cabinet official most of the country was exposed to, mostly

---

* *Orange curtain*: Slang for the dividing line, culturally and geographically, between Los Angeles and Orange Counties in Southern California.

on television, during Trump's one-term presidency. Maybe that's because, with reporters at least, the secretary was quite guarded and often abrupt.

Five weeks before Pompeo exited the State Department, I met with him in the secretary's ornate office at Foggy Bottom to conduct an exit interview for the *Washington Examiner*. Officially, I was getting twenty minutes. When I joked after the initial coronavirus elbow-bump greeting that I better dive right in because I presumed his press aide was going to pull the plug on schedule at the twenty-minute mark, a tactic I've used with other politicians to disarm them into giving me more time, Pompeo didn't bite. "They will; it will happen," he said, deadpan.

And sure enough, they did. Toward the end of our conversation, I told Pompeo that tracking down extensive biographical information on him had been difficult, "which I'm sure makes you happy," I said.

He simply chuckled, apparently pleased. To be fair—and maybe this was Pompeo revealing some of that supposedly trademarked charm—as I was packing up to leave, he reminded me that I had mentioned at the beginning of the interview that I would ask him a lighthearted question at the end if there was time. I had practically forgotten, as I had focused intently on squeezing in as many sober, newsworthy questions about Trump's foreign policy, and his tenure at State, as I could before they cut me off. But Pompeo reminded me. "You said you had a fun one, or something, that you wanted to ask?" he said, offering me a few more minutes.

"Basketball," I said.

Pompeo played varsity basketball at Los Amigos High School in Fountain Valley, California. During an address to the American Association of Christian Counselors in October 2019, he mentioned in a moment of self-deprecating humor that as a kid, he was convinced that "I was destined to be in the NBA."

I asked Pompeo if there was any truth to that, however ridiculous he might think it in hindsight.

"Early," he confirmed. "Before I realized [that I was] too slow."

Pompeo grew up a UCLA Bruins fan in the latter half of the heyday of the school's basketball program under legendary coach John Wooden. He was mesmerized by the roster of Hall of Fame players the university produced and the ten national championships it garnered from 1964 to 1975, seven of them in a row.

"I watched every game on TV," Pompeo said. "I'm still a huge Bruin fan. It's been hard times."

He's no faux fan. It has, indeed, been thin gruel for UCLA basketball for several years, not counting the school's Cinderella run to the 2021 Final Four, which had yet to unfold. Perhaps remembering he still aspires to a political future after the Trump administration, Pompeo was quick to add, "We're Wichita State Shockers fans now; season tickets to the Shockers."

———

So how did Pompeo, who graduated first in his class from the US Military Academy and retired from the Army with the rank of captain, and then matriculated through Harvard Law School, become the most trusted cabinet member to a populist Republican president completely unbound by the guideposts of Reagan Republicanism? That is the secretary's political superpower—and why he is a formidable contender to succeed Trump atop a party still very much in thrall of its twenty-first-century savior.

Raj Goyle, the Democrat whom Pompeo defeated in 2010 on his way to being elected to represent Kansas's Wichita-area congressional district, might have said it best. As he explained to the New Yorker for an article written by Susan B. Glasser and published in August 2019, "Pompeo's singular ability is in navigating power...On that I give him massive respect, the way he mapped Wichita power, the way he mapped D.C. power, the way he mapped Trump."

Pompeo is entirely self-made and periodically remade. Relationships are his currency.

Pompeo hardly knew a soul in Kansas, his mother's home state, when he parachuted into Wichita with Brechbuhl, Bulatao, and Michael Stradinger to launch Thayer Aerospace, an airplane parts manufacturer they formed by buying and combining three separate aviation industry firms. The business never became the success Pompeo and his West Point pals might have imagined. Pompeo, however, was the toast of Wichita, no small feat for an outsider who landed there by way of California, New York, Massachusetts, and Washington, where he was working as a downtown attorney before he got bored with practicing law. With Thayer Aerospace as his platform, Pompeo established profitable business relationships, some of which turned into reciprocally loyal political relationships with Kansas's key Republican power players. His wife, Susan, started out as his banker. Some, like the Koch brothers, whose multi-billion-dollar firm Koch Industries is headquartered in Wichita, became both business and political benefactors to him. Charles and his late brother, David, helped smooth some of the financial turbulence Pompeo experienced in business, investing in his firm at a critical juncture. They also assisted diligently in a political rise that began with a failed bid for Kansas Republican Party chairman (he lost to future Trump booster Kris Kobach) but recovered nicely thereafter.

Pompeo was elected Kansas committeeman to the Republican National Committee, and after that, representative of Kansas's Fourth Congressional District. From there, four years at Trump's side as one of the most powerful and prominent Republicans in the country. As it happens, Pompeo used his tenure as RNC committeeman, an otherwise overlooked political post, to forge a fruitful alliance with Wisconsin Republican Party chairman Reince Priebus. Some years later, the future RNC chairman would be tapped to serve as Trump's first White House chief of staff, a position that gave him a strong voice in administration staffing during the 2016–2017 transition period. Among the hiring recommendations he made to the 45th president: Mike Pompeo.

What is Pompeo's genius? The libertarian-leaning Koch brothers (David died in 2019) could not and cannot stand Trump. Charles Koch finds the former president's behavior repulsive and key planks of his agenda at odds with true conservative governance. The direction of the party under Trump, especially on matters of trade and immigration, was a critical reason the Koch network of political groups, which for nearly two decades had funneled hundreds of millions of dollars into Republican politics, soured on partisan engagement and decided to cut off the spigot and reduce its support for the GOP. But they still like Pompeo. Here is a Republican who developed a reputation as Trump's closest, most loyal aide save for Jared Kushner, the president's son-in-law, a relationship encapsulated by the headline on Glasser's story in the *New Yorker*: "The Secretary of Trump." Yet Pompeo is still the odds-on favorite to receive strong backing from Charles Koch and his network if he runs for president in 2024.

In 2016, the secretary endorsed Marco Rubio in the crowded Republican presidential primary and worked hard for his nomination. The choice was logical. Both were products of the Tea Party wave that swept Republicans to power in Washington in 2010, Barack Obama's first midterm election (although Senate Democrats hung on to power that year). Both were products of working-class families and adherents of Reagan-era Republicanism, an optimistic conservatism that sees (or saw) the United States as a land of boundless opportunities for socioeconomic advancement for Americans and new immigrants. Both were hawkish internationalists who believed US global leadership was essential to American national and economic security.

As he stumped for the Florida senator, on Fox News and around the country, the pugnacious Pompeo did not pull punches. In taking aim at Trump, the clear front-runner in the race, the Kansan delivered some of the most stinging rebukes of Trump in a campaign brimming with stinging rebukes of his future boss. At one point, Pompeo texted his good friend Alan Cobb, a Republican operative in Kansas and an early and energetic Trump supporter who is now president of the Kansas Chamber of Commerce, and asked him to "please tell your man, for the sake of your kids and grandkids, to find another shiny object."

During Kansas's Republican nominating caucuses, where Pompeo spoke on Rubio's behalf, he unloaded a double-barreled verbal assault on Trump as the front-runner looked on from backstage, wondering exactly who his critic was. "You know, Donald Trump, the other day, said that, quote, if he tells a soldier to commit a war crime, the soldier will just go do it. He said, they'll do as I tell them to do. We've spent seven and a half years with an authoritarian president who ignored our Constitution. We don't need four more years of that."

That was then. As the winds of change blew the Republican Party into a celestial orbit around Trump Tower, Pompeo listened—and pivoted. Republican VIPs who had already made the great migration and whose friendship Pompeo had courted and nurtured over many years helped the onetime Trump critic make a seamless transition. Pompeo's buddy list included Cobb and his classmate from West Point, David Urban, a Washington lobbyist and Trump's top campaign lieutenant in Pennsylvania. Urban, a consummate Washington insider, has already pledged to Pompeo that he will support his old friend for president should he seek the White House in 2024. Also on this list were friends made in Congress: Vice President–to-be Mike Pence, the Indiana Republican who overlapped with Pompeo in the House of Representatives in 2011 and 2012; and Representative Devin Nunes, the California Republican who chaired the House Select Committee on Intelligence from 2015 to 2019. And don't forget Reince Priebus, the relationship Pompeo collected at the RNC, circa 2008–2010. With their help, Pompeo avoided the penalty box for having said mean things about the forty-fifth president—a mortal sin in Trump World—and emerged as the ultimate Trump insider despite continuing to harbor disagreements with the president's foreign policy agenda that persist to this day. Those disagreements ran deep.

Pompeo's six years on Capitol Hill were defined by the attention he paid to foreign policy and national security issues. He served on the House Select Committee on Intelligence, a post that requires an appointment from the Republican leader, and was a member of the panel's subcommittee on the CIA. Pompeo also sought and was appointed to the select committee, created by then–House Speaker John Boehner of Ohio, to investigate the September 11, 2012, terrorist attack on the US consulate in Benghazi, Libya, that left ambassador Christopher Stevens and four other Americans dead.

In all that time, Pompeo never complained about the so-called endless wars being waged around the globe by the American military or issued demands to bring the troops home, as Trump said regularly, "where they belong." He never chastised President Barack Obama for refusing to pursue personal negotiations with dictator Kim Jong-un to reduce the threat of North Korea's growing nuclear weapons program. Pompeo never advocated for the United States to pull up stakes in Afghanistan and make peace with the Taliban. In September 2013, Pompeo even joined forces with fellow Republican hawk senator Tom Cotton of Arkansas to author an op-ed in the *Washington Post* urging GOP support for Obama's request that Congress authorize military force in Syria to punish dictator Bashar al-Assad for deploying chemical weapons against his own people.

Yet as Trump's top diplomat, Pompeo has been the face of every one of the president's foreign policy initiatives: détente with the Taliban, the Afghanistan pullout, ridiculing American global leadership as some endless war, the two glitzy summits with Kim Jong-un that legitimized his dictatorship but failed to lead to the mothballing, let alone dismantling, of North Korea's nukes. (Pompeo, pointing to Pyongyang's relaxation of "long-range" missile testing, argues that engagement with Kim was a success.)

Pompeo has played point each time, with nary a leak hinting at frustration or resistance given a lifetime of hardwired philosophical differences. When I interviewed Pompeo, I wanted to know how he survived so long in the circle of trust, given principled disagreements with Trump on the issue set he cared deeply about and was charged with managing.

"I've been asked this question a couple of times. I always think it an odd one," Pompeo told me. "What I've done in the administration is the things I've done all my life, which is that I understand my role, my place, I know what my duty is. And every day I get up and execute that as best I can. And that means being part of a team, so part of the president's national security team, versus CIA director—now as secretary of state. I know who the boss is. I know who got 306 electoral votes and who didn't, that was him, not me."

That's only half the story.

It doesn't paint a full picture of Pompeo's impact on Trump's transactional, unmoored foreign policy. It doesn't fully explain how he flourished for four straight years working for a president who went through three chiefs of staff plus a fourth, acting chief of staff; two defense secretaries plus a third, acting secretary of defense; two homeland security secretaries plus a third, acting secretary of homeland security; four national security advisers; and two attorneys general plus two acting attorneys general.

And those were just the most notable positions to change hands multiple times because Trump was fickle, or underlings couldn't abide by his policy directives—or both. Although they clashed from time to time, Pompeo and Trump saw eye to eye almost as often. Moving the US embassy in Israel from Tel Aviv to Jerusalem; pulling the United States out of the Joint Comprehensive Plan of Action, the deal the Obama administration and American allies signed with Iran to freeze the terrorist regime's nuclear weapons program; ordering a military strike against Qasem Soleimani, leader of Iran's Quds Force; bypassing the Palestinians and brokering peace treaties between Israel and Arab nations, known as the Abraham Accords; providing lethal aid to Ukraine to bolster its defenses against Russia; cracking down on the Chinese Communist Party. These are some of their more notable areas of agreement.

When I asked Pompeo, he didn't deny the existence of disagreements with Trump, nor did he downplay their differences of opinion by ticking off the above list to prove the existence of common ground between them. Pompeo said he was always blunt with the president about his views and direct with strategic recommendations. But the secretary was pragmatic, accepting that his job was to advise, not decide. When he lost the argument or failed to persuade Trump, he didn't look for a work-around, he implemented.

"I give him my best wisdom," the secretary said. "He then says, 'Yep, go do this, don't go do that'; and then we bust our tail to try and execute that on behalf of him. And you know, I think in that sense he has respected that effort. Because he has always known I'm going to tell him the truth as best I know it. When I think we've got it wrong or we made a decision that wasn't right, I'm going to walk in and be crystal clear about what it was, provide him with an alternative as best I can. And then he knows when he makes a decision, I'm going to go do my best to execute it."

———

In March 2019, Pompeo traveled home to Kansas for, as it turned out, one of the several domestic trips he took as secretary of state to speak publicly with American voters and convene privately with business and political leaders. On this late winter afternoon, Pompeo was in Overland Park, in eastern Kansas's Johnson County, to deliver a keynote address to an overflow crowd who gathered for an event focused on economic innovation in the American heartland hosted by the Global Entrepreneurship Summit. Before taking the stage, the secretary was hanging out in the green room with his buddy, Cobb, who was going to introduce him. As the two took the service elevator up to the ballroom of the Sheraton Overland Park Hotel, Pompeo marveled at how far he had come since embarking on a political career that he had to build from scratch, without the benefit of a politically connected family, a vast personal fortune, or, at least initially, a GOP establishment champion. "Alan," Pompeo asked. "Would you ever have imagined twenty-two years ago, when we met, that you'd be introducing the secretary of state, and that it would be me?"

Pompeo's shift to Trump despite ideological misgivings should not be surprising, either then or now. The secretary always harbored political ambitions beyond the House of Representatives. He twice considered running for Senate, in 2014 and 2016, and considered taking on entrenched incumbent Republicans to do it, but in both instances was dissuaded from sparking messy primary fights. Pompeo's ambition radiated so bright, some Republican insiders involved in Kansas politics in the secretary's early years there are convinced he vocalized plans to run for president someday. That recollection persists, even though the only evidence I could unearth was to the contrary, à la Pompeo expressing amazement to Cobb that he had made it as far as Foggy Bottom.

"He always wanted to run for president," a Republican operative involved in Kansas politics back then told me in the spring of 2020. "I mean, that was his thing."

As Pompeo sought to negotiate Trump World, with the goal of landing a substantial administration post, he identified CIA director and secretary of the Army as two positions he was interested in that he believed he was qualified to apply for. Pompeo had graduated first in his class at West Point. He was steeped in national security policy during his six years in Congress. On intelligence matters, he had made a name for himself through work on the special select committee formed to investigate Benghazi. Cobb recommended Pompeo work his relationships with Pence and Urban. Pompeo's subsequent rise, and staying power, is viewed as so successful that his crossover from tongue-lashing Trump opponent to praise-lavishing Trump confidant has—like victory—many fathers.

———

Once upon a time, the cabinet secretary was the fast track to the executive mansion. Six of the first fifteen presidents preceded Pompeo at the State Department, including a few you might have heard of: Thomas Jefferson, James Madison, James Monroe, John Quincy Adams, Martin Van Buren, and James Buchanan. But that gravy train ran dry nearly a century ago. Not since Herbert Hoover was elected president in 1928 after serving the previous eight years leading the Department of Commerce has the cabinet been a springboard to the White House. George H. W. Bush served as ambassador to the United Nations under President Richard Nixon and director of the CIA under President Gerald Ford, two positions elevated to cabinet level by some presidents but not others. But in any event, Bush's ascension to the White House in 1988 had everything to do with the fact that he served eight years as Reagan's vice president and virtually nothing to do with his impressive résumé. In 2016, Democrat Hillary Clinton hoped to turn her tenure as the first secretary of state under Barack Obama into a winning presidential campaign. She was thwarted by Donald Trump—and, no doubt, her use of a private email server to conduct official government business that landed her in hot water with the FBI.

All of this is to say, the path Pompeo is taking toward a possible presidential bid is fraught with risk. Because of how inexorably Pompeo is tied to Trump, he risks being saddled with all the president's negatives without enjoying any of the upside—the upside being Trump's unique ability to turn out low-propensity voters who participate in elections just once in a generation, when motivated by an unusually compelling candidate. Think H. Ross Perot; think Trump. For a center-left version, think Obama.

Worse, Pompeo risked irrelevancy. That was the essence of the pitch Senate Majority Leader Mitch McConnell made when he recruited Pompeo to run for an open Kansas seat in the US Senate in 2020. Pompeo would have cleared the field of Republican primary challengers and won the general election in a walk. In the twenty-first century, the US Senate is a great platform for the presidency. Pompeo turned McConnell down flat. Publicly, the secretary said it would be irresponsible of him to resign from the Trump administration in the aftermath of the assassination of Iran's terrorist in chief, Gen. Qasem Soleimani, so ordered by the president. The Quds Force leader oversaw Tehran's violent efforts to undermine the interests of the United States in the Middle East. He was responsible for the deaths of hundreds of American soldiers in the region. With the possibility of military and diplomatic turbulence ahead, Pompeo's reasoning was plausible. But in reality, the secretary never had any intention of running for Senate in 2020, despite the appearance of interest and consideration, culminating with his announcement that he would spend the 2019 holiday season mulling a campaign with his family. Pompeo might have been swayed by the urgency of boxing out Kobach. The polarizing immigration hawk, defeated by a Democrat in his bid for governor in 2018, said he would drop out of the US Senate race if the secretary ran. Soleimani's elimination in an American military strike, then, provided Pompeo with the permission slip he needed to make the decision he intended to make all along. It carried with it the added benefit of leaving McConnell, and other party insiders pushing him to run for US Senate, unable to try and change his mind without appearing consumed by petty politics at the expense of national security imperatives.

At the same time, Pompeo had every intention of keeping up his "most interesting" noncampaign campaign for the 2024 presidential nomination, with a full slate of domestic travel, roundtables, and dinners on tap for 2020. But then the coronavirus pandemic disrupted many of those plans, as it did for so many others—not to mention Trump's plans for a second term.

———

In the late winter of 2020, Pompeo was preparing a domestic tour of sorts to speak in churches. Eventually derailed by the coronavirus pandemic, tentative plans were on the books for him to address congregants in California, Florida, Georgia, and Texas.

Now look, maybe Pompeo was simply planning to share the good news of Trump foreign policy to interested Americans who, naturally, might have an interest in American foreign policy. Of course, if a prominent Republican was looking to build grassroots support for a presidential bid from the ground up—um, how to put this delicately?—the first constituency you might look to is the churchgoer, a crucial component of the Republican Party's governing coalition and a key voting bloc in GOP presidential nominating contests. There's a reason why Ted Cruz kicked off his 2016 presidential bid on the campus of Liberty University in Lynchburg, Virginia, rather than somewhere more personal, like, say, Texas. Not much had changed four years later. Exit polls from the Associated Press showed that the more often a voter attended church, the more likely he or she was to support Trump over Biden. Among monthly churchgoers, Trump beat Biden 53 percent to 45 percent; among those who attend church a few times a month, that lead stretched to 54 percent to 45 percent; and among weekly churchgoers, Trump romped, defeating Biden 61 percent to 37 percent. In October 2019, as Trump was navigating the beginning of an impeachment inquiry into allegations that he solicited dirt on Biden from a foreign government, Pompeo traveled to Nashville for a speech to twelve thousand people gathered for the annual American Association of Christian Counselors conference. It was a campaign speech hiding in

plain sight. But it also revealed Pompeo to have more range as a politician than commonly understood during a Trump administration tenure
defined by staredowns with reporters and brusque, one-note answers to
predictably combative questions.

In his remarks in Nashville, the secretary showed emotional depth,
humor, and...humility. Pompeo's Republican admirers swear by his retail
skills. They weren't making it up. Study his twenty-five-minute address
to the American Association of Christian Counselors, and it's suddenly
believable that presidential candidate Pompeo just might be able to pull
off the trick of embracing elements of Trump's agenda while subtly dis-
pensing of Trump the man, all without looking like a conniving hypo-
crite. Here's how Pompeo framed his remarks that day:

> I want to use my time today to think about what it means to be a
> Christian leader, a Christian leader in three areas: First, is disposi-
> tion: How is it that one carries oneself in the world. The second is
> dialogue—talking. How is it that we engage with others around
> the world. And, third, decisions, decisions that we make. How do
> we make choices; upon what basis?

The pulpit wasn't the only stop on Pompeo's inventive, noncampaign
campaign. In January 2020, he parachuted into rural Sumter County,
Florida, home of The Villages, a massive retirement community that
has constituted the bedrock of the Republican Party's growing strength
in this perennial swing state during the Trump era. (In 2016 and 2020,
Trump garnered a massive majority of the vote there—68.8 percent and
67.8 percent, respectively. In 2018, a midterm year in which Republicans
barely captured a Senate seat and hung on to the governor's mansion,
Senator Rick Scott won the county with 70.8 percent and Governor Ron
DeSantis received 69.6 percent.) Not a bad place for Pompeo to stop by
and make friends. They loved him back, with about three hundred packing a hall at the Sumter County Fairgrounds to hear him speak, despite

the out-of-the-way location and minimal advance notice, both of which were a deliberate part of the planning in order to gauge just how much juice the nation's chief diplomat had with rank-and-file voters. Pompeo is expert at knowing his audience, a skill that did not fail him here.

"For too long, we weren't winning. Now, we have a president who's getting it done. Is anybody tired of winning yet?" he said.

There also was a stop in South Florida to meet with a group of Cuban American doctors. Just prior to Election Day 2020, with Trump embroiled in a knife fight with Biden in Wisconsin for its decisive eleven Electoral College votes, Pompeo headed to the midwestern battleground to deliver a speech to the legislature from the well of the state senate. Notwithstanding the convenient political timing, Pompeo's remarks, very appropriately, focused on the Chinese Communist Party, and the Trump administration's policy for rebuffing Beijing's malign activities in the United States in an attempt to influence American policy toward China. All the while, Pompeo was quietly playing a mean inside game, meeting privately with business executives in an array of industries, political operatives, Washington lobbyists, and wealthy Republican campaign contributors.

To commemorate Veterans Day 2019, Pompeo spoke at the Citadel, a military college in Charleston, South Carolina, a key early primary state on the presidential nominating calendar and host of the first such contest in the South. Nothing out of the ordinary, especially as the secretary is an Army captain, retired. But Pompeo shrewdly tacked on an extra meeting to the trip, with O'Donnell reaching out to Matt Moore, the former chairman of the South Carolina GOP, to have him organize a private meeting for the secretary with three to four dozen of the state's top Republican activists—donors, operatives, business owners, and industry executives.

In the spring of 2020, Pompeo was scheduled to headline a private dinner for wealthy GOP donors as part of the Republican Jewish Coalition's annual spring conference in Las Vegas, an event that became another in a long line of pandemic casualties.

In DC, Republican lobbyist Scott Weaver, who backed Rubio in 2016, has been something of a Sherpa for Pompeo, organizing dinners and helping to connect him with senior K Street lobbyists and industry executives who help inform his job as secretary of state. The meals are very conversational, with Pompeo opening things up with some brief remarks before asking questions of his guests and letting them do most of the talking. Like all good politicians, he studies up on the guest list in advance so that he knows who they are and is prepared to ask questions that are poignant.

The crowning achievement of Pompeo's "friend-raising" empire was the Madison Dinner. It was the brainchild of Pompeo's wife, Susan, and named for Founder James Madison, the fourth president and fifth secretary of state who hosted salons with foreign diplomats and VIPs during his tenure at State. Pompeo's Madison Dinners proceeded quietly for a couple of years, without catching the attention of the national press corps, until NBC News reported on the existence of the events in late May 2020.

Before the coronavirus forced Madison Dinners on hiatus over the spring and summer of that year, I attempted to land an invitation in order to relay firsthand for this book, in vivid detail, the flavor of the guest list, the pageantry of the evening, and the experience of watching Pompeo work the room. Correspondents Josh Lederman, Laura Strickler, and Dan De Luce of NBC News, without attending but through good old-fashioned shoe-leather reporting, beat me to it. Per their review of "master guest lists," roughly 30 percent of the invitations went to corporate executives, about 25 percent went to mostly conservative media figures, and another 30 percent went to mostly Republican political operatives or government officials. The rest of the invited were comprised of diplomats, academics, or officials in some capacity that would seem directly related to Pompeo's job as secretary of state.

Among the eyebrow-raising VIPs: country music star Reba McEntire; Governor Chris Sununu of New Hampshire, a key early primary state; race car driver Dale Earnhardt Jr.; Raytheon CEO Thomas Kennedy; Brian Kilmeade, cohost of Fox News's marquee morning show, *Fox & Friends*; former Major League Baseball commissioner Peter Ueberroth; American Gaming Association president Bill Miller; pro-life activist Marjorie

Dannenfelser, who leads the conservative group Susan B. Anthony List; Chick-fil-A fast food restaurants chairman Dan Cathy; Matt Schlapp, a lobbyist, chairman of the American Conservative Union, and organizer of CPAC; his wife, Mercedes Schlapp, co-CPAC ringleader and veteran of both the Trump White House and Trump's 2020 campaign; and Laura Ingraham, host of Fox News's *Ingraham Angle*.

Among the diplomatic guests and guests with a national security portfolio were Saudi Arabia's ambassador to the United States, Princess Reema bint Bandar; National Security Adviser Robert C. O'Brien; and Representative Lee Zeldin of New York, a member of the House Foreign Affairs Committee. Other invited guests have included AOL cofounder Steve Case plus wealthy Republican campaign contributors Paul Singer, who runs a hedge fund; Ken Langone, cofounder of the Home Depot; and real estate mogul Harlan Crow. After cocktails, guests are seated for an hourlong dinner and informal conversation with the secretary of state and his wife, who is the keeper of their guests' valuable contact information.

The political implications of the Madison Dinners are unmistakable, especially given Pompeo's ambitions—a point highlighted by his (mostly) Democratic critics. But there is nothing necessarily untoward about Pompeo's attempt to expand his circle of relationships. He spent six years in Washington as a parochial congressman from south-central Kansas; he worked for a president with even fewer contacts in Washington when he assumed office in January 2017.

His four immediate predecessors at State—John Kerry, Hillary Clinton, Condoleezza Rice, and Colin Powell—might not have entertained business, political, and media figures in the ornate eighth-floor reception rooms of the Harry S. Truman building that were named for Benjamin Franklin, Martha Washington, and John Quincy Adams. But having spent decades in Washington and immersed in national politics and government service before being confirmed by the Senate as America's top diplomat, they did not need to.

———

Which brings us back to Pompeo's "most interesting" noncampaign campaign.

At first blush, taking a pass on the US Senate would seem foolish for a would-be president. How is Pompeo supposed to compete with Tom Cotton, Ted Cruz, Ron DeSantis, Kristi Noem, Marco Rubio, Rick Scott—even Tim Scott—without a public stage to keep him top of mind in a political culture that prizes immediacy and a news cycle that moves swiftly? It is impossible for a senator to move two feet without a microphone or camera being shoved in his or her face. For every major or minor issue that arises, every reporter and Sunday show producer wants a piece of them, providing daily opportunities to create the viral moments that drive grassroots support, which drives internet fund-raising, which is (increasingly) the mother's milk of competitive presidential campaigns.

On the other hand, Pompeo can spend the next few years in control. Of his agenda, his public schedule, his life. There's an expectation in Congress that lawmakers take a public position on the big and the small— on everything. There are thorny votes for bloated government spending bills, imperfect compromises. A senator from Kansas might be inclined to cooperate with a Biden administration on an agriculture package, given how important the industry is to the state's economy. A Republican hawk, which Pompeo is, might find himself compelled to endorse a Democratic president's hard-line position on some matter of foreign policy. If you can imagine: In 2013, then-representative Pompeo collaborated with Cotton in a very public effort to convince fellow Republicans to support Obama's request for congressional authorization to use force against Syria. Dictator Bashar al-Assad had used chemical weapons against his own people amid an ongoing civil war, violating a "red line" for military action established by the forty-fourth president. Pompeo believed the threat to US credibility for failing to act outweighed the political complication of backing a president who years later elicits more boos at Republican events than the current (Democratic) president.

"No matter the president's party or his past failures, all Americans should want, and help, him to succeed when it comes to our national security," he and Cotton wrote in a joint op-ed in the *Washington Post* published on September 3, 2013.

Republican primary voters don't always take kindly to this sort of cross-aisle cooperation—er, governing—even when a lawmaker is standing on principle and supporting good, conservative policy. Pompeo (and Cotton) was bailed out from such political "folly" when a Congress that included a Republican House and majority Democratic Senate declined to put the authorization request on the floor for a vote.

These are the sorts of dilemmas he will be free to avoid with Biden in the White House. Meanwhile, Pompeo has managed to hold on to the establishment cred he had when he entered the Trump administration, positioning the secretary as a bridge between two alien worlds that need each other to win presidential elections. As CIA director, and then secretary of state, Pompeo did not have the luxury of building a shadow campaign organization—a political nonprofit, super PAC, or something like that. The job didn't afford him the ability to surround himself with a team of overtly political operators. But through intermediaries, Pompeo has spent four years planting seeds, seeds that may sprout at a later date with just a little bit of water. Brechbuhl, Bulatao, and Kimmitt have subtly made the rounds of Washington, apprising Republican power players of Pompeo's work as Trump's chief diplomat and soliciting feedback on his work product.

Simultaneously, they were busy establishing key relationships and accumulating intelligence on an evolving GOP. What might the 2022 elections look like? What about 2024? Pompeo and his close-knit team of advisers were making preparations for a campaign, and they weren't really bothering to hide it.

"Over coffee, they're kind of leading you down a path of: 'How do you think Mike is doing?'" the veteran Republican insider in Washington told me. "Ninety percent of the people they're talking to are not foreign policy experts."

By the time Biden was inaugurated and Pompeo left the State Department, he had been fielding questions about running for president in 2024 for nearly two years. His domestic travel and networking with political and corporate leaders—even his decision to set up a personal Twitter account—didn't stoke speculation about his future ambitions so much as reveal them. When I asked Pompeo about it in that exit interview, he, refreshingly, declined to wave me off.

"When I hear people talk about these opportunities, I always thank them for being kind, for thinking that I might be qualified," the secretary said. "I have just loved—I've been serving the country now for ten years, six as a member of Congress, four years in the administration; I was a soldier for five years. That service has been an important part of my life and my wife's life. We'll leave that now for a bit and then the Lord will tell us what's next." Pompeo served in one of the Army's armored cavalry divisions, patrolling the border of the old Iron Curtain in Europe, what had been the demarcation between the US-led West and the Eastern bloc, dominated by the now-defunct Soviet Union. That experience shines through in Pompeo's approach to China, a rising communist power of a different sort.

When I caught up with him again a few months later in Orlando, Florida, a couple of hours after he delivered a rather well received speech on the main stage at CPAC, Pompeo was leaning into the 2024 question with more abandon. CPAC 2021 came five weeks after Trump left office and functioned as the first conservative gathering where 2024 hopefuls could test-market their wares, in person, with political consumers. Pompeo showing up was acknowledgment enough of his interest in running for president. While there, he conferred with House Minority Leader Kevin McCarthy, and the two agreed that the former secretary of state would spend the 2022 election cycle traveling the country raising money and stumping for Republican candidates to aid the party's effort to recapture a majority in the House of Representatives. A few months later, Pompeo unveiled CAVPAC, a political action committee he said was dedicated to supporting Republicans running for office in 2022. With Pompeo's decision to use the new group to get involved in campaigns for state legislature, in battlegrounds like, for instance, New Hampshire, there was a distinctly 2024 flavor about it.

Suddenly, the path Pompeo was taking looked familiar—similar to the one paved by Nikki Haley, the other veteran of Trump's cabinet eyeing a White House bid. Meanwhile, Pompeo joined the Hudson Institute, a conservative think tank, and incorporated a new firm, Kansas CNQ LLC, as a receptacle for income from paid speeches, both essential elements in the script followed by major political figures during their post–government service, pre–campaign for higher office, interregnum period. It had been but two and a half months.

But with all of this in mind, I asked Pompeo again: What about 2024?

He embraced the question:

"I care deeply about America. America has been enormously good to me and my family. I have an obligation to stay in the fight and I intend to do it."

The very next day, before leaving Orlando, Pompeo stopped by a Baptist church to mingle with locals at Sunday services. No big deal, just a little retail politicking in a key media market of a crucial battleground state.

———

If Pompeo does run for president and he actually wins, he may have a vested interest in the actual loser actually conceding.

So I asked a former secretary of state who had traveled the world extolling the exceptional virtues of American democracy what he was doing on January 6, 2021, and how it made him feel to see the US Capitol overrun with supporters of an outgoing president who would not accept defeat. Pompeo was in his office at the State Department that day, due northwest from Capitol Hill and clear on the other side of town. As he watched the shocking breach of the Capitol unfold on his television screen, he started reaching out to colleagues in the Trump administration to discuss what action needed to be taken to quell the unrest and restore security. Pompeo told me he was "troubled" by the violence and "bothered" by the attacks on the US Capitol Police, the force that protected him during his tenure in Congress. And he hopes prosecutors throw the book at the rioters. The former CIA director also hinted at a concern about the intelligence failure.

"How could the Capitol Hill police not have protected us from what they knew was going to be a large gathering?"

But what about the hit to America's prestige internationally? How are presidents, and Pompeo's successors at the State Department, supposed to make the case that in a competitive global marketplace the United States offers the better model, and makes a better partner, than a rising communist China? Doesn't Trump's refusal to accept the results of the 2020 election, citing claims of massive fraud, and the subsequent insurrection at the Capitol, enable Chinese autocrat Xi Jinping to make a credible case that American democracy is in decline, if not a mirage?

"I actually think that what took place on the sixth gives every [American] leader, everybody who's still at the State Department, a chance to talk about how American democracy is different," Pompeo said. "In another country, they might well not have retaken [the Capitol]. It might be that the junta, that the military would still own and control it. I've seen this time and time again. That didn't happen in the United States."

Pompeo was right, in so much as "All's well that ends well." But the secretary took the events of January 6 far more seriously, and found the failed insurrection far more problematic, than he has been willing to let on for public consumption. In the days after the mayhem, White House officials and members of Trump's cabinet resigned. Talk of a second impeachment and a possible removal via the Twenty-Fifth Amendment swirled. The speculation in Washington was that no one was minding the store in the Oval—that the president had simply checked out, angry that his ouster was indeed a done deal, and humiliated by what occurred on his watch. Pompeo was concerned enough about the message this mess was sending abroad that he decided to send a subtle clarifier to American adversaries, assuring them a firm hand remained on command and control of the government's national security apparatus and, if need be, capabilities.

On Friday, January 8, two days after the Capitol riot, Pompeo tweeted a picture of himself, Director of National Intelligence John Ratcliffe, and National Security Adviser Robert C. O'Brien in discussion around a table in an unnamed but formal-looking federal office. "Honored to work alongside [Ratcliffe] and @WHNSC Robert O'Brien," Pompeo wrote. "Great patriots who work every day to make America and the world safer and more prosperous."

———◆———

CHAPTER SEVEN

"That Day"

Donald Trump was sulking in the White House, refusing to concede to Joe Biden, stubbornly clinging to wild conspiracy theories that would somehow, some way, deliver him another four years in the Oval Office. **Mike Pence**, ever the dutiful soldier, didn't say a word to the contrary. "Trump-Pence" fund-raising emails, some issued in the vice president's name, were spit out by the hour, and by the dozen, appealing for resources to finance an "election defense fund" to produce victory where none could possibly exist after all legal votes had been counted. In some instances, the votes were recounted, and then recounted again, as Trump and his most fervent supporters wailed on Twitter to "#StoptheSteal." Like so much of the last four-plus years, it seemed an odd juxtaposition for Pence.

The gracious midwesterner is an institutionalist who believes elections have consequences. Before finally winning a seat in the House of Representatives in 2000, the future forty-eighth vice president of the United States lost—twice, in 1988 and 1990. It never occurred to Pence to cry foul about the results. It occurred to him to take an introspective look at why voters kept rejecting him and to hone his craft. Over the next decade, Pence would run a conservative think tank and host a talk radio program. He immersed himself in public policy and interacted with a call-in audience of mostly Republican voters, three hours a day, five days a week. Ten years later, after a third campaign in which defeat would have permanently doomed his political aspirations, Pence enjoyed the thrill of victory. The outcome was unfettered by preposterous claims of fraud or theft. In the late twentieth century, it simply did not occur to an American politician to do anything other than accept, gracefully, the agony of defeat. It certainly would not have occurred to Pence to do anything but.

Winning, too, carries responsibilities. Some may be politically inconvenient. That did not stop Pence from taking them seriously and honoring them. A dozen years after his breakthrough victory and the distinguished career in Congress it spawned, Pence earned a spot on the short list of potentially formidable Republican presidential candidates. He ran for governor of Indiana instead. After Obama was reelected the same year, Pence was stuck greeting the Democratic president on the tarmac, with hand extended in front of the cameras, whenever Air Force One touched down in his state.

Well, not stuck. Pence was compelled by respect for the office of the presidency and an inherent sense of duty and commitment to American political tradition. As it happens, this once innocent bit of ceremony has been known over the past twenty years to come back to bite the politicians who honored it. In the heat of a primary campaign for nomination or renomination, making nice with the opposition makes for an easy attack ad that suggests a lack of "fight"—among the most prized candidate attributes of late. And so even though it had become rote for Pence to steadfastly cling to his boss in public more than four years after Trump plucked him from an uncertain reelection campaign for governor to be his running mate, his de facto participation in this ultimate undermining of American institutions and traditions was glaringly out of step with the vice president's character. It was such that he initially froze any actions that might be interpreted as acknowledging the results of the 2020 election, acknowledging that Joe Biden was going to be the president of the United States at noon on January 20, 2021. That included making inquiries with Realtors back in Indiana so that he and his wife, outgoing Second Lady Karen Pence, could find a place for them to live after they moved out of the vice president's residence on the grounds of the Naval Observatory in Northwest Washington, DC, to make way for Vice President Kamala Harris and Second Gentleman Doug Emhoff.

But quietly, sequestered from the cameras and the hamster wheel of Beltway gossip, Pence already had a plan in motion.

————

The early days of the post-2020-election period were marked by Trump's ahistorical non-concession. In laymen's terms: It was bizarre. Adding to the upside down of it all, even as the outgoing president insisted that he wasn't going anywhere, he was furiously dropping hints that he planned to seek the White House again in 2024. Initial assumptions were that Trump would freeze a field of presidential primary candidates otherwise expected to be as crowded as a New York subway car in prepandemic rush hour. Oh well. Not only were several Republican climbers continuing their White House preparations apace; Pence, the epitome of the loyal No. 2, was among them. As Trump tweeted through November and into December that the "rigged" 2020 election was "far from over," Pence's top advisers were sketching out a deliberate and strategic blueprint for the post vice presidency. It would keep the conservative stalwart front and center in the Republican consciousness over the next couple of years. It would prime the pump for a campaign for the GOP nomination for president from Pence's planned home base and political headquarters—Indiana—when the time was right. Job One would be to stand up a political nonprofit organization, a 501(c)4, that includes as advisers Trump World insiders and is adroitly constructed to promote Pence without getting him crossways with the forty-fifth president or the legion of loyalists clamoring for the return of their king. Advancing American Freedom launched in April 2021, ahead of Pence's first trip to South Carolina as an ex–vice president. The group's advisory board included a cross section of Republicans, including, as planned all along, some key Trump administration veterans, such as former chief White House economic adviser Larry Kudlow and former White House counselor Kellyanne Conway, plus all-around Trump cheerleader Newt Gingrich, former Speaker of the House of Representatives.

Federal law limits electioneering by political nonprofits. Their primary usefulness is policy advocacy. But they happen to be the perfect vehicle for the politician who needs to stay in the public eye, and stay relevant, during an extended period prior to running for the office that is the apple of their political eye. That is especially true because they allow for one critical aspect of political activity: building the proprietary lists of grassroots supporters and small-dollar contributors that are increasingly the lifeblood of viable presidential campaigns. (Since he joined the Republican ticket in the summer of 2016, every name, email, cell phone number, and other piece of information Pence helped Trump collect for his two presidential campaigns—of which he was an integral part—generally belongs to Trump. Nothing nefarious—that's life as the understudy.)

The policy aspect to all of this was critically important to the plans Pence was making for his next chapter, despite the fact it was likely to be overshadowed by the sexier, political component to the nonprofit's mission that will more obviously suggest a nascent presidential campaign is afoot. To stay simpatico with Trump and his acolytes, Pence planned to spend the next few years using his group to defend the exasperated ex-president's "America First" legacy by doing battle with Biden, Harris, congressional Democrats, and anyone else who might undo it, either through the legislative process or in the courts. What MAGAmaniac could possibly have any problem with that?

As the calendar flips from 2021 to 2022, phase II of the Pence postelection plan is likely to take shape in the form of a resurgent Great America Committee, the political action committee the former vice president unveiled soon after he and Trump were sworn into office in 2017. Through this overtly political vehicle, Pence planned to raise money and campaign for Republicans up and down the ballot—gubernatorial candidates, congressional candidates, even those running for office at the state and local levels. Party efforts to recapture a narrowly divided US Senate after a brief, two-year interregnum, and reclaim the House of Representatives after four years out of power, are going to be a magnet for 2024 Republicans. Even in Trump's shadow, the jockeying will be fierce, but Pence begins with a head start: He's already a known quantity. Early in Trump's presidency, the president was generally uninterested in mundane party-building activities outside of playing host of his traveling rally road show; his vice president filled the void with gusto. Whether Trump mounts a third White House bid in 2024 or not, Pence had a plan to put himself in position to pull the trigger on a presidential campaign, and he was executing.

———

So much ink has been spilled about Pence and his odd-couple political marriage to Trump.

Pence voted for Democratic president Jimmy Carter in 1980. Four years later, Ronald Reagan had turned him into a conservative Republican. Like so many Republicans of his era, Pence modeled his political persona on the Reagan model. Pious, principled, polite. Pence's calling card for years was: "I'm conservative but I'm not angry about it."

Yet this happy warrior went ahead and hitched his ride to a trash-talking, transactional populist with little regard for the truth whom Pence, presumably, never would have tolerated in his personal or professional life. As the story goes, Pence subjugated himself to Trump, sidelining integrity earned over the course of a career to assure and reassure wary Republicans and a skeptical public that it was safe to hand the nuclear codes to a master social media troll. Pence no doubt contributed to the myth with fawning praise, lavished on his boss for public consumption.

"The greatest privilege of my life is to serve as vice president to a president who's keeping his word to the American people; assembling a team that's bringing real change, real prosperity, real strength back to our nation," Pence said in June 2017 as Trump presided over a meeting of his cabinet with cameras rolling, setting an obsequious tone for the rest to follow.

The vice president was at it again six months later, just after the US Senate voted to approve what would turn out to be Trump's signature legislative achievement—passage of a $1.3 trillion tax overhaul. Only this time, Pence hammed it up for effect:

"I know I speak on behalf of the entire cabinet, of millions of

Americans, when I say, 'Congratulations and thank you.' Thank you for seeing through the course of this year an agenda that truly is restoring this country...And I'm deeply humbled as your vice president to be able to be here."

The Trump toady is a unique political species that mushroomed throughout the Republican Party—and, really, the broader conservative ecosphere—during the latter half of the 2010s. For four of those years, Pence delivered an Oscar-worthy performance as the quintessential idolator. But underneath the aw-shucks, dear-leader routine Pence played so well for public consumption was an assertive, shrewd politician who maximized his relationship with a president who knew a whole lot less about how to run a government—and party politics—than his vice president. It was like that from the beginning. Pence and Trump weren't exactly on a first-name basis when the flamboyant New Yorker plucked the self-effacing Hoosier to be his running mate. They had met briefly some years earlier, once when Pence traveled to Florida for events in his capacity as a congressman representing Indiana's Sixth Congressional District, and later, in 2011, as he ramped up his bid for governor, while on a fund-raising swing through New York.

Fast-forward five years, and Pence, in the middle of running for a second term as governor, huddled with Trump and a close adviser, former New Jersey governor Chris Christie, in Indiana. Trump, the leading candidate for the Republican presidential nomination, sought Pence's endorsement as he looked to close out Texas senator Ted Cruz in Indiana's crucial primary. The governor ultimately backed Cruz. The two were aligned ideologically and shared a penchant for bucking party leadership on Capitol Hill—Cruz then and Pence during his early years in Congress. But Pence came away from his meeting with Trump impressed, finding a lot more substance to the man than was apparent by the Ringling Brothers act he perpetuated in public.

So, in a bit of cunning, underestimated at the time as Pence's trademark cautiousness, the governor watered down his endorsement of Cruz with a heavy dose of high praise for Trump.

"I like and respect all three of the Republican candidates in the field," Pence said, referring also to the supremely unlikable John Kasich, then Ohio's governor. "I particularly want to commend Donald Trump, who I think has given voice to the frustration of millions of working Americans with a lack of progress in Washington, DC. And, I'm also particularly grateful that Donald Trump has taken a strong stand for Hoosier jobs when we saw... the Carrier Company abruptly announce leaving Indiana, not for another state but for Mexico. I'm grateful; I'm grateful for his voice in the national debate."

Wait, wasn't this a Cruz endorsement?

Criticized at the time as, well, chickenshit, Pence's backhanded endorsement of Cruz and deft massaging of Trump's ego even as he spurned the notoriously sensitive strongman revealed a keener understanding of his future boss and astute sense of where the Republican Party was headed than most GOP insiders of his ilk had.

It's difficult to overestimate how those two early, failed campaigns for Congress shaped Pence.

Rather than mark the 1990s by climbing the political ladder to stake his claim as the next Ronald Reagan, Pence spent the decade wandering the wilderness. For a young, aspiring politician talked about in Republican circles as a rising star, the experience was humbling. It matured him. By the time Pence sought the House of Representatives a third time, the politician in a hurry, motivated by ambition, had been replaced by a methodical plotter driven by faith in God and a desire to serve. There were still stars in his eyes. Pence fashioned himself the leader of a conservative insurgency at a time when Republicans controlled most of Washington and a pragmatic party establishment reigned virtually unmolested by outside forces in the media and grassroots circles.

In 2001, toward the end of his first year in the House of Representatives, Pence voted against President George W. Bush's bipartisan education reform legislation, the No Child Left Behind Act, which then had the support of most Republicans and was well received by voters. The next year, just his second on Capitol Hill, Pence resisted strong-arming by the Bush White House and House GOP leaders and voted against the president's popular expansion of prescription drug coverage for seniors as provided for under Medicare. A few years later, Pence ran for and was elected chairman of the Republican Study Committee, serving from 2005 to 2007. Before there was a House Freedom Caucus, the RSC was *the* caucus to join for conservatives who wanted to push Republican leadership to embrace more far-reaching legislation and mix it up more aggressively with the Democrats.

Then, in 2006, just after Democrats won control of Congress for the first time in a dozen years, Pence challenged John Boehner of Ohio for minority leader. He got clobbered, earning just one-fifth the votes of his peers compared to the future House Speaker. Two years later, Boehner invited Pence to run for Republican Conference chairman, the No. 3 ranking in the leadership pecking order when the party is in the House minority. Pence accepted and, facing no opposition, was installed with unanimous support. During this period, Pence at key moments exhibited the sort of unwavering loyalty to colleagues, and resolute commitment to task, that would spark so much derision from critics years later when practiced in service to Trump. In late 2002, Pence stood for Jim Ryun and supported the Kansan's bid to become Republican Conference chairman in the 108th Congress. It was obvious that Ryun would fall short—and he did, finishing a dismal third out of three candidates. But Pence had made a commitment to his friend and fellow conservative; Ryun at one point was ranked the most conservative member of Congress. So Pence defied House GOP leadership, who was whipping for the eventual runaway winner, Ohio representative Deborah Pryce, and spoke on Ryun's behalf before the vote.

Eight years later, soon after being elected Republican Conference chairman himself, a US Senate seat opened up in Indiana unexpectedly when Democrat Evan Bayh announced he would forgo reelection and retire at the end of 2010. The party faithful wanted Pence to run.

Republican insiders encouraged him to mount a campaign. There were even calls for Pence to seek the White House in 2012. Obama was up for reelection that year and the economy was limping along a bumpy road to recovery from the Great Recession. The Republican field was wide open.

Pence would have been formidable. Despite joining the GOP leadership team in the House of Representatives, Pence's prominent clashes with the party establishment over the years had cemented his bona fides with a grassroots activist base that was growing rebellious and feeling more and more disenchanted with its leaders in Washington. But Pence had made a commitment. Just a couple of months before Bayh announced his retirement, the future vice president had accepted Boehner's invitation to run for House Republican Conference chairman. He had asked colleagues to support his candidacy for leadership. He did not feel comfortable walking away.

Six years later, embroiled in an uncertain race for reelection as governor, Pence wouldn't be so cautious about an opportunity to advance when Trump came calling. This time, he was ready to maneuver.

———

Mike Pence never lost faith—in himself or Trump.

It was a Thursday in the middle of July 2020, four months before his career as vice president would be cut short in a particularly pointed rebuke of Trump. In public and private polling, the Republican ticket was in a world of hurt. The pandemic was raging early that summer as coronavirus ravaged states that had survived the initial spring wave relatively unscathed. The economy was still cratering, as businesses big and small reeled from government-enforced lockdowns intended to slow the spread of COVID-19. Civil unrest tore apart communities across the United States, as Americans protested racial injustice, and criminals looted and rioted, in the aftermath of the death of George Floyd.

But Mike Pence was serene, confident, and very optimistic. That much became clear to me as I trailed the vice president across central Pennsylvania, toward Philadelphia, while on assignment for the

Washington Examiner. Earlier that year, before the pandemic froze regular political activity, Pence's political team got wind of a couple of plush, armor-plated touring buses manufactured for the federal government during the Obama administration but that had spent the Trump years mothballed. Taken with the idea of hitting the 2020 campaign trail in a couple of billboards on wheels, Team Pence had the vehicles mechanically prepped, painted blue, and emblazoned with the slogan "Trump-Pence, Keep America Great, 2020" alongside smiling pictures of the president and vice president.

After months of delay due to the pandemic, Pence kicked off his first bus tour of the reelection campaign in Pennsylvania, the commonwealth that mattered most. That day, there was no hint of the anxiety that he had every right to feel. As Pence wound his way through rural Lancaster County's two-lane roads, the bus stopped at one point and the vice president exited to greet supporters who were lining nearly every inch of road with official and homemade Trump-Pence campaign signs. After pocketing an easy $1 million for the campaign at an outdoor fund-raiser on the grounds of a local farm owned by a wealthy Republican donor, Pence sped off to a roundtable at a technology firm. He ended the day in Philadelphia with a scorcher of a speech (by Pence standards, at least) to police officers and their family members at a Fraternal Order of Police lodge in which he accused Biden of turning his back on law enforcement and siding with the anarchist mobs ravaging American cities.

Afterward, I boarded the bus for a chat with Pence as we made our way to the airport for the ride back to Washington on Air Force Two. The vice president was giddy; he was energized. The support he witnessed along the back roads of central Pennsylvania, and the response from the audience at each stop, had him absolutely convinced there was only one way the reelection campaign would end. And Biden being declared president-elect once a sufficient number of votes had been counted did not figure into that equation.

"I don't put a lot of stock in the polls," he told me, as chief of staff Marc Short, press secretary Katie Miller, and top political adviser Marty

Obst looked on. "I sense people are more enthusiastic today than they were four years ago."

What struck me about Pence over the next forty-five minutes was how effective he was as a messenger for Trump. The forty-fifth president was the showman; he sparked a movement that turned unlikely voters into Trump voters and occasional Republican voters into regular Republican voters. His showing in 2020, more than 74 million voters, was the most ever for a sitting president—pretty good, except for the fact that Biden did better. But Pence softened Trump's rough edges and translated his populist stage rants into recognizable conservative policy, something that mattered for a good bit of the coalition that carried the two of them into the White House in 2016 and nearly did so again four years later.

As Pence's bus rumbled toward the airport, I tried to pin him down on myriad controversies stoked by Trump; I probed for daylight between them on topics that Pence most certainly must have approached differently given their two starkly different political pedigrees. In light of current events, I asked about Trump's stubborn insistence on equating monuments to the Founders with memorials to Confederate traitors in his admonition against removing such statues from the public square. Our conversation made clear there simply was no separating Pence from Trump, no matter the subject, no matter the controversy, no matter the inherent disagreement between the two. At best, Pence would redirect. He is rather adept at explaining how Trump didn't mean what you thought he meant, but rather meant something that makes a lot more sense and is a whole lot more acceptable.

Failing that, Pence will admit that he was wrong and Trump was right (apparently). Toward the end of the interview, Pence volunteered that a Biden administration would "surrender" to China. So I asked the vice president: Wouldn't the United States be in a better position to contain Beijing had Trump implemented the Trans-Pacific Partnership, the multilateral trade deal between Washington and a collection of Asian nations that was negotiated by Obama just before he left office and would have bound China's neighbors more tightly to the United States?

"Let me tell you something," Pence countered. "I was on a learning curve with all of this myself. When I was in Congress, I supported virtually every trade agreement that ever kind of came before the Congress. One of the things, that in one of our very early conversations, one of the things that the president said to me during the campaign was that these multinational trading agreements are not in America's best interest because you lose leverage."

The vice president's remarks were heartfelt. They also amounted to a strategic choice that Pence decided on very early on to maintain a seat at the table that for four years quietly afforded him immense leverage to operate more independently than most vice presidents.

From the moment Pence was hired as Trump's running mate, in the summer of 2016, he has operated with an unusual degree of autonomy, politically and as a policymaker. This unique partnership unfolded both by design (Pence took the initiative) and circumstance (Trump's inexperience and disinterest). From day one, Pence demanded from the Trump campaign authority to pick his team and surround himself with loyalists who understood what made him tick and would prioritize his success.

The vice president would spend more than four years navigating all manner of controversy and scandal generated by Trump—reckonings big and small that put him directly at odds with Trump. And that was on top of the occasional policy choice made by the president that ran afoul of what his vice president believed in, and had advocated, over thirty years in the public eye. What did Pence do? Without expressing a hint of hesitation or regret, he saluted and carried out his orders. It was a deliberate, strategic choice, made over and over again.

———

Trump let Pence have the run of the place. When Pence asked for autonomy over his team upon joining the 2016 campaign, Trump said yes. When Pence asked for autonomy over his itinerary—where to campaign, when to campaign, how to campaign, Trump said yes. When Pence filled gaping holes in the MAGA agenda with mostly conventional, conservative

Republicanism instantly recognizable and comforting to skittish GOP voters, Trump went along with it. The former president is seemingly so domineering and the former vice president seemingly so compliant, it obscured a mutual partnership under which Pence exercised inordinate political power.

Trump was the senior partner, protocol Pence was always careful to observe. In showing deference, Pence obtained from Trump the green light to act independently. He alluded to this dynamic in our interview, recollecting about the 2016 campaign, "I'll never forget one of our first conversations. He told me, 'You go north, I'll go south. You go east, I'll go west.'"

As usual, Pence framed his role in the decision-making process as subordinate to Trump's wishes. In reality, Pence proactively drove campaign strategy, at times steering the ship completely. In part, that is because Pence injected into Team Trump decades of political experience that the principal lacked (his unique political abilities and achievements notwithstanding). And he brought forth a group of experienced, battle-tested advisers who could run circles around a threadbare Trump campaign that amounted to a group of loyalists numbering barely enough to field a basketball team's starting five.

Along with senior strategist and future chief of staff No. 2, Nick Ayers, top fund-raiser Marty Obst, future chief of staff No. 1 Josh Pitcock, and future chief of staff No. 3 Marc Short, the first thing Pence did upon joining the Trump campaign was to pore over polling and data analytics and, superimposing the information on the calendar, map out a strategy for where, when, and how to deploy himself to bolster Trump's (and his) prospects against Hillary Clinton, the Democratic nominee, and her running mate, Senator Tim Kaine of Virginia. To head off any friction, Pence kept Trump in the loop. In those early days after accepting the vice presidential nomination in Cleveland, Pence used the telephone, Trump's favorite mode of communication, to cultivate first a working relationship, and then a friendship with his new boss. In what would become a hallmark of Trump's interaction with Republicans on Capitol Hill unaccustomed to dealing with presidents interested in dealing with them, he and Pence typically began and ended every day with a telephone call, often trading phone calls several times in between. Pence's reciprocation was crucial. It helped him earn Trump's trust, which in turn allowed him to accrue more power within this new, political division of the Trump Organization.

Pence's decision to stick by Trump through scandal, particularly the *Access Hollywood* row, a choice made after considerable deliberation with his wife, cemented that trust, and Pence's power base. When Trump's son-in-law and chief adviser Jared Kushner summarily dismissed Chris Christie from the presidential transition effort and incinerated the extensive work he had put in to prepare Trump to staff his administration, Pence was put in charge. In fact, it was Pence who played a key role in Trump's decision to hire onetime critics and potential 2024 rivals Nikki Haley and Mike Pompeo for prominent positions in his administration.

———

The vice president doesn't really have anything to do, not officially, anyway. He (and now she) presides over the US Senate as president of the chamber but is virtually powerless to influence the proceedings. In the case of a deadlocked vote on legislation or a president's nominee to serve on the judiciary or in the executive branch, they cast the tiebreaker.

That's hardly enough to fill a workday, except on rare occasions when American voters have sent to Washington a Senate split evenly among the two major political parties. How symbolically divorced from the executive is the office of the vice president? For payroll purposes, they are employees of the legislative branch. Vice presidents were irrelevant through much of American history, except when called upon to fulfill their prime function. That has steadily changed in the modern era. Recently, some have been especially consequential, acting as governing partners and wielding authority within administrations. Ironically, an increasingly nationalized political environment has diminished a running mate's ability to deliver critical Electoral College votes to a presidential campaign. Pence's immediate predecessors, Biden and Dick Cheney, were picked despite hailing from states, Delaware and Wyoming, that are each worth three electoral votes. (Indeed, twice this century, in 2000 and 2016, the Democratic and Republican nominees, respectively, lost their home states, outcomes unthinkable a generation ago.)

The evolution of the vice presidency is due in no small part to enterprising politicians uninterested in spending four, or eight, years as a withering houseplant that its owners neglect to water. They demanded a seat at the table as a condition for joining the ticket. And with Trump, the table was practically barren as he readied to take the oath of office, and for several months afterward. He was a rookie politician with few Washington allies and virtually no idea how government worked. The forty-eighth vice president filled the void. In fact, Pence assumed so much power and influence—it was just sitting there for the vacuuming—that Trump World insiders who watched events unfold say he took on the role of de facto prime minister.

Pence initially served as a West Wing gatekeeper for corporate and political interests with business before the administration, a dynamic that receded but never really faded even as Trump gained a firmer grasp on governing and developed close personal relationships with Republicans on Capitol Hill. That was in part due to the fact that professional Washington was familiar with the vice president and his team. In turn, Pence and his lieutenants understood the political pressures and limitations Republicans faced as members of Congress that were often lost on Trump.

The business community sought out Pence for a very basic reason. As explained to me by a Republican lobbyist friendly with the Trump White House, "I have corporate clients who would say, 'Oh, we really need to get to Pence because he's going to be the sane guy in the room.'"

It wasn't necessarily Pence's fault that this was the prevailing sentiment. Trump doesn't take kindly to criticism. When problems arose, many allies of the administration preferred to go to the vice president with their complaints.

"My rule of thumb when I was governor, in particular, was, if I agreed with the president, I said it. If I had a problem with him, I called Mike Pence," Scott Walker, former Wisconsin governor, told me.

The vice president and his office was the only place to go on the White House grounds where a corporate executive, politician, or lobbyist was guaranteed to get an audience to air their concerns and get answers, even if those answers were "No." Pence embraced it, both the attention it attracted from power brokers in business and politics and the influence it afforded in Washington.

Meanwhile, the vice president stood up a distinctly separate political operation inside the White House and launched a political action committee that only he controlled. Pence is a devout Christian and often speaks publicly (and privately) of politics and his political future being in God's hands—a belief that is heartfelt. But underneath, Pence is an interested political tactician with a keen eye for strategy who is an active member of his political team's decision-making process. So, immediately following the 2016 campaign, Pence convened with Ayers and Obst to develop a blueprint for his political operation as vice president, what to focus on and how to deploy himself. The first decision Pence made was to bypass the White House political shop headed by Bill Stepien, who would emerge as one of the president's most trusted aides and, in July 2020, manager of his reelection campaign. His second big move was greenlighting GAC—Great America Committee. The group was a standard, hard-dollar political action committee, the sort of leadership PAC popular with members of Congress.

According to federal guidelines, these kinds of PACs can accept contributions of only $5,000 annually from individual donors. It was unusual for a vice president to raise his own pot of money. Normally, the No. 2 executive operates through the auspices of the national party committee. Pence wanted to avoid interference from the Republican National Committee and, frankly, anyone else. Great America Committee offered an efficient way to finance expensive travel on gas-guzzling Air Force Two, which, incidentally, saved the RNC money, and by extension, saved

Trump money. But the key to understanding Pence's decision to form his own political action committee was that he wanted control. Having served in the House of Representatives for a dozen years, in the minority and majority, under Democratic and Republican presidents, he knew what awaited Trump, and the GOP, in the 2018 midterm elections. Pence wanted to chart a course to resist the blue wave he feared might build over the next two years unfettered from meddlers inside the party: where he traveled, where he raised his money from, who he campaigned for. Among his first moves was to put together a joint fund-raising committee tying Great America Committee to House Majority Leader Kevin McCarthy.

Being able to promote his connection with the vice president helped the California Republican raise money for his colleagues. It also promoted the vice president (but more on that in a moment). Great America Committee raised $20 million that election cycle, giving most of it away in direct donations to House Republicans and spending the rest on the vice president's extensive campaign travel. How extensive? Pence hit the road for 160 political events in 2017 and 2018. That's an average of nearly seven per month, or nearly two per week. That's not counting the events Pence headlined in Washington. Prior to launching GAC, Pence and his team ran it by Trump and his chief White House adviser, son-in-law Jared Kushner. They pitched the PAC and the vice president's planned political activities as a vehicle, and strategy, to protect the president's political flank and shield the future of his legislative agenda from a Democratic takeover of Congress in the next election.

That's not to whitewash the fact that Pence had his own agenda. Pence wanted to be master of his fate; the brain trust he surrounded himself with certainly did. There were ancillary benefits to this approach to bolstering Trump's political interests—of which they were well aware. This unorthodox setup put Pence on the front lines of Republican politics at a time when Trump had little interest in party-building activities, and the GOP establishment, from elected officials to donors to grassroots activists, hardly knew the president personally and was still coming to terms with his surprising victory. These people desperately sought a conduit into the

White House. Or at least they wanted to maintain the same open lines of communication they had always enjoyed with prominent Republicans in Washington. Pence designed it so that he was their point man and could travel to meet with them personally. Ditto for the populist elements of the MAGA coalition Trump activated in 2016 but with whom Pence was unfamiliar, having matriculated from the Republican Party's traditional wing.

In doing so, the vice president was cultivating relationships across the GOP, old and new, laying the foundation for a hoped-for strong second term under Trump and a 2024 presidential bid. That included meetings like the one he held with the American Opportunity Alliance in early 2019 as a part of his assumed role as Trump's ambassador to wealthy Republican donors, a community with which the president was initially antagonistic but grew more friendly with over time—and vice versa. The AOA is a press-shy organization of Republican billionaires led by hedge fund mogul Paul Singer that meets regularly with GOP candidates and incumbents— by invitation only. Pence was the sort of conservative they were familiar with, comfortable with. That included meetings like the one he held with about fifteen influential Republican activists, operatives, and campaign contributors in Columbia, South Carolina, a crucial early primary state, also in early 2019. That included headlining a big fund-raiser in 2017 for Governor Chris Sununu of New Hampshire, host of the first presidential primary and second contest overall on the nominating calendar.

———

On the outside, it appeared to some as though Pence was building a wall to keep out crazy, that he was prepping for a political future that might arrive sooner than originally scheduled.

Perceptions were fueled by a White House generally engulfed in chaos, stoked almost minute by minute by the guy at the top, especially, but not limited to, the first two years of the administration. Leaks, infighting, paralysis, confusion, staff turnover. As if that wasn't enough, just shy of four months after Trump was inaugurated, the Department of Justice

appointed Robert Mueller, the former director of the Federal Bureau of
Investigation, as special counsel in charge of the federal investigation into
allegations that Trump and his campaign conspired with Russia and its
strongman leader, Vladimir Putin, to defeat Clinton.

Yet beneath all that smoke, there was little daylight visible between
Trump and his vice president. Pence wouldn't stand for it, much to the
chagrin of some longtime allies. After the 2016 election, Trump and
Pence were welcomed to the White House by Obama and Biden in a show
of détente for the cameras; part of the uniquely American democratic
ritual—quaint, apparently—in which the outgoing administration, especially one of the opposing political party, assists in the peaceful transfer of
power.

During their powwow, Biden offered Pence a piece of advice: Demand
facetime with the president; schedule a weekly lunch. Pence followed
Biden's counsel—and then some. He spent nearly as much time in the
Oval as Trump, making sure to attend meetings big and small and be
present for discussions, consequential and trivial, often with Ayers by his
side. Pence read Trump into everything. That included asking the president for his seal of approval before moving forward with Great America
Committee, and updating him on details of his conversations with CEOs
and key political figures. Pence, a close associate recounted, was preoccupied with proving his loyalty to the president.

That's understandable, if off-putting. Trump himself is preoccupied
with loyalty—loyalty to him. Get that part right and he'll overlook almost
any perceived transgression. For four years, the president existed under
a cloud of personal and political scandal of the sort which ran afoul of
the reputation for integrity that Pence built, and nurtured, over decades
in public life. Pence wouldn't budge, couldn't be goaded. Critics called
it fealty. Supporters called it smart politics. It was an amalgamation.
Distancing himself from Trump, never mind some kind of betrayal, public or private, was unthinkable.

"That is just not who he is," a Pence admirer said. "That is biblical for
him." It endeared him to Trump and strengthened their bond.

However. A vice president doesn't run his own show, surrounded by hard-nosed campaign operatives loyal to *him*, out promoting *him*, without drawing attention—and scrutiny. In this case, the attention of the Washington press corps and scrutiny from Trump partisans suspicious of Republican establishment figures like Pence that were so prevalent in the president's orbit in the beginning of his presidency.

First came reporting from the *New York Times*, with a story published on August 5, 2017, in the early days of the Russia investigation, when many prominent Republicans speculated the probe might sink Trump's presidency, possibly before the end of his term. In "Republican Shadow Campaign for 2020 Takes Shape as Trump Doubts Grow," reporters Jonathan Martin and Alexander Burns detailed the formation of Great America Committee, Pence's robust political activity, and the authority over that activity he had seized as early as his invitation to join the 2016 ticket. "Some in the party's establishment wing are remarkably open about their wish that Mr. Pence would be the Republican standard-bearer in 2020," they wrote.

Politico struck nearly eight weeks later with "Pence Group Rakes in Corporate PAC Money," a three-byline story that focused on the vice president's proprietary fund-raising operation. "Skeptics say there's no good reason for the vice president to build his own political outside group unless it's to further his own political ambitions," wrote Maggie Severns, Matthew Nussbaum, and Ben Lefebvre.

The stories kept coming. Fast-forward to mid-May the following year. The *New York Times* hit again with "Pence Is Trying to Control Republican Politics. Trump Aides Aren't Happy." This time, Maggie Haberman joined Burns and Martin for a piece that cast Pence as an increasingly assertive figure who was hoarding political power at the expense of the president, granting favors and making decisions that reverberated across the GOP. "Republican officials now see Mr. Pence as seeking to exercise expansive control over a political party ostensibly helmed by Mr. Trump, tending to his own allies and interests even when the president's instincts lean in another direction."

Two days after this story broke, *Vanity Fair*'s the Hive, where I am a contributing writer, published a piece I had been working on for several weeks: " 'Pence Is Not Stupid': As Trump Sinks, G.O.P. Insiders See a Shadow Campaign Taking Shape—Could Pence's Ambition Make Him the President's Next Mortal Enemy? Or Will His Well-Oiled Political Operation Allay Trump's Concerns—At Least for Now?"

Everything Pence was doing—the broad strokes, at least—had been approved by Trump from the very beginning. The vice president objected to these stories strenuously, publicly, insisting there was no hidden agenda nor actions taken based on lack of faith in the president's political staying power. His aides were frustrated. If they had a Pence 2020 campaign in mind, the last thing they would do is try to seed the effort with a harddollar PAC that could only accept money in dribs and drabs—because doing so would be so obviously ineffective. Everybody knows political empires are built with super PACs and 501(c)4s. The reporting nonetheless caused problems for Pence. A media-obsessed and particularly *Times*-obsessed Trump read stories of his White House being in disarray and his impending demise, framed as Pence to the rescue, and he wasn't happy. A Republican operative who understood Trump and liked Pence laid out the risks for the vice president when I interviewed him for my *Vanity Fair* story.

"Sometimes [the vice president's] political organization moves so quickly, it creates the appearance that the vice president is purposely getting out in front of Trump," I wrote, paraphrasing the operative's concerns.

"It looks like he's trying to outflank the president, but really he's just steady and competent," this Republican insider told me. "It's a dangerous thing for the vice president."

Pence saw the writing on the wall. He decided to dial things back. The work continued apace—a full political calendar and heavy fund-raising through Great America Committee. But Pence moved quieter and shifted to a collaborative approach with the White House political shop and Trump's political advisers. The hope was that this new approach would tamp down on the rumor mill and put a stop to suggestions that Pence harbored concerns about Trump and was driven by ulterior motives.

By January 2019, as preparations for what was officially the "Trump-Pence" reelection campaign intensified, some Republicans were asking what happened to a vice president, former governor, and former congressional leader who had carried himself with such confidence, who had acted so consequentially. One friend, Indiana Republican David McIntosh, whose retirement from Congress made way for Pence and who now runs the Club for Growth, an influential conservative advocacy group, sent to the vice president through intermediaries his recommendation that it was time to assert himself again by picking an issue, something that would resonate with voters, and lead on it. Pence wasn't interested. He had concluded that his singular priority should be in an attendant role to Trump and his political and legislative priorities.

By the beginning of 2020, as the reelection campaign accelerated further, many Republican insiders—donors, operatives, and the like—had concluded that Pence was an honorable man and an effective vice president, but ultimately a "cheerleader," not an "executive leader." Their conclusions fomented doubts about Pence's 2024 viability at precisely the time when Trump's second-term prospects looked brightest. The president had been impeached, but it was a political flop for the Democrats. During the trial in the US Senate to adjudicate two articles of impeachment approved by the House of Representatives, Trump enjoyed some of the best approval ratings of his presidency. Meanwhile, the Democratic Party seemed poised to nominate for president socialist Vermont senator Bernie Sanders.

Then came two unexpected events with far-reaching ramifications, political and otherwise. Biden won in South Carolina and defeated Sanders in key primaries on the Super Tuesday that followed, quickly solidifying his position as the presumptive Democratic nominee. And the deadly coronavirus, which first emerged in Wuhan, China, struck the United States, enveloping the country in a pandemic that one year later had killed more than five hundred thousand Americans. Both developments would, in their own way, impact Pence, the latter more immediately. Trump tapped Pence to oversee the White House COVID-19 task force. The vice president played point in coordinating the efforts of an unwieldy collection of federal agencies while working with governors—especially governors who had a rocky relationship with Trump—to satisfy the needs of their states. Maryland governor Larry Hogan said Pence was a rock star amid the Trump administration's often chaotic federal response to the pandemic. In an interview, the prominent Trump critic, who is considering a presidential bid of his own in 2024, put it this way: "The one thing I complimented them on, mostly Mike Pence, but the administration, was they did do a tremendous outreach."

Hogan wasn't the only Republican to take notice of Pence's competent leadership of the task force. Some of the party insiders who had come to doubt Pence were reminded of his political acumen and leadership skills. As it turns out, Pence would have another opportunity to showcase his executive abilities before the year was out.

———

To prepare for the vice presidency, Pence read multiple biographies of vice presidents who had come before him. Two made a lasting impression and would influence his approach to serving under Trump. From Republican Calvin Coolidge, elected in 1920 as the twenty-ninth vice president, Pence learned that his primary function was to advance the president's policies as a member of the president's team. Emphasis: *his* policies, *his* team. From Republican George Herbert Walker Bush, elected in 1980 as the forty-third vice president, Pence learned how to handle differences of opinion with the president: Air your disagreement once, in private, and keep it confidential. That explains why Pence never spoke up in cabinet meetings to express even a hint of skepticism of anything regarding Trump. Presuming the cabinet would leak like a sieve, Pence stayed tight-lipped and waited for a moment alone to share his concerns with the president.

None of what Pence had gleaned from Coolidge and Bush, the rules of conduct he had established for himself over the past four-plus years, was applicable to January 6. This was a choice for the vice president to make and an action for the vice president to take. There was no way to keep a disagreement with Trump private.

We tend to forget, because until recently there was no need to remember, but there are three steps to the presidential election. In early November, the people vote. In mid-December, the Electoral College votes. In early January, Congress certifies the vote. Enter the vice president.

Under the Constitution, the vice president's job is to preside over the joint session of Congress and count state-certified Electoral College votes in his capacity as president of the US Senate. As long as there are not competing, certified slates of electors from the same state, or slates of electors submitted that have not been certified, there is nothing else for the vice president to do. Trump, instigated by a cast of advisers-cum-conspiracy theorists, had other ideas. If the Congress could be persuaded to block ascertainment of legal, state-certified Electoral College votes, Pence, so one of their theories went, could unilaterally send the rejected slates from so-called problem states back home. There, friendly, majority-Republican legislatures would use their so-called authority to reverse the initial vote, and Trump wins. Or: By unilaterally throwing out supposedly objectionable state-certified electoral votes, Pence could force a vote of the House of Representatives to decide the election. In such case, each state's House delegation gets one vote. Since Republicans control a majority of state delegations, Trump wins. All Pence had to do, Trump seemed convinced, was locate the intestinal fortitude to seize for himself this extraordinary constitutional power to decide the outcome of the election, over the will of American voters, that had been hiding in plain sight since the founding of the republic.

"Unfortunately, I think the president had some really, really bad advice, and the way that the White House was structured at that point was that those people giving that really, really bad advice were given carte blanche access to the president, and I think there were no safeguards in the way the White House was being run at that point," Marc Short, Pence's chief of staff from March 2019 until he left office, told me about a month later over a quiet lunch near the Capitol.

Pence saw it coming. He was troubled by it; he aimed to do something about it to make it less likely that a future president would ever be tempted down this road again. The options before Pence appeared binary: satisfy Trump and reject enough state-certified electoral votes to overturn the election—and, by the way, ignite a constitutional crisis. Or, rebuff Trump. Show up on Capitol Hill on January 6 and do what vice presidents before him have always done, even vice presidents who as presiding officer of the joint session were forced to certify their own defeat as the Democratic or Republican presidential nominee, ascertaining the winner by reading aloud the certificates of the Electoral College vote submitted by the several states and DC.

Pence created a third option.

Pence does not deny the existence of voter fraud, nor that it occurred in the election that made him a one-term vice president. In our interview the previous July, Pence said he shared Trump's concern that massive irregularities could result from coronavirus-inspired changes to the voting rules in many states that encouraged participation by mail and made it easier to do so.

"We believe in an absentee ballot system where people will request a ballot and give a basis for why they will not be participating in person," Pence told me. "But we're going to continue to oppose efforts around the country for a mass distribution of mailed ballots, because we think it's a potential for tremendous voter fraud."

But Pence is a constitutionalist. Every single legal challenge to Biden's victories in more than half a dozen states brought by the Trump campaign and its allies failed in court for one reason or another. Recounts in almost as many states failed to make a dent in Biden's tally of 306 electoral votes. The Electoral College met, it voted, and in every single state plus DC, the results were legally certified. By Republican officials, too. Also a critical metric that influenced Pence: No state submitted competing slates of certified electors. Especially after all of that but not only because of all of that, the notion—the conspiratorial theory—that the vice president was invested by the Framers of the US Constitution with the power to dictate presidential elections and held in his hands the authority to do so all these years struck Pence as plainly preposterous. He told Trump as much, informed and armed by reams of information on history and constitutional precedent researched and compiled by his general counsel, Gregory Jacob, a Justice Department veteran and longtime Washington attorney recruited to the vice president's office from white-shoe law firm O'Melveny & Myers. "We researched all of those, and I think very fastidiously wanted to be respectful of new perspectives that we were brought, but always felt strongly that no limited-government conservative would ever advocate that one person could unilaterally choose what electors to accept or reject and would ever be given that sort of power by our Founders. Nor would we ever want anyone to have that power," Short said.

In one particular meeting, on January 4, the conversation grew heated. Pence had been campaigning in Georgia that day in advance of a pair of Senate runoff elections on tap for the following day when a call came in to Air Force Two asking him to return to the White House. When he arrived, Trump was being briefed in the Oval Office by John Eastman, a prominent conservative law professor then at Chapman University in Southern California. "He's a respected constitutional attorney, you should hear him out," Trump said. In fact, Eastman was very well respected in conservative circles—and well known. He wasn't some Kraken crackpot. That Eastman was advising Trump of Pence's apparently extraordinary until-then-unknown powers left Pence and his team flabbergasted. In that January 4 meeting, the vice president listened courteously, as was his habit. But he held firm, as was also his habit, reiterating his position on the matter that he had relayed to the president, unwavering, so many times before in several cordial meetings that had gone unreported, maybe because none had erupted in a shouting match.

Facilitated by White House chief of staff Mark Meadows, Trump in the weeks leading up to January 6 was increasingly surrounded by people telling him what he wanted to hear: that Pence was empowered to reject electoral votes. All that was required was the political will to act. As the day of the joint session of Congress drew nearer and Trump latched himself tighter to this cockamamie theory, Pence began to fret that the forty-fifth president wouldn't be the last losing chief executive to be tempted by it. A future vice president, he thought, might not share his view of the Constitution and his conclusion that his role in the congressional certification of electoral votes was purely mechanical.

So Pence instructed Jacob to research the matter extensively and prepare documentation, in the form of a formal "Dear Colleague" letter that he would make public. "It was such a boneheaded analysis and so we wanted to have our record make that clear, too," Short said, emphasizing the significance of the letter for posterity.

The vice president's goals were twofold: Control the narrative in a stormy news environment and, more important, place a constitutional vise on his successors, and on Trump's that—like a precedent established in a Supreme Court decision—would hamstring them from traveling down this road for time immemorial.

"It is my considered judgement that my oath to support and defend the Constitution constrains me from claiming unilateral authority to determine which electoral votes should be counted and which should not," Pence wrote in the letter, issued just before the opening of the joint session on January 6.

At that moment, Trump was addressing a massive crowd of grassroots supporters who had gathered near the White House for a "#StoptheSteal" rally aimed at pressuring Congress and the vice president to reject certification of the November 3 election.

"If Mike Pence does the right thing, we win the election," Trump told the adoring sea of supporters. "He has the absolute right to do it."

Trump's speech on that January 6 morning was really no different from any other Trump speech. The media is fake; my presidency is beyond reproach; the election was stolen. The usual, but with a caveat. More than a half dozen times in seventy minutes, the forty-fifth president turned his attention to the forty-eighth vice president, assuring the crowd, without reservation, that he possessed constitutional authority to deliver his administration a second term.

"I hope Mike has the courage to do what he has to do," Trump said, despite already being fully aware of the vice president's decision on that matter.

"I hope he doesn't listen to RINOs [Republicans in Name Only] and the stupid people he's listening to."

Within a couple of hours of those remarks, Pence would be in hiding in an undisclosed location at the US Capitol. The building was under siege by a violent mob of grassroots Trump supporters, many of whom walked from one end of Pennsylvania Avenue to the other intent on using force to prevent the Congress from certifying that Biden would be inaugurated the forty-sixth president two weeks hence. The rioters were chanting, "Hang Mike Pence." In the middle of this shocking insurrection that was playing out as Americans all over the country watched on their television screens, Trump essentially called Pence a coward, expressing unhappiness that the vice president had done exactly what he told the president he was going to do when the counting of the electoral votes commenced.

"Mike Pence didn't have the courage to do what should have been done to protect our Country and our Constitution," Trump tweeted.

Much has been learned since then about how Pence conducted himself in those hours; much was witnessed. The vice president refused to leave the Capitol, wouldn't even wait out the mayhem in his secure automobile, as the Secret Service suggested, because he didn't trust that the agents wouldn't put their foot on the gas and speed him to safer confines.

With Trump taking little action to quell the violence, instead tweeting out oddly encouraging messages to the mob (that included the obligatory, though totally weak, admonishments to disperse), Pence filled the gap. He led. The vice president conferred with top Pentagon officials to accelerate deployment of security forces to the Capitol and kept in constant contact with Democratic and Republican leaders in the House and Senate: House Speaker Nancy Pelosi, Senate Minority Leader Charles Schumer, House Minority Leader Kevin McCarthy, and Senate Majority

Leader Mitch McConnell. What did Congress need, he wanted to know, so that the joint session could resume that very day, a prospect that in the middle of the siege seemed very much unlikely. Pence was determined to climb back onto the rostrum of the House of Representatives that day and finish certifying a presidential election, the results of which would oust him from office after one term.

When order was finally restored and lawmakers were returning to their respective chambers to finish debating the objection to Arizona's electoral votes and get on with the rest of the process, Pence asked McConnell if he could first say a few words from the dais about what had happened. The majority leader agreed. "As we reconvene in this chamber, the world will again witness the resilience and strength of our democracy," Pence said in remarks that lasted two and a half minutes. "Now let's get back to work." Republicans, in Washington and around the country, took notice.

Pence awoke the morning of January 6, 2021, possibly the least formidable heir apparent vice president to a president in a very long time. The Republican apparatus and a majority of the party's wealthy donors could have pledged their banners to Pence. Yet even if Trump had won a second term, it wouldn't necessarily have mattered all that much. Pence had two strikes against him wholly of his own making, and they created unique difficulties. He had never actually run for president. That may sound like a small thing, but in the eyes of ambitious Republicans with 2024 circled on their calendar, it added up to one less reason to stand down in deference to the vice president, reelected or not.

Pence's public relationship with Trump was the other problem. The forty-fifth president demanded that subordinates bend the knee. Pence tended to comply, both out of a sense of duty to the job and a matter of self-interested strategy. Stroking Trump's id enabled Pence to wield power and maneuver independently. None of that was apparent to Republican insiders who were not otherwise predisposed to back a Pence 2024 campaign. They saw a toady missing the stuff leaders are made of. Ditto grassroots conservatives. They appreciated Pence's loyalty as much as anyone short of Trump himself. The impression that loyalty left with them—that the vice president is by nature a follower, not a fighter—was problematic. Republican primary voters value fight in their leaders even more than unquestioned loyalty to Trump. Trump didn't make them this way, he simply proved in their eyes, by winning the presidency and coming damn close a second time around, that fighting is more than cathartic, it is effective, productive. On January 6, 2021, Pence flipped the script. To be crystal clear, he would much rather this particular opportunity to do so not arisen in the first place. But as Pence openly defied Trump, refusing to be bullied into an unconstitutional power grab, as Pence took command, practically in the middle of a war zone, while his boss shirked responsibility, doubts harbored by institutional leaders in the Republican Party, and by some in the broader conservative movement, melted.

Ironically, the Republican voting base saw the hard-nosed politician who had inspired so many grassroots conservatives to encourage a temperate Indiana congressman to run for president a decade earlier. They will have to see more of that, still—much more, if Pence is to dominate a 2024 primary. Pence would bristle at that assertion. Who over the past twenty years has fought harder in the public arena for conservative principles and policies, against Republicans and Democrats? In the age of Trump, being a workhorse is not enough.

"That is a part of leadership Mike's going to have to think through and make a slight change in how he does things, and projects things," one Republican ally said.

In the days after January 6, the telephone in the office of another Pence ally started ringing. Republican donors; county GOP chairmen, conservative activists, about two dozen in all, they all wanted to send word that (1) Trump's treatment of Pence on that day, especially after four years of loyal service, was appalling; and (2) if he runs for president in 2024, count them in.

"I had one person in Iowa that was upset," conceded this conservative operative. "Everybody else was like, 'You did the right thing; you made us proud'—including a few hardcore Trump supporters."

Every vice president who has ever run for president in the shadow of the president who made them has been faced with a dilemma: charting an independent course and promising change while simultaneously campaigning to maintain course and block the change promised by the opposition party. Pence was always going to have to untether himself from Trump, eventually. January 6 accomplished that. In the process, it saved the vice president from having to manufacture independence from Trump by criticizing an element of the so-called America First agenda or admonishing the forty-fifth president for his crass behavior. Now, Pence is free to promote the achievements of the Trump presidency without reservation. When inevitably asked in the midst of a presidential campaign if he would be separate and distinct from the last Republican president, all Pence needs to do is raise his eyebrows and say, "Really?"

There is another crucial aspect of the long-term political impact of January 6 that could be serendipitous for Pence.

"Boy, does he have a story to tell," said his ally who fielded calls of support for the vice president in the immediate aftermath of the insurrection. "How he chooses to tell that story will tell you a little bit about what he might want to do."

And that's the big question for Pence, really: What story does he want to tell?

On some days since the former vice president left office, he tells the story that he and Trump are still bosom buddies, yukking it up, like in the before times, when everything was copacetic between the two of them. MAGA-mates forever-and-a-day. Other days, Pence sends encoded messages of disbelief and discontent. Trump's loyal lieutenant can't quite bring himself to sing his own, unapologetic version of B. J. Thomas's "Another Somebody Done Somebody Wrong Song" (although his team of enforcers certainly have no problem doing so). But in those moments when Pence is feeling enough is enough, he lets his hair down and lets Trump have it, in the distinctively nonaggressive way he tends to let people have it, when he feels thusly compelled.

In early June 2021, Pence headlined the Lincoln-Reagan fund-raising dinner for the Hillsborough County Republican Party in Manchester,

New Hampshire. Pence devoted much of the speech to lionizing all that Trump (and the Trump-Pence administration) had accomplished in just four years, to the clear delight of the GOP activists who had packed the ballroom to hear the former second-in-command speak. Toward the end, though, the former vice president added this little coda in direct response to the fact that Trump will not stop telling anyone who will listen that he chickened out on January 6 and colluded in Biden's theft of his second term. "January 6 was a dark day in the history of the United States Capitol," he said. "President Trump and I have spoken many times since we left office—and I don't know if we'll ever see eye to eye on that day."

Interestingly, nobody booed or hissed.

CHAPTER EIGHT

Bless Your Heart

In the winter of 2016, as the South Carolina primary drew near, Nikki Haley made a last-minute decision to host her own version of *The Apprentice*. She would offer a select group of Republican presidential contenders not named Donald Trump the chance to audition for her endorsement. Instead of the mock boardroom where Trump had grilled contestants on his hit reality television show for NBC before quitting to seek the White House, Haley would evaluate finalists for her backing, much sought after, over cocktails and an intimate family dinner at the governor's mansion in Columbia, the state capital.

The second-term governor had been reluctant to wade into the unwieldy nominating contest before South Carolina voted and when it voted. At its most crowded, the Republican presidential primary included more than a handful of candidates she counted as friends, plus a wild card front-runner in Trump. The hospitality and branding mogul had donated to Haley's gubernatorial campaigns, and she referred to him as a friend. But it became increasingly apparent as Trump's campaign picked up steam after its mid-June 2015 launch that he was not her cup of conservative tea.

In case there was any doubt, Haley went out of her way to make that fact abundantly clear with her rebuttal to President Barack Obama's final State of the Union address the evening of January 12, 2016, and subsequent round of interviews the next day. The South Carolina primary, third on the nominating calendar and first in the South, was six weeks away. Some weeks earlier, House Speaker Paul Ryan of Wisconsin and Senate Majority Leader Mitch McConnell of Kentucky approached Haley about delivering the Republican Party's televised response to Obama. Haley was still debating internally how vocal to be in the primary, or whether she wanted to have any say at all after nearly a year of nonstop, exhausting tumult in her state. The State of the Union rebuttal assignment is thankless, no matter the president. The task has tripped up rising political stars of both parties. (Why else, exactly, would a top congressional leader farm it out?) From the perspective of Ryan and McConnell, Haley was a sensible pick for the gig. She is a woman and not white, making her something of a valued commodity among high-ranking Republican officials (and aspiring 2024 presidential candidates). Crucially, the governor had distinguished herself that year and caught the attention of the nation as she led South Carolina through a racially charged police shooting (in April) in which a white officer shot a black man in the back, killing him; and the mass shooting of black church congregants by a twenty-one-year-old avowed white supremacist (in June), two days after Trump announced for president. The grisly massacre of nine African Americans gathered for a Bible study session inside the Emanuel African Methodist Episcopal Church in Charleston, among the oldest black churches in the country, had a deeply emotional impact on the governor. She responded swiftly with a meaningful gesture as grand as it was overdue. Haley wanted to retire the Confederate flag from its honored perch on the statehouse grounds, and she wanted to do it in a way that would make it nearly impossible for the legislature or a future governor to bring it back.

It was legislatively complicated and fraught with political risk for an ambitious governor who valued her close relationship with South Carolina's conservative grass roots. But Haley was determined; and she pulled it off—in July, no less. Through it all, Haley was unwavering, showcasing her skill as a communicator and displaying an advanced level of political sophistication for a forty-three-year-old small-state governor with a relatively thin political résumé. The episode transformed that little-known small-state governor into an admired household name. Perhaps as important to Ryan and McConnell as Haley's notoriety and charisma, maybe more important: Haley was an available, acceptable choice because she had not endorsed a GOP presidential candidate, although like many Republicans, she had recently criticized Trump for proposing to ban Muslims from entering the United States on the basis of their being Muslim.

She accepted their invitation on the condition that her speech not be subject to edits, vetting, or other forms of approval, conditions she would demand over and over again as prominent Republicans of all sorts came calling with invitations for her to lend her political voice to their political effort. The Speaker and the Senate majority leader agreed. In her *Obama* rebuttal, Haley didn't hold back.

"During anxious times, it can be tempting to follow the siren call of the angriest voices. We must resist that temptation," she said about midway through, dropping the line that would lead every news story about her speech that night and the next day and foreshadowed her decision to jump into the primary with both feet with an endorsement of one of Trump's rivals. That was who Haley was talking about with her admonishment, right?

"Yes. Mr. Trump has contributed to what I think is just irresponsible talk," she told NBC's *Today* the following morning.

Asked about her comments again later that day, Haley didn't back down, telling ABC News's Jonathan Karl, "I was given an opportunity by Speaker Ryan and Senator McConnell to be able to say what I think."

Haley was born to Sikh parents who immigrated to the United States, legally, from Punjab, India, by way of Canada. She was born and raised in Bamberg, South Carolina, in rural Bamberg County, in the southwestern part of the state. For thirty years, her father was a professor at Vorhees College, an historically black institution. Haley had lived the immigrant experience. She appreciated the vitality immigration brought to American society, infusing the nation with people from around the globe seeking freedom from the tyranny of authoritarian regimes and an economic system that did not limit the financial rewards of hard work. Understanding the difference between where they came from and their new home like only an immigrant can, many of these new arrivals practically deify the

United States. In that context, it's no wonder that Trump's populist rhetoric, often casting immigration as a drain on the country's resources and disparaging immigrants as crafty socialists or hardened criminals, rankled Haley—especially in the middle of a year during which she was spending most of her time attempting to soothe racial and cultural tensions in South Carolina.

The governor's simmering frustration with Trump boiled over with the candidate's December 2015 proposal—in the aftermath of an Islamic State–inspired jihadist terrorist attack in San Bernardino, California, that left fourteen people dead—to order a "total and complete shutdown of Muslims entering the United States until our country's representatives can figure out what is going on."

Haley had finally heard enough and ended her self-imposed embargo on commenting about Trump, whose campaign was largely built on hyperbole about the mortal dangers posed by immigrants.

"It's an embarrassment to the Republican Party," Haley said during a news conference two days later, the *Post and Courier*'s Andrew Shain reported, responding to a question she instructed her press aides to plant with the assembled journalists. "It's absolutely un-American."

For Haley, Trump's behavior was reaching a tipping point. But… what to do? There was the option of following the lead of Senator Tim Scott, the black Republican Haley had appointed to the US Senate after Jim DeMint resigned a couple of years earlier. Scott made sure he was involved but avoided picking sides by offering to host a town hall meeting for any interested GOP presidential contender. That didn't appeal to Haley. Even though her first endorsement experience, in 2012, didn't end well—eventual Republican nominee Mitt Romney was clobbered in the South Carolina primary by former House Speaker Newt Gingrich—Haley always leaned toward making a statement. But…who to endorse?

After the New Hampshire primary, there were five candidates left from a field that once numbered seventeen. Trump wasn't an option; stopping him was the whole reason Haley was doing this. Ohio governor John Kasich? No way. Nobody liked Kasich, least of all Haley. Ben Carson, the famous neurosurgeon who would serve as Trump's secretary of housing and urban development? Unappealing.

That settled it. Haley would meet with Jeb Bush, the former Florida governor and a close friend who had mentored her during her maiden run for governor in 2010 but whose prospects looked especially grim; Texas senator Ted Cruz, whom she did not know but whose antiestablishment message and battles with Republican leaders in the US Senate reminded her of herself, giving him an initial advantage; and Florida senator Marco Rubio, whose familiar, up-by-your-bootstraps immigrant story and optimistic message about American exceptionalism tugged at her heartstrings, making him a real contender.

The dinners were scheduled to occur in succession roughly one to two weeks before the vote and the South Carolina primary edition of *The Apprentice* was picked up as a limited series. Target audience: demographic of One.

———

What's remarkable about this part of Haley's backstory, years after the fact, is not whom she endorsed, or why. We already know (Rubio, because he most impressed her and she concluded he was best equipped to derail Trump, who was on the verge of running away with the race after stomping the competition in New Hampshire). What's remarkable is what the two runners-up for Haley's seal of approval, Bush and Cruz, presumed about her intentions, related to an endorsement, as each polished off his meal and exited the governor's mansion after two different meetings on two different nights. It reveals much about Haley's style and capabilities as a political operator as she seeks a major leadership role, if not *the* leadership role, atop an unsettled and evolving Republican Party rife with competing factions and crosscurrents.

Cruz arrived in South Carolina with a win under his belt yet stuck in a rut. The senator had topped Trump in Iowa, a big victory that generated zero momentum in New Hampshire, where he finished a distant third. Cruz needed to breathe life into his campaign heading into Nevada and Super Tuesday. A strong finish in South Carolina could do that. Cruz had always wanted Haley's endorsement. Now he needed it. The senator showed up for dinner at the governor's mansion ready to wow. With him was aide Jason Johnson, a Republican strategist in Texas. Überconsultant Jeff Roe helmed the campaign and made all the operational decisions. But it was Johnson who had a close, personal, and professional connection to Cruz, vested with the authority to call him by his first name and keep him grounded.

The governor's husband, Michael Haley, joined the gathering, and at least one of their children was lurking about. Haley was concerned about Cruz's likability issues. Otherwise, she appreciated the senator and was sort of leaning toward endorsing him because she saw in him a fellow traveler. Cruz had defeated a sitting GOP lieutenant governor (a very powerful position in Texas) in a primary on his way to being elected to the US Senate; Haley had defeated the longest-serving lawmaker in the legislature in a Republican primary on her way to winning a seat in the South Carolina House of Representatives. He had scuffled with entrenched, reform-resistant Republicans as a freshman member of the US Senate; she had done the same as a junior member in the statehouse. As their conversation progressed, they developed a rapport. It was clear that Haley and Cruz saw eye to eye on the key issues of the 2016 campaign, and he made a compelling case as they examined polling and other data that he was the only candidate left in the race who could topple Trump. Haley wanted to know how Cruz planned to win South Carolina, and he laid out a detailed digital and grassroots strategy. And he made it all about her. Endorsements don't really matter anymore, Cruz explained—and Trump was living proof of that. But the senator told Haley that she was a rare exception to the rule. Without her, Cruz declared, Trump might well be the nominee. Cruz and Johnson thought they hit it out of the park.

Haley, although blatantly noncommittal, was legitimately impressed, and let it show. Reading between the lines, Team Cruz concluded that the governor was disinclined to back Rubio, the senator's main competition. They walked away certain the dinner had achieved one of two outcomes:

Either Haley was going to endorse Cruz, or she was going to remain neutral. The Cruz campaign spent the ensuing days trying to reach Haley's aides to firm up plans for the endorsement. They found out the governor was backing Rubio from news reports.

Episode two starred Bush, brother of the forty-third president, George Walker Bush, and son of the forty-first president, George Herbert Walker Bush.

Bush limped into South Carolina after getting steamrolled in the Iowa caucuses and flattened in New Hampshire, finishing a disappointing fourth in the "first in the nation" primary. At this point, it was up or out. The establishment scion wasn't giving up without making one last stand. Bush had been backchanneling with Haley for months. Careful to avoid playing favorites, the governor gave her old mentor friendly tips for navigating South Carolina amid a Lindsey Graham campaign that was obviously going nowhere but which had nonetheless locked up the state's big-time establishment donors and political operatives. Bush was subtly courting his onetime student, planting seeds he hoped would flower into an endorsement at the right time, or at least protect his campaign from getting whacked by Haley endorsing a rival.

As he transitioned to South Carolina, post–New Hampshire, Bush was as pleased as he could have been under the circumstances. Almost everyone knew he was a dead man walking. But Graham had dropped out and joined his campaign, bringing a lot of veteran South Carolina Republican insiders with him. They, in turn, were working on Haley to deliver her endorsement. And Bush could still hope that his big brother might work some magic when he traveled to South Carolina to headline one of his campaign rallies, a rare occurrence post–White House for the only Republican president since Ronald Reagan to win reelection, and the only Republican nominee since his father to win the national popular vote. Then Bush received the invitation to dine with Haley and her husband.

So he headed over to the mansion with top aide Brett Doster. Doster, a Republican strategist in Florida who got his start in politics carrying around Bush's luggage as he campaigned for governor, ended up functioning as the campaign's senior emissary in South Carolina. Throughout the evening, Haley again was blatantly noncommittal. But Bush and Doster liked the signals they were getting. The governor suggested, they were convinced, that she wasn't enthralled with Bush's remaining competitors. Plus, Haley wanted to know why Bush was running. What was his vision? What would he want his legacy to be? Then, delicately, around the edges, without being explicit, where did Bush think their views aligned and how might she fit into a third Bush administration?

Plus, she asked the ex–Florida honcho for a favor. Haley wanted to get a picture with Bush 43, with her family, too. Do you ask for that if you're about to say "thanks but no thanks"? On their way out the door, Bush and Doster deemed the meeting a success. Their thinking was, they had accomplished their objective, in that either they had won Haley over or she wouldn't pick sides. The first thing they did was get on the horn and schedule Haley's private photo line with Dubya. George W. Bush was flying in to South Carolina to headline a campaign rally for his little brother in Charleston. But before that, he was stopping in Columbia to appear at a closed-door Bush campaign event for military veterans. It was there that Jeb Bush arranged for the governor and her family to meet with his big brother and take some pictures. A couple of days after he delivered on Haley's request, the governor called to let him know she was endorsing Rubio. (Political operatives connected to Haley dispute this account of how her meeting with Bush 43 came about. They told me that he and the former first lady invited the governor to the veterans event directly. They also emphasized that Haley had her own relationship with the former president and his wife, and that as the sitting governor, it was typical for her to greet visiting political dignitaries of his stature. The notion she engaged in an endorsement ruse to manipulate Jeb Bush into scheduling a meeting with his brother is preposterous, they said.)

Two dinners; two candidates. Two polar opposite candidates, in fact—one an insurgent in his midforties, the other an establishmentarian in his early sixties. And yet, one conclusion; the *same* conclusion. Each was confident he had won Haley's endorsement. At the very least, each felt assured that if he didn't receive the governor's backing, nobody else would. Years later, Republican operatives who had worked the Bush and Cruz campaigns, respectively, were absolutely convinced that Haley knowingly misled their candidates. But here's the thing: The governor did not make any explicit declarations during either dinner. She never told Bush or Cruz that she would either endorse them or no one. Nor did Haley tell either that she had decided against endorsing Rubio, her third and final dinner guest, whom she had yet to size up.

From Haley's perspective, both Bush and Cruz were missing some key ingredients—tangible and intangible. There was a reason she hesitated to pull the trigger. Blocking Trump from the GOP nomination was the overriding reason Haley had jumped into the primary in the first place, and the staid Bush simply wasn't going to defeat the swaggering populist. Cruz was energetic, prepared, precise. Like Haley, he was a fighter. The governor didn't feel like they clicked. It was as if the senator was too prepared, too precise, too...tactical. Haley simply wasn't that, as would become apparent at a much later date.

But the governor was taken with Rubio. She liked Rubio's wife, Jeanette, who accompanied Rubio to the dinner, and she was impressed when the former senator took some time after they arrived to introduce himself to the wait staff and spend time chitchatting with them. (Rubio's parents had worked in the service industry; this was a common occurrence.) Haley offered her endorsement on the spot, before Rubio left the mansion. She was clear and unequivocal about it. Rubio proceeded to finish second, albeit a distant second, behind Trump in the South Carolina primary, which Team Haley considered a success considering his embarrassing fifth-place tally in New Hampshire just eleven days prior. Throughout, Haley revealed some truly hard-to-come-by political talent, abilities that separate presidents from presidential candidates. The governor managed to make Bush and Cruz feel nearly as good upon the conclusion of their dinners, without getting what they came for, as Rubio must have felt upon the conclusion of his, getting exactly what he came for.

It explains Haley's knack, oft discussed during her tenure as US ambassador to the United Nations, for thriving as a member of Trump's cabinet without losing her dignity. The governor is a Republican hawk who never soft-pedaled her criticism of Russia and dictator Vladimir Putin's attempt to undermine American interests at every turn, drawing a sharp contrast with her boss, very publicly, especially in the early days of his administration. Yet Haley never seemed to run afoul of Trump's onerous demands for loyalty bordering on fealty, and would leave the cabinet of her own accord, her relationship with the president intact (for the time being, as it turned out).

"Nikki is a very charming, direct person—she is," a Republican operative and veteran of South Carolina politics told me. "But she's great at not making any commitments."

———

It had reached the point where the Conservative Political Action Conference stopped sending Haley invites.

The American Conservative Union's three-day grassroots bonanza of energy and activism is a must-do for upwardly mobile Republican politicians. Yet South Carolina's governor, who clearly qualified as such, didn't seem much interested in attending. Not since March 2013, a bygone era in the Republican Party, had Haley bothered to show up. And even then it was to deliver short introductory remarks for the GOP's defeated 2012 presidential nominee, Mitt Romney, not to deliver her own keynote. So, CPAC stopped asking.

Well, things change. Early in 2020, about a year after resigning as UN ambassador, Haley reached out to Matt Schlapp, ACU chairman and the czar of CPAC, looking for her invitation to that year's conference. It was an obvious move. Haley unveiled Stand for America, a political nonprofit organization, in February 2019, fresh off of her departure from Trump's cabinet at the end of the previous year. Ostensibly, Haley launched the group as a geeky policy clearinghouse. Haley is a big advocate for old-school free-market capitalism—lately out of favor in the Republican Party—and confronting China, lately in favor in the GOP, to blunt the ruling Communist Party's naked attempt to supplant the United States as the globe's preeminent superpower. Her new group was pushing Congress and the administration to support legislation that revolved around those twin policy pillars. But naturally, Stand for America served a dual purpose. Haley's nearly two-year sojourn at the United Nations had solidified her standing as a national figure who could speak with expert authority about a broader breadth of complex national and international issues than was the case when the ambassador was simply a recognizable, albeit effective, two-term governor of a small southern state. With Stand for America, Haley hoped to entrench this newly expanded prominence, parlay her association with Trump into a position of influence within the GOP, and build a strong foundation for a 2024 presidential bid, should she choose to pursue the White House.

The traditional wing of the party—military hawks, wealthy donors, fiscal conservatives—was already watching with intrigue as Haley plotted her rise. But it takes at least some portion of the Republican base to win a GOP primary, a fact Haley understood as well as any in her party. And it was obvious even then that the Republican base in the sort-of-but-not-exactly post-Trump era would remain enthralled with the forty-fifth president and looking to him for cues. Ditto the party's populist faction, the once junior partner in the Republican coalition elevated by Trump. CPAC was, and is, a key venue for connecting with these critical Trump ground troops—perhaps *the* key venue. Attending offered the ambassador a major opportunity to make inroads with this community on a national level and forge lasting connections that she could bring with her into a presidential campaign. After all, CPAC didn't pick up the nickname "T-PAC," as in "Trump Political Action Conference," nor proudly flaunt it, for nothing. Haley's decision to reengage with the conference after several years was a smart play.

However, when the ambassador's representatives called conference officials looking for her invitation to the 2020 gathering, held that year, as most years, just across the Potomac River from Washington, DC, they were told not to expect one. Hint: "Since you weren't interested in us, we moved on—and we're doing just fine." That's when Haley reached out to Schlapp and turned on the charm, which is among her biggest assets and often rather effective. In a telephone conversation, the ambassador waved off her presumed ambivalence to CPAC to miscommunication and staff error and told Schlapp she wanted to work together. He relented. Sort of. The fifty-three-year-old Schlapp has worked in Washington for more than twenty-five years. An experienced operator, he was political director in the George W. Bush White House and ran the Koch Industries government affairs office in Washington. The firm, an industrial juggernaut owned by a conservative family that has piqued the ire of liberals everywhere, is headquartered in his hometown of Wichita, Kansas. Later, Schlapp branched out with his own lobbying firm, Cove Strategies, signing some of the biggest brands in America as clients. It's been successful. Schlapp was a fierce Bush partisan and still talks fondly of his time in Dubya's White House. He also embraced Trump enthusiastically, making him something of a rarity in Washington. For the past half dozen years, Schlapp's passion has been CPAC, and he has nurtured the event like a sixth child. (He and his wife, Mercedes Schlapp, a Republican operative who also worked in the George W. Bush White House, have five daughters.) Schlapp, attuned to the cultural sensibilities of the prototypical grassroots conservative, tinkers with the guest list every year, as a form of high political art, to give the CPAC audience what it wants, sometimes before they know what they want themselves.

But it's a two-way street. Schlapp wants guests to treat the conference with reverence and show an appreciation for the community it attracts. So, Haley. That she finally decided the event had value, and that the audience might want to hear from her wasn't quite enough. Schlapp, basically, decided to test her commitment. In 2020, he declined to offer the ambassador an invitation to speak to the crowd from the main stage in the expansive ballroom of the Gaylord National Harbor Resort and Convention Center in National Harbor, Maryland, on the banks of the Potomac River. Instead, Schlapp offered Haley an opportunity to speak off the cuff at "the hub." Basically, a podium set up in the middle of a downstairs hall, where vendors selling conservative-themed goods and conservative groups looking to sign up members set up booths to hawk their wares. Haley accepted, and wowed the crowd with a stem-winder.

But Haley's CPAC admissions test started even before that, with a special invitation to the private cocktail party at the Schlapps' lavish Northern Virginia home that marks the unofficial kickoff of the annual conference. Schlapp and his wife had dreamed up the event as a way of expanding the CPAC experience by catering to the more refined attendees and, in some instances, financial supporters. The invite-only guest list features influential conservative insiders, wealthy business executives, Republican donors, aspiring and elected politicians, media personalities, CPAC VIPs, and more, who get to spend an exclusive evening hobnobbing and getting to know each other. The event is closed to the press and, by design, isn't advertised.

Haley impressed. She showed up early and stayed late. She worked the room, introducing herself and chatting with guests. She showed her appreciation for CPAC and, incidentally, made connections with prominent figures whose support would come in handy as she laid the foundation for a (potential) presidential campaign. It wasn't the first time Haley had angled to take her brand national.

––––––

The so-called fake-news media, and the liberal intelligentsia. The supposedly out-of-touch industry of Republican professionals in Washington, and every poll-obsessed homegrown political pundit from Wall Street to Sunset Boulevard. Throughout the summer and fall of 2016, they weren't alone in presuming Trump couldn't win, wouldn't win, that he was about to be KO'd by Hillary Rodham Clinton. Haley presumed the same.

In the closing weeks of that campaign, the shrewd second-term governor, all of forty-four, quietly took steps to claim leadership of a Republican Party in turmoil. Or at least a Republican Party that surely would be the day after the election. Haley was preparing paperwork to launch an outside political organization, aptly dubbed "Haley Leadership Fund," and directed her political team to chart an aggressive public relations strategy to position her as a leading voice in charge of cleaning up the mess left by Trump, to begin the moment Election Night vote crunchers had seen enough and called the race for Clinton. Haley's statement reacting to her nominee's loss was drafted early. An embargoed interview with

Time magazine advancing her vision for rejuvenating the GOP was in the can. As the first woman elected president of the United States, Clinton would dominate the cover, with a picture of Haley adorning the upper right corner as the face of what would be next for the Republican Party. Interviews with NBC's morning show, *Today*, and with the major television networks' marquee Sunday morning public affairs shows, were on the calendar for the morning of November 9 and the weekend that followed. Major speeches to Republican-aligned groups were in the planning stages. An outline of Haley's scrapped statement offers clues to the message she would broadcast, and the image she would cultivate, in her bid for party primacy before Trump upended her meticulous plans.

"Although neither I nor the majority of my state voted for Hillary Clinton, I congratulate her on her historic victory. She will be our next president and I wish her every success moving our country forward after this difficult election. After three consecutive presidential defeats, my fellow Republicans must make changes. Our conservative principles hold the essential keys for America's prosperity and security. But our policies must be updated to fit today's challenges and our message must become more inclusive and inspiring."

Trump had radicalized Haley; or at least, he activated her.

The governor had been wary of getting involved in another presidential primary. The last one didn't end well for her. Four years prior, the newly minted Tea Party superstar governor endorsed front-runner Mitt Romney for president. Republicans in South Carolina took one look at the genteel former Massachusetts governor and promptly said "no thanks," instead throwing their support behind Newt Gingrich, the imperious former House Speaker, powering him to an upset victory.

But Haley's uneasiness with Trump eventually wore down her hesitation to risk diminishing her political brand by endorsing another loser. His rhetoric in the intervening months magnified her concerns with a populist campaign that from the moment Trump descended an escalator into the tacky, gold-tinted lobby of his signature Fifth Avenue skyscraper was laced with a subtle but unmistakable dose of white ethnonationalism. So Haley decided to make a last stand against a runaway Trump nomination by endorsing Rubio.

It didn't work. Still, Haley was generally satisfied. The way she looked at it, Rubio left South Carolina still kicking, with a fighting chance to derail Trump. And the governor had thrown down a marker about what the Republican Party should be about—and what it should look like: less old, less backward, less white, and less grievance; more aspirational, more ethnically diverse, and more tolerant.

That was the message Haley planned to arm herself with when she traveled to the tony Waldorf Astoria hotel and resort in Orlando, Florida, near Disney World, to join other Republican governors for a postelection Republican Governors Association business meeting. Long scheduled for the week following Election Day, the assumption was that the confab would function as a postmortem dive into the severe challenges the GOP faced after losing a third consecutive presidential election, an insult the party hadn't suffered since Presidents Franklin Delano Roosevelt and Harry Truman ticked off five victories in a row from 1932 to 1948. The steakhouse at the Waldorf Astoria, the Bull & Bear, with its extensive menu of adult beverages, was a suitable venue to mull over how Republicans had managed to lose the national popular vote in six of the last seven presidential elections. The RGA meeting that November was also where Haley was set to climb the next rung on the ladder of the party's hierarchy: Months earlier, she had locked up the votes to be elected as the group's vice chairman.

I had booked my trip to cover the RGA months earlier; I wanted to make sure I had a front-row seat for all of it. Should Trump lose, an outcome I was convinced was far from certain (but that's another story), there would be no clearer window into the recriminations and reassessment of the Republican Party amid the wreckage of Trump's teardown and early 2020 jockeying by Haley and other Republicans who see presidents in the mirror. Republican governors with White House ambitions typically use the RGA as a stepping-stone. Under the agreement the governors negotiated for leadership of the group over the four years leading into Hillary

Clinton's presumed reelection bid, Haley would serve the first two as vice chair and the second two as chairwoman. In both roles, Haley would travel the country stumping for Republican gubernatorial candidates in early presidential primary states. Big races were on the horizon in Iowa, New Hampshire, and Nevada. So were contests in crucial White House battlegrounds that voted later in the presidential nominating calendar and mattered in general elections: Arizona, Florida, Michigan, Ohio, Wisconsin, and Pennsylvania. Haley might have increased her national profile, but she was still a small-state governor with a limited pool of ardent supporters. The South Carolina governor's RGA responsibilities would expose her to the group's lucrative Rolodex of political benefactors, wealthy Republican donors who finance presidential campaigns.

Coincidentally, the RGA fund-raising she had done some years back connected her to one such donor in New York—a flamboyant real estate developer who ended up host of his own reality television show and had for years flirted with running for president. After Haley won reelection in 2014, this donor, Donald Trump, sent her a brief note of congratulations: "You're a winner."

Campaigning on behalf of gubernatorial candidates would also put Haley in front of conservative activists who could fuel a White House bid with crucial grassroots energy. The opportunity to spend the next four years juxtaposing herself with Clinton was a bonus.

And then Trump won.

And so as I made the rounds at the RGA in Orlando in mid-November 2016 and tried to pin down Republican governors on the hostile Trump takeover of their party, the mood was a mix of hope, uncertainty, and bewilderment as they grappled with the strange new world they were living in as now-anachronistic Reagan-era conservatives. During a news conference with Governors Susana Martinez of New Mexico, Rick Scott of Florida, Scott Walker of Wisconsin, and Haley, a colleague of mine asked the group to address Trump and the Republican Party's at least stated, long-standing commitment to improve relations with ethnic minorities and win more of their votes. The South Carolina governor tried to reconcile the dichotomy between the kind of politics she practiced and the kind of politics Trump practiced, this way: "It goes back to what every elected official needs to remember in the Republican Party, which is, communication and tone matter, the power of your words matter," she said, acknowledging the divided nation the election left in its wake. "For all the governors, we realize that the second we get elected, our job is to lift up everybody, whether they voted for us or not."

Pressed again to address her differences with Trump, Haley embraced an approach that would become the go-to approach for Republicans in Washington over the next four years: recasting Trump as the political figure they wished him to be, rather than the political figure he was so obviously choosing to be. It's an approach impossible to sustain, as Haley would find out *even after* Trump lost reelection; *even after* he was no longer president.

> So far, President-elect Trump has done well. I hope he continues to do that. I hope he continues to be disciplined in his comments and what happens. I don't know what we can expect out of communication. I'm hopeful because of the tone that he's had since he's been elected, and I hope that he can continue to be that same person using that same tone that includes everyone and doesn't make anybody feel any sort of division whatsoever.

Haley never had a chance to say much more than that. In the middle of a closed-door RGA executive committee meeting, as her colleagues were installing her as vice chairman, the governor received a text message from Trump Tower in New York, where President-elect Trump was presiding over his transition to power and vetting potential staff and cabinet picks. It was Reince Priebus, the incoming White House chief of staff and outgoing Republican National Committee chairman. Priebus was interested in unifying the GOP after a pretty nasty family feud of an election. Adding Haley to the cabinet, Priebus thought, could help him do that.

The governor had done little to hide her disappointment with Trump's nomination and unyieldingly provocative behavior, disloyalty the president-elect usually refused to countenance. But what Priebus saw was a prominent Trump antagonist from the establishment wing of the party who had quieted her criticism down the stretch of the campaign *and* focused on the positive aspects of Trump's victory.

Plus, Haley was a legit rising star in the party, and Trump liked that sort of image in members of his supporting cast. Upon reading the text, Haley quietly excused herself from the executive committee meeting and stepped outside to call Priebus. He told Haley that despite her complete lack of foreign policy experience, Trump wanted to meet to discuss offering her the plum post of secretary of state. At first, Haley attempted to hold them off a few days, explaining she was in the middle of RGA business. But the news of Trump's interest in bringing her into the administration was already leaking to the national press corps. Priebus, who was scrambling to assemble candidates for the State Department for the president-elect to interview, was insistent. Haley canceled the rest of her Orlando itinerary and hurriedly slipped out of the Waldorf Astoria to board a plane for New York. The prospect of Haley going to work for Trump would no doubt thrill her mother, who enthusiastically voted for the future forty-fifth president that fall. Indeed, she had privately disagreed with her daughter's decision to endorse Rubio in the South Carolina primary.

———

For four years, from the moment Haley answered Priebus's text message until enough votes had been counted to project Biden as the forty-sixth president of the United States, no Republican of consequence in America navigated the minefield of Trump better than his first ambassador to the United Nations.

Working in the Trump White House made formidable business and political professionals—hard-nosed and accomplished in their own right—look like abject fools. Some managed to escape by merely looking weak and duplicitous. Either they found themselves slathering Trump with praise like an insecure, lovesick schoolboy (some members of his cabinet turned this into a form of high art), or they made sure it leaked to the press that they thought Trump was a first-rate idiot whose shambolic leadership was on the verge of turning the United States into a third-rate power if not for their intervention.

Not Haley. For instance, she could sit for an interview on Sunday morning and call the forty-fifth president's appeasement of Putin misguided without insulting him and eliciting a nasty tweet in response. During Trump's tenure, nobody in Washington other than Haley ever figured out how to thread that needle. It's no wonder so many Republican insiders looking ahead to 2024 and the challenge of stitching together the Reagan and Trump wings of the party were casting their gaze in her direction. Haley's team, lorded over by enigmatic Republican strategist Jon Lerner, a devout Jew who is a pollster by trade, is almost maniacal about emphasizing the ambassador's supposed ambivalence about running for president. But about this they are transparent—if Haley decides to pull the trigger, "she wants to be ready."

Team Haley likes to present Stand for America as an earnest little policy group. As an advocate for good old-fashioned Reagan-era free-market capitalism and fiscal discipline, it is that. Same goes for the group's nostalgic promotion of the sort of internationalist foreign policy that pervaded the Republican Party for decades, urging the projection of American power to confront a rising China much the same way the United States stood athwart Soviet expansionism all those years ago. But the founding of this earnest little political nonprofit, smack in the middle of Trump's first term, with his plans for a 2020 reelection campaign already in motion, also marked the beginning of Haley's unapologetic participation in the 2024 sweepstakes. A helpful way to understand what the ambassador was doing with Stand for America is to think of a shorthand description I coined to crystalize its purpose for friends or relatives who would ask me what she (and other 2024 contenders) was up to: AEI—not to be confused with the conservative Washington think tank the American Enterprise Institute, but rather Alliances, Exposure, Infrastructure.

After leaving Trump's cabinet, Haley used Stand for America to build alliances with prominent Republicans across the party and across the country, generate public exposure to grassroots conservatives and the broader

GOP electorate, and build a political infrastructure to function as the foundation for a 2024 presidential campaign apparatus. To wit, Stand for America wasn't some post office box or unattended website monitored haphazardly by a rotating cast of interns. Haley hired serious, experienced political operators to manage the organization day-to-day and, significantly, to *grow* it. She tapped serious, experienced political strategists to sharpen its activities and shepherd that growth. For the crucial post of executive director, Haley brought in Tim Chapman from Heritage Action for America, the bare-knuckled campaign arm of its button-down cousin, the Heritage Foundation, a conservative Washington think tank closely associated with the Republican Party and located steps from the US Capitol.

Chapman, more comfortable anonymous and behind the scenes, is an expert in organization and coalition development. He spent the previous decade building Heritage Action for America from scratch, turning it into an influential grassroots advocacy group with national reach. The last two of those ten years he served as executive director, succeeding Needham, the other driving force behind Heritage Action for America, after he departed to become Rubio's chief of staff.

Chapman got results. As the end of his second year at the helm of Stand for America approached, Haley had amassed an email list of grassroots donors that exceeded five hundred thousand, her organization's email updates on policy initiatives were reaching more than one and a half million people, and she was presiding over a full-time staff of five, including the group's policy director, Leslie Dewees, who followed her from the United Nations. Plans were already in motion for additional hires (more on that in a moment). Haley wasn't a creature of Washington, which, though that sounds like exactly what voters want, can hamper a presidential campaign. Institutional support is crucial; allies are critical. Just ask Cruz. So Chapman leveraged relationships he cultivated over two decades to introduce the ambassador to a range of influential and well-connected Republicans—in Congress and elsewhere. She willingly made herself available, participating in a variety of virtual and in-person events.

Haley was a featured guest of the Republican Study Committee, a significant caucus of mainstream House conservatives that counts former vice president Mike Pence as a past chairman. For ninety minutes, the ambassador discussed and fielded questions about US-China policy from the seventy-five representatives on the call. She spoke via conference call to House Republicans on Energy and Commerce, among the most powerful committees on Capitol Hill, at the invitation of the panel's top Republican, Representative Cathy McMorris Rodgers of Washington State. And in March and April 2021, the ambassador traveled to Washington, DC, for meetings with Republican women elected to Congress just a few months earlier. Those meetings are ongoing.

Haley also invested her time and energy traveling the country to campaign for Republican congressional candidates on the 2020 ballot—then got right back to it the day after the election, stumping for the Republicans running in a pair of Senate runoff elections in Georgia. Some prominent politicians who lend their notoriety to down-ballot candidates are diva-difficult and pay minimal attention to the individual they've signed up to help. Haley was attentive, thorough. In the 2020 election cycle, Republican consultant Jeff Burton was advising a few of the party's congressional candidates in Texas. Population shifts, suburban realignment, and Trump had conspired to take the formerly ruby-red bastion of conservatism that elected and reelected Republicans with regularity into a legitimate battleground trending toward the Democratic Party. Burton's candidates, one incumbent and two challengers, were running in competitive districts in Austin, Dallas, and Houston, respectively, and needed all the help they could get.

As we chatted over Zoom at the beginning of the coronavirus pandemic, about six months or so before Election Day, Burton marveled that Haley was the only oft-mentioned 2024 contender who had reached out and offered her assistance.

"Nobody outside of Nikki Haley has reached out to us at all," he told me. What especially struck Burton was the extent of the information Haley's team gathered on candidates she supported. In one instance, the ambassador was headlining a virtual fund-raiser for a group of female congressional contenders that included Genevieve Collins, the Republican challenging

Democratic representative Colin Allred in the Dallas-area Thirty-Second Congressional District. Haley was a draw; the event raised almost a quarter of a million dollars, and Collins pocketed $40,000 for her campaign, hardly chump change for a House race. But prior to that, Collins's campaign had to spend thirty-five minutes on the telephone with Haley's team answering dozens of granular questions about the candidate and the contest—the top issues, political dynamics, her views of Trump, his performance in the district in 2016, Senator Ted Cruz's performance in the district in 2018, Allred's strengths and weaknesses, etc., etc., etc. Almost none of it was relevant information for Haley's role as a fund-raising headliner.

"My campaign manager was tearing his hair out," Burton said. He figured it was possible Haley was "just super high maintenance and wants all this information, even though she'll never use it." More likely, Burton said, "they're collecting all of this information for a purpose later on."

To build on this effort, and formalize it, Haley paired Stand for America with an affiliated political action committee, going public with the new organization in January 2021, the same day the House of Representatives impeached Trump a second time. To run Stand for America PAC, the ambassador tapped a talented Republican operative with immediate, real-world experience running tough campaigns. Betsy Ankney had just finished a two-year stint as political director of the National Republican Senatorial Committee, the Senate GOP's campaign arm. The Ohio native spent the previous four years working two very tough assignments, serving as campaign manager for Wisconsin senator Ron Johnson's nail-biter reelection victory in 2016 and Bruce Rauner's ouster from the Illinois governor's mansion in 2018. Haley's political action committee was unveiled as a full-service operation focused exclusively on helping Republicans win majorities in the House of Representatives and the US Senate in 2022. The plan was to recruit, fund, coach, campaign, and advertise for Republican congressional candidates Haley believed would help the party accomplish that goal. Never mind that this exclusively political component of her expanding platform—and Ankney, the woman she placed at the helm—could transition seamlessly into a 2024 presidential campaign. It was about this time that Haley's execution of her flawlessly choreographed political balance beam routine began to falter.

Like any upwardly mobile presidential contender, Haley had plenty of detractors. The Trump wing of the party is suspicious of her, and certain elements of the Reagan wing of the party fear she is Jeb Bush 2016 2.0—all hype and no heft. If you're still not sure what I mean, plug "Jeb Bush" and "please clap" into your favorite internet search engine. But as Haley tripped over Trump's refusal to accept his defeat, those doubts for the first time spread beyond the usual suspects.

"At the United Nations, I often found that many countries agreed with US policies in private but would not say so in public. One wonders if President-elect Joe Biden has a similar view of President Trump's foreign policy successes."

With those words, written at the top of an op-ed for the *Washington Post*, Haley publicly acknowledged the outcome of the November 3 election for the first time. The article was published on December 16, 2020, two days after the Electoral College voted in the fifty states and District of Columbia and four days after the US Supreme Court rejected a lawsuit Texas and other Republican-led states had brought in a Hail Mary bid to undo Biden's victory. The ambassador is a specialist in subtlety, and this was her subtle way of declaring further resistance to the election results, by Trump or any other Republican, unwarranted—and unhelpful. It was all downhill from there.

Haley never bought the conspiracy theories about the 2020 election.

Yes, she thought, there were small, isolated incidents of fraud and other irregularities. No, she did not approve of some last-minute changes Democrats implemented in some states to ease access to mail-in and other forms of remote voting in response to the deadly coronavirus pandemic. And she was on board with the massive legal effort Trump undertook to reverse the results, believing it a legitimate part of the electoral process and useful for bringing closure to a divided country. But after watching Trump strike out in court again, and again, and again, Haley was ready to turn the page from a president whom she would have happily served again, in a second term, had opportunity knocked. It was time, finally, to hold Biden accountable and help Republicans reclaim power in Congress in the 2022 midterm elections.

For Republican leaders and Republicans with leadership aspirations, this was easier said than done. Trump was not ready to let go (never has been), and GOP voters were with him (are with him). Haley was the exception. Staying in Trump's good graces without muzzling her own voice or rejecting blatant truths was her superpower. Until, like kryptonite, a collision of unforeseen events rendered the ambassador powerless.

After receiving Trump's endorsement, Ronna McDaniel was a shoo-in for reelection as chairwoman of the Republican National Committee. It was unusual, to say the least, for an outgoing president to meddle in the RNC, especially after being ousted by a Democratic challenger. Trump's play was obvious—to control the national party apparatus postpresidency. This caused McDaniel heartburn. When Trump was president, she naturally answered to him as the leader of the party and the president who appointed her to the chairman's post. With Trump retired and an open presidential primary looming in 2024, McDaniel was supposed to be neutral and ensure the party treated all contenders equally. To prove she would not be beholden to Trump, who was already signaling interest in seeking the White House again four years hence, the chairwoman invited a handful of Republicans who hoped to succeed him atop the party to address the annual RNC winter business meeting. And in what would turn out to be a rather consequential coincidence, McDaniel moved up the meeting from its usual late January date to January 6, 2021, in Amelia Island, Florida, near Jacksonville. The entire party, basically, would already be in Georgia campaigning for the Republicans running in a pair of Senate runoff elections on January 5, so why not let them hop the state line and save them an extra trip to Florida later in the month? (And why give RNC members more time to reconsider electing her to a third term as chairwoman?) Weeks earlier, Haley had been invited to address RNC members on Thursday, January 7, and she planned to deliver a valedictory lauding Trump for all that he accomplished in just four years.

No big deal. That was what this crowd wanted to hear, and Haley believed it all, in any event. The ambassador wasn't counting on an insurrection at the US Capitol the day before, one that Cruz would later describe as domestic terrorism. Nor did Haley assume the president's blasé reaction to criminal acts committed by his grassroots supporters, who marched on Capitol Hill because they believed his claims that a presidential election had been stolen. What to do? Haley decided to do what she had always done before. Speak honestly about her differences with Trump over his handling of the postelection period and how his rhetoric impacted the events of January 6—and then get right back to her regularly scheduled programming with a speech extolling the virtues of his presidency. No rationalizing but no virtue signaling.

It didn't work; Haley lost control of her message. Maybe it was the way her speech was reported, or the political stakes. Haley's remarks were closed to the press. In the portion that leaked and made national headlines, attributed to people in the room, she walloped Trump.

"President Trump has not always chosen the right words. He was wrong with his words in Charlottesville, and I told him so at the time. He was badly wrong with his words yesterday. And it wasn't just his words. His actions since Election Day will be judged harshly by history," Haley declared. "It's deeply disappointing."

Those remarks didn't go over well in the room. But it wasn't a disaster. Maybe if the rest of Haley's remarks had been given equal billing, Trump and his acolytes would have been more forgiving. Maybe the ambassador wouldn't have faced charges of flip-flopping to appease Trump in subsequent interviews, during which she appeared to temper her criticism but was really just rehashing that speech.

"I am one who believes our country made some truly extraordinary gains in the last four years," Haley said. "President Trump and Republicans deserve great credit for that. We should not shy away from our accomplishments."

Haley wasn't simply a victim of political circumstance, or bad luck. Trump's behavior postelection had to have weighed on her more heavily than she let on. How else to explain the ambassador, among the GOP's more deliberate communicators, choosing to bare all to reporter Tim Alberta, both before and after January 6, for a *Politico Magazine* feature about her political career—past, present, and future—appropriately headlined "Nikki Haley's Time for Choosing."

In scanning the piece for the quote that best represents just how unabashedly she unloaded on Trump, it was impossible to pick just one, or two, or even three. I settled on this one:

> We need to acknowledge he let us down. He went down a path he shouldn't have, and we shouldn't have followed him, and we shouldn't have listened to him. And we can't let that ever happen again.

After the story hit in February 2021, Haley attempted a business-as-usual posture. She plugged Stand for America policy initiatives, beat up on the Biden administration the same as any Republican who hopes to take his job in 2024, and did her best to ignore her feud with Trump (or Trump's feud with her), tweeting about his February 28 speech at CPAC: "Strong speech by President Trump about the winning policies of his administration and what the party needs to unite behind moving forward. The liberal media wants a GOP civil war. Not gonna happen."

But it was evident to anyone paying attention Haley was struggling. She was laboring to regain her political footing and wrestling to rediscover the confidence as a communicator that had carried her so far and made her so incredibly imposing as a presidential contender. Two months after the *Politico Magazine* story dropped, Haley was visiting South Carolina State University to review upgrades to the Orangeburg campus when she stopped to field questions from reporters. Meg Kinnard of the Associated Press wanted to know if Haley would stand down in 2024 if Trump seeks the White House. Tactically, Haley's answer was the smart one. The surest way to lure Trump into the race is declare him irrelevant. But the meek tone in the ambassador's voice suggested insecurity of the kind that can self-immolate a presidential campaign before it ever gets off the ground.

"I would not run if President Trump ran," she said.

But just as the 2024 prognosticators began writing Haley off, something happened: She kept on going. And Republicans responded. I traveled to Iowa in late June of 2021 to check things out for myself.

There, I discovered that the former ambassador was as in demand as she ever was. During a weekend swing that lasted a couple of days, Haley's schedule was booked solid. She headlined fund-raisers for the state's Republican members of Congress; she helped Governor Kim Reynolds blow the doors off a fund-raiser for her 2022 reelection bid with the well-heeled set at a lakeside event in north-central Iowa; and she sold out the annual Lincoln Dinner fund-raiser for the Iowa Republican Party near Des Moines, which was attended by more than five hundred GOP activists who traveled from all over the state to see her. It's as if her feud with Trump, still quite popular there, never happened.

Haley's dry stump speech needs work, and she didn't leave the audience jumping on tables, clamoring for more. But she can still go off the cuff and tell a story with the best of them.

In interviews with conservative activists after Haley's address, she won plaudits for her positions on key issues, especially the hard line she is taking on China. And, more important, the consensus was that her row with Trump over his handling of the postelection period was not a disqualifier. If Haley mounts a 2024 bid and shows up in Iowa in a play for caucus queen, Republicans will at least give her a look. "I feel like I heard her heart and got to see the knowledge that she's acquired," one grassroots Republican who holds Trump in high esteem told me after Haley's speech, in a report I filed from the Hawkeye State for the *Washington Examiner*. "If anything, I think it shows that she has her own opinions, her own thoughts, and has the guts to present them, and let it fall as it may."

Think she isn't looking ahead? Here's what Haley said when Iowa GOP Chairman Jeff Kaufmann asked this former South Carolina governor if she was committed to protecting Iowa's position as host of the first nominating contest on the party's presidential calendar: "I'm fine with Iowa being first in the nation as long as you keep South Carolina 'first in the South.' You mess with us, we'll mess with you."

It might be easy to forget how tenuous Trump's hold on the Republican Party appeared in July 2016 on the eve of the presidential nominating convention in Cleveland. It's in this context that Pence, Trump's peace offering to suspicious Republican regulars, asked Haley to nominate him at the forty-second quadrennial Republican convention.

The governor's validation of the Trump-Pence ticket, on the penultimate night of the convention, could help unify a fractious party and smooth the sharpest edges of Trump's polarizing image with a broader voting public reluctant to give him control of the red button. Haley's speech could improve Trump's chances against Clinton in November; it could help Pence become the next vice president. Pence sent his invitation to Haley through top political aide Nick Ayers. Haley and Ayers knew each other. The Georgia-based political superoperative was executive director of the Republican Governors Association in 2010, the year she was elected governor after outpacing better known, more politically connected candidates in the GOP primary. There was a relationship there. Team Haley deliberated.

The governor had a genuine affection for Pence and was encouraged by his addition to the ticket. Personal rapport aside, the Indiana governor was Haley's kind of Republican. Under normal circumstances, saying yes to Pence would be more than just easy; it would be a no-brainer—for personal and political reasons. But some Haley advisers were resistant to Pence's request. Taking the stage in Cleveland came with unavoidable implications—that either Haley didn't believe a word of the concern she had been expressing about Trump, or she had simply changed her mind and decided he was a righteous dude. The governor tried to thread the needle. Her camp told team Pence she would deliver the keynote address nominating him for vice president as long as she was guaranteed full autonomy over the contents of the speech; zero vetting by the Trump-Pence campaign. Haley promised not to talk around Trump. She would endorse the nominee, and not in a backhanded way that was disrespectful or controversial. Haley's terms were presented as nonnegotiable. The Trump campaign balked. Campaigns typically reserved the prerogative to review a convention speaker's remarks and redline objectionable text, and Trump-Pence was no different. They wanted the final say. When Haley, adamant, refused to budge, Pence pivoted, turning to a close Republican ally from Indiana, Eric Holcomb, the lieutenant governor.

So began a brewing rivalry.

The notion that Trump would fire Pence was (mostly) ridiculous. As a matter of personal principle, trading in a devoted governing partner for a shiny new model would not solve Trump's problem with women, who would look askance at such coldhearted disloyalty. As a matter of party politics, dumping Pence could cost Trump his coalition, dependent as it was on traditional Republicans never quite at ease with the defiant populist but who took solace in the fact that this particular vice president maintained an office in the West Wing. Maybe Trump understood all of that; maybe he just liked Mike, which in fact he did. Either way, the president would make clear to all who asked, publicly and privately, that he intended to sign Pence to a second four-year contract. "Based on every conversation I've had with the president, at no point has Pence ever been considered for being replaced. None whatsoever," a Trump World insider told me a few months before the 2020 election. "He's earned his capital with Trump."

With Trump, yes, but not so much with a few of the president's senior advisers, voices he listened to. One such discussion unfolded in the Oval Office in front of Secretary of State Mike Pompeo and senior White House advisers Jared Kushner and his wife, Ivanka Trump, the president's eldest daughter. Nobody had the forty-fifth president's ear, or trust, the way Kushner and his wife did. And the West Wing power couple, as well as Brad Parscale, who was eventually deposed as Trump's 2020 campaign manager but who at that time wielded enormous influence inside Trump World, were pushing for the president to swap out Pence for Haley. "There were several in the room and it got raised in the room and it was bantered about in a serious way," a Republican insider familiar with this particular discussion recalled. "It wasn't just something that was offhand, dismissed."

The vice president's close-knit team of no-nonsense political operatives treated the threat seriously, maneuvering to quash it by quietly and not so quietly reminding Trump and his inner circle why Pence was so valuable. "I think you're underestimating the value the vice president brings to the ticket," Marty Obst, the senior Pence political adviser, who ran the vice president's political action committee, privately told Parscale. In another instance, Pence chief of staff Marc Short sent that message publicly, telling *Politico's* Alex Isenstadt in a prepared (i.e., deliberately worded) statement in August 2019, "The vice president has enormous respect for Nikki Haley, and she was an excellent ambassador for the Trump-Pence agenda during her one year at the U.N." Emphasis on "one year." The rumors festered such that Haley was, after a while, compelled to bat them down. In the summer of 2019, the ambassador tweeted a picture of her and Pence sitting side by side at the UN General Assembly with the comment, "Enough of the false rumors. Vice President Pence has been a dear friend of mine for years. He has been a loyal and trustworthy VP to the president. He has my complete support."

About the same time the Haley-for-Veep rumors first flared, Team Pence went knives out.

Operatives for the vice president began keeping close tabs on the ambassador's political movements, real and perceived, maneuvering to outflank her. It didn't go unnoticed in the White House, where even rank-and-file staff were plainly aware of the angst Haley's rise was causing inside Pence's operation. "She occupied real estate in their head," a Republican who worked in the West Wing at the time recalled. There were some Republican players in Trump's inner circle who chalked up the tension to natural, even healthy, competitiveness. "It's like quarterbacks on a football team," one told me. Ambitious politicians who attain high office, and are reaching higher still, tend to size each other up and exercise what power they have to protect their sixes. The zealousness with which Pence's band of hard-charging advisers approached this task began to leave the impression that there was something more afoot—that the vice president, or at least his aides, were borderline obsessed with Haley.

In July 2019, Haley traveled to Aspen, Colorado, for a Republican Governors Association business meeting. Republican Governors Association events are a magnet for high-rolling GOP donors and well-connected party operatives of all kinds. The crowd presidential contenders like to have in their corner. And this crowd is always looking for an excuse to spend some time in Aspen, a tony resort community nestled in the picturesque Rocky Mountains about two hundred miles southwest of Denver. Six months out of the Trump administration and already a top-tier contender in the unfolding 2024 shadow primary, Haley was booked as the main attraction.

The Republican Governors Association had tapped the ambassador to deliver an evening keynote address during a private dinner for the assembled GOP glitterati. It was a prime opportunity for Haley to further establish herself as a national Republican leader—and fill the coffers of Stand for America, her new-ish political nonprofit that would lay tracks for a 2024 presidential campaign and keep her in the public eye. In fact, Haley was doing just that. Nick Ayers, the Republican strategist and former Pence chief of staff, accompanied the ambassador to Aspen to facilitate fund-raising meetings with GOP moneymen. To headline a closed-door breakfast banquet the following morning, just hours after Haley's keynote, the Republican Governors Association invited the vice president of the United States.

After Haley was announced as the dinner speaker, Pence's representatives reached out and offered to lend a hand. The breakfast slot was what was available. They accepted. But it wasn't long before Team Pence took issue with the second-in-command playing second fiddle to a former ambassador and sought to turn the tables. So it seemed, at least. At the eleventh hour, Pence decided to wedge a Trump Victory fund-raiser into his Aspen itinerary. Now, this was not at all unusual. The vice president was among the most active fund-raisers in the Republican Party and an in-demand headliner. What struck more than a few of the Republican operatives in town for the governor's conference out of the ordinary was the scheduling of the Pence fund-raiser.

The vice president was flying in on Air Force Two from Denver, where he was raising money for the party. It's certainly possible that Pence's schedule required him to fly in to Aspen and hold his high-dollar fund-raiser practically on top of Haley's keynote. It's also certainly possible that the vice president was playing power politics. The affluent party insiders, compelled to show up for Pence and forced to rush back to the Republican Governors Association to avoid missing Haley, placed their bets on the latter. "We wrapped up the VP's event and we all had to race back over to get to the Haley event," a Republican donor who begrudgingly attended both explained. Added another GOP financier who did the same, "There was some real [expletive] hostility on the ground around that." It wouldn't be the last time.

Nearly eight months later, the Republican Jewish Coalition spring donor conference in Las Vegas was shaping up to be one of the more important gatherings of a critical election year.

Billionaire gambling magnate and coalition benefactor Sheldon Adelson, who died in January 2021, was hosting the mid-March 2020 gathering at the Venetian, his luxury hotel and casino on the Las Vegas Strip. Trump was headlining. But he wasn't the only draw. Joining Trump were more than a dozen top Republicans, among them members of Congress and a handful of aspiring 2024 contenders. One of them, Secretary of State Mike Pompeo, was to be the featured guest at a more intimate dinner with a select group of the organization's top donors, on Thursday evening, the day before the conference opened.

Speaking slots are so coveted that Republican Jewish Coalition events function as a shadow primary campaign trail all their own. And not just for aspiring presidents, but wannabe senators and governors, too. I remember back in the spring of 2015, when the GOP universe was fixated on the unfolding Republican presidential primary, watching then congressman Ron DeSantis of Florida work the room of donors as an attendee with a future run for statewide office of some sort in mind.

In an effort to play fair, and ensure that regular attendees hear from a variety of Republican leaders, current and future, the Republican Jewish Coalition typically rotates invitations to its various annual conferences. In addition to Trump, the program offered a laundry list of some of the most talked-about and influential Republicans that year: Texas governor Greg Abbott, Senator Joni Ernst of Iowa, former US ambassador to Israel David Friedman, Senator Lindsey Graham of South Carolina, House Minority Leader Kevin McCarthy, Republican National Committee chairwoman

Ronna McDaniel, Senator Martha McSally of Arizona, South Dakota governor Kristi Noem, Senator David Perdue of Georgia, Senator Thom Tillis of North Carolina, Senator Todd Young of Indiana (who was chairman of the National Republican Senatorial Committee), Pompeo, and... Haley.

And Pence? Pence was invited. Of course he was invited. Pence was the sitting Republican vice president and possessed an exemplary record on the issue the Republican Jewish Coalition cares most, though not exclusively, about—the security of Israel and maintaining strong relations between the United States and Jerusalem. Pence accepted the invitation, RSVPing early, without a commitment from the Republican Jewish Coalition for a prime speaking slot. Haley did the same. Through a series of scheduling snafus and conflicts, the only day and time that worked for the vice president... and the only day and time that worked for the former ambassador... was Friday night. To accommodate both, the coalition offered to turn that evening's dinner event into a double bill, with Pence and Haley addressing conference attendees back-to-back. Haley didn't complain. Pence, on the other hand— or his team, at least—wasn't thrilled. They said as much. Representatives of the vice president went back and forth with Republican Jewish Coalition officials over who would speak first, whose speech would be deemed the honorific "keynote" speech. In other words, who would be treated as the more important Republican in the room. Amid all of that jockeying, Pence suddenly discovered that he had a scheduling conflict and canceled his appearance. Possibly. He was the vice president; duty surely called from time to time. Or: Pence simply did not want to share the stage with Haley.

His absence might have been glaring had the conference not been canceled because of the coronavirus. The day it was set to begin, Trump declared a national emergency. His campaign put the kibosh on in-person campaigning and shifted to a virtual footing as the president urged the closure of all but essential businesses across the country in an effort to arrest the pandemic.

CHAPTER NINE

Florida Man

On a warm, humid evening in early May, the week before Mar-a-Lago would close down for the summer, **Donald John Trump**, former president of the United States, and his wife, Melania, strode together onto the patio for dinner to a standing ovation.

There was no particular reason. The forty-fifth president, gone from the White House nearly three months, hadn't accomplished anything new that day, at least not publicly. Nor had there been some startling new development lending credence to his dubious claim that the 2020 election was stolen, that he was the rightful commander in chief. This is simply how Trump is welcomed by diners at Mar-a-Lago each time he walks to his reserved table, cordoned off by velvet red stanchions, to enjoy a meal at his private Palm Beach social club.

On this Wednesday evening—Cinco de Mayo, in fact—the expansive courtyard patio was packed. Donald Trump Jr., the former president's eldest son, and his girlfriend, former Fox News personality Kimberly Guilfoyle, occupied one ten-top toward the center of the patio, joined by acquaintances who included Pam Bondi, the former Florida attorney general and chief spokesman for Trump during his first impeachment. Wealthy members and guests, dressed in South Florida chic, were savoring one last evening rubbing elbows with Republican royalty before Trump packed up and headed north to his country club in Bedminster, New Jersey, for the season.

Much earlier, as I waited patiently for my appointment with Trump tucked away in an empty interior dining room, Mar-a-Lago wait staff assembled to review instructions for the upcoming dinner service. It was buffet night, and the stations would be manned by servers sporting red "Make America Great Again" baseball caps, with a giant "45" on one side and an American flag on the other. There would be a seafood station, a pasta station, a meat and poultry station, a salad station, and a dessert station that featured "world famous" Trump chocolate cake. Drinks would flow from an ample outdoor bar.

Among the expected guests that night, the manager detailed, were members of the billionaire Nolet family, as in the famed Dutch distillers of spirits like Ketel One Vodka and Nolet's Gin. Mar-a-Lago doesn't serve Nolet's. But the manager had some brought in for the occasion, and he emphasized that the Nolets were only to be served gin from this special stash of their family's liquor, which, he assured, tasted better than what was usually on offer behind the bar in any event. In one final note to the staff, the manager acknowledged it was Cinco de Mayo but said there would be no specially themed dishes or drinks to commemorate an annual holiday popularized by the Mexican American community. In other words, no Mar-a-Lago version of the Trump Tower Grill "taco bowl" the future forty-fifth president somewhat infamously promoted in a tweet on a Cinco de Mayo five years earlier.

When I arrived at Mar-a-Lago around 4:30 that afternoon, the first thing I noticed was that almost nobody was wearing face masks. True, it was Florida. The coronavirus pandemic was in recession, and even before that residents of the Sunshine State weren't all that receptive to wearing masks. But even my West Palm Beach hotel required them in the common areas, as did, it seemed, every place of business I frequented in town, so it was jarring to walk into the lobby and be told I could take it off indoors. Relieved, I ripped it off and shoved it in my pocket. It was ninety degrees out and I had been vaccinated (Johnson & Johnson) six weeks prior.

Mar-a-Lago is like Trump Tower's sophisticated cousin. Where the lobby décor of the kitschy Manhattan skyscraper is dominated by over-wrought gold-colored, gleaming brass fixtures and marble flooring, the interior of Trump's waterside Palm Beach club, though featuring a similar color scheme, is elegant and admirably restrained. After checking in, I was escorted to the lobby—the "living room," they called it, presumably because it was once a living room. Envisioned as a palatial residence on a seventeen-acre parcel of the barrier island that makes up Palm Beach proper by original owner Marjorie Merriweather Post, the Post cereal heiress, construction of the 126-room, 110,000-square-foot Mar-a-Lago was completed in 1927. Post willed the property to the US government when she died in 1973. Trump picked it up for a cool $10 million a dozen years later. It's easy to forget that before the polarizing former president peddled conspiracies, he was a pretty darned good hospitality industry executive who was good at making people—*all* people—feel welcome, special. I thought of that as Nick Luna, a former White House aide who stuck with Trump in retirement, stopped by to greet me.

"Are you excited about your interview with the president?" he asked, smiling, as though I had arrived at the resort spa for my deep-tissue massage. "I'm sure it's going to go great."

After a few minutes, they would move me into that side dining room because, as I would soon see, Trump was about to sit down in the living room for a chat with former congressman Mark Walker, a Republican candidate for the US Senate in North Carolina, where his daughter-in-law, Tarheel State native Lara Trump, also was mulling a Senate bid. Walker was there for meetings and, Trump would tell me later, to ask for an endorsement.

Mar-a-Lago really was, as the former president aptly described, the "Grand Central Terminal" of Republican politics. And so is Palm Beach. During the pandemic, wealthy Republicans from New York, the Midwest, and California flocked to the tony winter enclave to live full-time. They were reeled in, no doubt, by the beach-resort lifestyle and relaxed coronavirus gathering limits, but they also made the move to escape the skyrocketing taxes—Florida has no state income tax—crime, and homelessness dominating the cultural centers of the mostly Democratic-run states they left behind. Republican politicians, looking to raise money, and seeking

Trump's backing for this or that endeavor, followed suit, spending more time in the Sunshine State than anywhere outside of the nation's capital.

"I'm meeting more politicians than I used to meet in Washington, because they all want the endorsement," Trump said.

Very unlike Washington, everywhere Trump moved inside the plush confines of his Palm Beach palace, he was treated like more than a president; he was feted like a king, by everyone he encountered, just for being him.

———————

Trump received me with a warm, coronavirus fist bump.

The former president, dressed in a tailored dark blue suit, crisp white dress shirt, and shimmering, solid turquoise tie (no pocket square), gave me a quick tour of the living room, pointing out elements of the interior design work. As we retired to the back corner of the dining room that had served as my holding space, Trump, a trace of the old hotelier emerging, generously asked if I'd like a "Coke." Diet, I told him.

Some Republicans had stopped consuming Coca-Cola products ever since the Atlanta-based beverage giant issued a public statement condemning a Georgia voting law, enacted in April 2021, with a statement suggesting it amounted to "voter suppression." Not Trump.

As we settled in, myself, Trump, and his aide, Margo Martin, who spent the interview listening attentively and typing away on her laptop, the former president asked me what the book was about.

"Well, it's about you," I told him, while showing him the homemade lapel pin I picked up from the elderly couple at CPAC that featured an American flag and the words and hashtag "We Are #74MillionStrong."

Trump relaxed. "Go ahead," he said.

As our conversation unfolded over the course of nearly two hours, it slowly became clear to me the former president was not simply convinced the election the previous November was stolen from him through a deliberate, far-reaching conspiracy—he believed discovery of the scheme was just around the corner and that his ouster could be reversed.

"Do you believe it's possible that the results of the 2020 election as they stand today could be undone?" I asked him.

Trump didn't blink. "Yes."

The rantings of a disgruntled loser may not seem to matter. Biden is the forty-sixth president. Twenty years ago, some of his fellow Democrats never accepted George W. Bush as a legitimate president, but that did not get in the way of Bush's exercising the full weight of his executive authority and winning a second term.

But it does matter. From a policy perspective, and especially in disposition, Trump displaced Ronald Reagan as the North Star of the Republican Party. Yet he is more than the party's new guiding light. Trump is the GOP's present and possibly its future. The former president is mystified, and a bit flummoxed, that so many Republicans believe he will not chase the White House a third time in 2024.

Some of his adult children, particularly Donald Trump Jr. and possibly Lara Trump, also plan to stick around. And in this immediate future, the forty-fifth president was interested in, above all else, litigating the outcome of his loss and forcing Republicans everywhere to contend with it. He wouldn't shut up about it, much as Republicans in Congress were desperate to shift the discussion to Biden and recapturing the majority in the House of Representatives and US Senate in 2022. My interview of Trump coincided with the dismissal of Wyoming congresswoman Liz Cheney as House Republican Conference chairwoman—No. 3 in rank in the House GOP leadership—for the twin sins of refusing to accept Trump's claims about the election and calling them out as "lies." Trump acknowledged that his fixation on the last election could doom his party's otherwise sunny prospects in the next election.

"It could be a problem," he conceded, although he quickly insisted, "It could be an asset."

Trump even accepted the premise that he might have cost his party control of the US Senate by tacitly discouraging Republicans from voting in two runoff elections in Georgia in January by arguing so aggressively that the state's system for counting ballots could not be trusted to render accurate results.

"They didn't want to vote, because they knew we got screwed in the presidential election," Trump admitted, even though he typically blames the defeats on Senate Majority Leader (now Minority Leader) Mitch McConnell for opposing his push for larger, direct payments to Americans as part of a year-end coronavirus relief package.

So I asked Trump: What might have happened if you told Republicans in Georgia that, despite some irregularities that deserved looking into, the state's voting system was reliable, so please go vote?

"I don't know," he said. "I did two rallies—very successful rallies. I did say a version of that, but not as strongly as you said, because I was angry with what happened there."

There wasn't a twinge of regret in his voice, perhaps because he has concluded that his power over the Republican Party is greater now as an ex-president than it was when he was president. "You would think that wouldn't be true," Trump said, stating the obvious. "What happened is the anger of the election. People aren't reading it right. It's the single biggest thing—not '22 or '24."

Don't tell Republicans in Congress. They are trying to concentrate on Biden and winning back power. They are adamant that the American Dream is under assault by the *actual* president and are doing almost everything they can think of to shift the political debate away from Palm Beach and in the direction of what is happening in Washington to avoid the topic of the last election and the inevitable risk of antagonizing Trump. Republicans in the House of Representatives ejected Cheney from leadership for the simple reason that she wouldn't get with the program. It's as though after five long, exhausting years, they have learned nothing about the forty-fifth president. He is already antagonized. (He always is.) As the GOP's singularly loudest megaphone, Trump is doing everything he can to make sure the party stands for him.

———

In early 2019, as Trump's two-year drive to win reelection was getting under way, senior staff at the National Republican Senatorial Committee, then under the chairmanship of Indiana senator Todd Young, reached out to their counterparts at Trump-Pence to schedule a get-to-know-you.

Kevin McLaughlin, executive director of the Senate GOP campaign arm, along with his top lieutenants, figured it was a good idea to touch base with the senior strategists at the president's reelection campaign and make sure they were all rowing in the same direction. Republicans in the US Senate were defending a three-seat majority and anticipated threats from all directions. Appointed senator Martha McSally was in trouble in Arizona; veteran incumbent senator Susan Collins was vulnerable in Maine. There were two seats in Georgia—Georgia!—to worry about. Sirens were blaring all over the country—red states, blue states, purple states. Senate Republicans knew the fate of their majority rested with Trump and the crew over at the NRSC wanted to do whatever they could to help. So, they departed the committee's sleek headquarters on the northeast side of Capitol Hill, a few blocks from the US Capitol, and crossed the Potomac River to a high-rise in the Rosslyn business district of Arlington, Virginia, that housed Trump's reelection campaign. The agenda was simple: Find out what the NRSC could do to help the president win a second term and determine where the two operations could work together. To that end, toward the end of the meeting, committee staff made a point of asking the assembled Trump campaign officials where they might collaborate. The question was barely floating in the air when Trump campaign manager Brad Parscale interjected. "Never," he said, use Trump's image or likeness "without our approval."

The NRSC staff turned to one another, mystified. The president was a public political figure, the face of the Republican Party. Naturally, they would never put words in Trump's mouth, in an advertisement or email fund-raising appeal, without having the script approved. But permission to use his "likeness"? They were flabbergasted by the demand and that it seemed to be the highest-priority ask of the Trump campaign in their meeting, given that so much was riding on the upcoming election. The

NRSC would ultimately ignore the request, although they would honor it for Trump's adult children, who sometimes helped out with down-ballot contests.

But the episode reveals the adversarial nature of the forty-fifth president's relationship with the Republican Party. Even four-plus years after Trump engineered a hostile takeover of the GOP and emerged as the undisputed leader of the (dreaded) Republican establishment, he was suspicious of the party he led and, frankly, he didn't have a very high opinion of it. That was why, after leaving the White House in 2021, he sent fresh cease-and-desist letters to the NRSC, now under the chairmanship of 2024 contender and Florida senator Rick Scott, and the National Republican Congressional Committee, under the chairmanship of Minnesota representative Tom Emmer, demanding explicit permission to use his image and likeness in political messaging. That was why Trump continued to roll out or support a collection of new, shadow political organizations that overlap with the party's infrastructure and threaten to compete with it for precious resources. In that regard, Trump is in line with so many Republican voters who share his contempt for the party they affiliate with, which is among the reasons why they love him so much. To support him is cathartic.

"I don't like everybody that's a Republican," the former president told me. "I don't think a lot of the groups have done a good job."

To spend time with Trump discussing the state of the Republican Party is to be briefed on his enemies list. You don't have to ask; details are provided as part of answers to questions only slightly related. Most, though not all, of the former president's intraparty opponents are rather consistent supporters of the majority of his legislative agenda. That includes **Liz Cheney**, who did so more than 90 percent of the time, according to tallies of her votes on the floor of the House of Representatives.

"Not the brightest person in the world," Trump told me of a congresswoman he is fond of calling a "warmonger" because she is a hawk on national security matters. "She's a psycho."

And so it went. Pennsylvania senator **Pat Toomey**, who is retiring in

2022: "Driven out of office because of his stupid, absolutely stupid stance on tariffs."

Maryland governor **Larry Hogan**, a 2024 contender: "He's useless... total, weak, stupid RINO... Has he looked in the mirror? That guy has zero chance."

Republican presidential nominee in 2012 and Utah senator **Mitt Romney**: "He's very unpopular in his state right now. If he had an election, he couldn't be elected dog catcher."

Georgia governor **Brian Kemp**: "I did two rallies for him in Atlanta [in 2018] and he ended up winning, *unfortunately*."

North Carolina senator **Richard Burr**, who is retiring in 2022: "Lightweight and a stupid person."

James Mattis, retired Marine general and Trump's first secretary of defense: "The world's most overrated general. I beat ISIS after he was gone."

Jeff Sessions, Trump's first attorney general: "No good."

Former Nevada senator **Dean Heller**, who lost reelection in 2018: "Very negative to me. And then at the end he came and kissed my ass, and I'd go out and do rallies for him. They'd have signs, 'Sir. He's not for you. He's not for you.'"

But of all the Republicans on Trump's naughty list, he was the most obsessed with **Mitch McConnell**.

Everyone else garnered a single mention. Well, not true; Cheney garnered two. The former president complained about the Senate minority leader, unprompted, no less than five times throughout the course of the interview; about once every twenty minutes or so, on average. Trump owes a great deal of his accomplishments that will endure to McConnell.

The Kentucky Republican, then still the majority leader, blocked Barack Obama from filling a vacancy on the US Supreme Court during the final year of his presidency. Without McConnell's ballsy move (Democrats, understandably, have a different word for it), the forty-fifth president would never have had the opportunity to appoint three justices to the high court, reshaping it with a conservative majority that could last for decades. McConnell also shepherded more than two hundred of Trump's nominees for lower federal courts to the bench, a startling number for a single term in office. That included fifty-four new judges on the thirteen circuit courts of appeals, short of the Supreme Court the most powerful legal venue for adjudicating constitutional disputes in the judicial branch of government. McConnell flubbed health care, failing to deliver fifty-one Republican votes for legislation that would have enabled Trump to keep his campaign promise to repeal and replace the Affordable Care Act, also known as Obamacare. But he was instrumental in negotiating the Tax Cuts and Jobs Act, the historic $1.3 trillion overhaul of the federal tax code that sparked an economic boom and was poised to power Trump to reelection before the onset of the coronavirus and his mishandling of the pandemic.

The point is, their collaboration was extensive—and fruitful. Once the Electoral College voted and McConnell received personal assurances from Attorney General William Barr that there was no credible evidence of voter fraud that would materially impact the outcome of the 2020 election, he publicly acknowledged the results and declined to oppose certification of Biden's victory. Trump, feeling betrayed, turned on him.

"Mitch McConnell is a total stiff, he should have fought for us in the election," Trump lamented, telling me that instead, McConnell argued that "now we have to get on with the government. What's he getting on with? He's getting on with getting horrible things passed by the Democrats."

Trump takes credit for McConnell winning reelection in reliably Republican Kentucky, a state the former president carried with 62.1 percent of the vote. It's laughable. McConnell routed Democratic challenger Amy McGrath by just under twenty points. But the former president apparently agrees with the hundreds of thousands of grassroots liberals who donated more than $93 million to McGrath because they mistakenly believed McConnell's career was on the rocks.

"Mitch McConnell was going to lose his race. I endorsed him; he went up twenty-one points," Trump claimed. "He's got no personality; he's got nothing going... He's a stupid person."

Trump, appearing quite sincere in his assessment, had Margo hand me a sheet with polling purporting to show McConnell in deep trouble until rescued by his endorsement. McConnell confidants will tell you that's blatant fabrication, if not active imagination. Throughout the 2020 election cycle, Trump and McConnell met regularly, with aides, to discuss the status of competitive Senate races. For each contest, the group would review the up-to-the-minute political atmospherics and examine the last three or four available polls, both public and private. For Republican incumbents who appeared in jeopardy at that particular moment, Trump would often launch into a soliloquy that could last up to ten minutes, explaining that the senator in question had criticized him and that was why he or she was losing. That's how Trump reacted in the summer of 2020 when polling showed Iowa senator Joni Ernst vulnerable to Democratic challenger Theresa Greenfield.

"Do all of you know Joni—the one time when she said that the phone call [with Ukraine president Volodymyr Zelensky] wasn't perfect?" Trump asked. "It was perfect; it was a perfect phone call." He repeated himself for what seemed like fifteen minutes before tying the diatribe to Ernst and declaring that the reason for her political troubles.

Never, in any of these meetings, was a poll presented that showed McConnell threatened in Kentucky; the closest survey ever passed around had the majority leader ahead by seven points. Trump was always offering to campaign for McConnell. It makes sense—Trump loves a crowd that loves him, and voters in Kentucky love Trump. McConnell always assured the president he *was* needed, but elsewhere, explaining that if Republicans were slipping in the Bluegrass State, they had much bigger problems than saving his seat. And Trump's polling sheet that suggested McConnell was behind until the president endorsed him? Nobody connected to McConnell or the NRSC ever saw it until Trump spokesman Jason Miller tweeted it out in February 2021, after the senator voted to acquit the former president on a single article of impeachment alleging that he incited the January 6 riot at the Capitol but denounced him none-theless for his role in fomenting the violence. When I asked Miller about this, he defended Trump's (and his) characterization of McConnell's reelection campaign, pointing to McGrath's fund-raising advantage and the fact that the former president outperformed the senate minority leader in every county but one, by an average of 6.07 percent. Meanwhile, Miller said, Trump only lost two Kentucky counties, while McConnell lost three. "His endorsement not only resulted in a much-needed fund-raising boost, but also a potential down ballot boost." Trump's conflict with McConnell is a perfect microcosm for the constant state of hostility that exists between the former president and the elected representatives of the party he still dominates. That simmering tension may not say much significant about Trump—after all these years, he is who he is, and he is consistent. But it explains a lot about top Republicans in Washington and elsewhere, who revolve in an uneasy orbit around Trump as if moons circling a careening asteroid. Their desperate desire to assuage the former president and keep him on their good side is driving actions and strategy at the highest levels and defining what the party is about in the near term.

The day before my get-together with Trump, Texas senator Ted Cruz, his seemingly long-ago bitter rival, stopped by Mar-a-Lago for dinner. Afterward, Cruz tweeted a picture of the two of them at the former president's reserved, cordoned-off patio dining table with the comment: "He's in great spirits! We spent the evening talking about working to re-take the House and Senate in 2022."

This is another example of the tired genre of social media posts, statements, and interviews prevalent during Trump's presidency (and postpresidency, apparently) in which Republicans declare him to be in a good mood and committed to the same goals they are committed to. Because somehow if Trump is happy, he won't blow up the party—and them along with it. Because somehow, if they say Trump is going to do the right thing—what they believe to be the right thing—he just will. After Biden defeated Trump in November but well before the insurrection at the

Capitol on January 6, McCarthy had sketched out an entire 2022 election strategy based on this pie-in-the-sky line of thinking. McCarthy's grand plan was to intimately involve Trump in House campaigns, consulting him on endorsements in primaries and inviting him to wield his considerable influence with GOP voters. The House minority leader aimed to keep Trump focused and in the fold by collaborating with him postpresidency in the same way he did when he was president—not deferring to the whims of the mercurial seventy-five-year-old but attempting to steer him in a productive direction.

A Republican takeover of the House of Representatives would be his victory, McCarthy would tell him, avenging the voter rebuke of Trump in midterm elections four years earlier that put Democrats in the majority. If a little odd for a party leader to grant so much power, or the appearance of power, to an unelected figure—especially a president ousted by the voters after one term—there was logic to this approach. McCarthy, a canny political strategist, is on the cusp of becoming Speaker of the House of Representatives after Republicans shocked political prognosticators by flipping fourteen seats in 2020 using this very same approach to elevate strong candidates in competitive primaries and juice GOP turnout in the general election. It was a massive turnabout that left the GOP just a handful of seats shy of the Speaker's gavel. McCarthy's plans would seem to have been scrambled when Trump's grassroots supporters ransacked the Capitol in a homegrown attack on American democracy that sent lawmakers—including McCarthy—fleeing for their lives.

Except they weren't. Initially, McCarthy held Trump responsible for the mayhem, publicly and privately. He didn't support impeachment. But his rhetoric in regard to what happened January 6, and in regard to the 2020 election, wasn't all that indistinguishable from Cheney's, and it caused a big schism in their relationship. The difference is that Cheney wouldn't let it go, adamant that Trump was shredding the fabric of American democracy and had to be confronted. Pragmatic, in a way. McCarthy was pragmatic in a different way. Biden's policies were plenty problematic and Republican voters were still with Trump. Splintering the party and passing on a chance to win the majority wouldn't solve the party's Trump problem—a problem a majority of his minority conference didn't believe existed. So he scurried down to Mar-a-Lago to smoke the peace pipe. From a certain vantage point, it makes sense. There was, and is, about as big of a Republican constituency to purge Trump from the party as there is for smaller government and deficit reduction.

You do the math. The former president has. He understands the power he has over Republicans in elected office. They fear him and he knows it. No amount of cheesy trinkets, like the NRSC's first-ever "Champion of Freedom" award, which committee chairman Rick Scott presented to Trump in April 2021, are going to tranquilize the former president.

"Even Ted last night, he came here," Trump remarked of Cruz, noting that even Republicans not running for office in 2022 are showing up to kiss the ring. "He wanted to have dinner. So I said, 'Ted, you're not even running.'"

Later in the interview, when Trump raised the subject of McCarthy's obsequiousness, I observed that the high-ranking California Republican was "preoccupied" with maintaining good relations between them. Trump rolled his eyes. "Yeah, he is."

———

At least as early as the summer of 2020, Trump was telling confidants he planned to run for president again in 2024 if Biden managed to beat him in the upcoming election.

The forty-sixth president is some kind of resilient, weathering more personal tragedy than anyone ought to have to endure. Biden lost his first wife and one-year-old daughter in a car crash when he was thirty, a few weeks after winning an upset victory in his first race for the US Senate in Delaware in 1972. Forty-three years later, at the tail end of his two terms as vice president under Barack Obama, Biden buried his namesake eldest son, Joseph Robinette "Beau" Biden III, forty-six, who died after a bout with brain cancer. The younger Biden's death cut short a political career on the rise. He was the Delaware attorney general and was expected to run for governor and eventually end up in the US Senate, like his father. Biden swelled with pride over Beau. Years earlier, in an interview for *Roll Call* about his son's first run for attorney general, then-senator Biden told me that watching Beau campaign gave him butterflies that reminded him of years gone by, when he would sit in the bleachers and watch his son play Little League baseball.

Politically, Biden's otherwise successful climb through the ranks in the US Senate—he was reelected six times and served as the ranking Democrat and chairman of the Judicial and Foreign Relations committees—was pockmarked with embarrassing presidential campaign flameouts. In 1988, Biden's first White House bid was barely off the ground when it was felled by a plagiarism scandal. In 2008, his second White House bid was felled by the fact that Democratic primary voters didn't vote for him in any measurable number. In 2020, Biden's third White House bid was practically broke and on the brink of collapse... Then he finally broke through with a big win in the South Carolina primary. The rest is...

But all Trump saw in Biden once he emerged as the Democratic nominee was a shriveled old man whose brain was on the fritz—unworthy competition who even in his prime was a third-rate political careerist.

"I will be so embarrassed if I lose to Joe Biden because I shouldn't lose to this geezer," the president mocked to a political adviser. "If I lose to this guy, I'm going to run against him in 2024 and I'll still be younger than he is today."

Not exactly. Biden won the presidency a few weeks shy of his seventy-eighth birthday. Trump would turn seventy-eight just under five months before Election Day 2024. In the spring of 2021, the former president sounded more like a future candidate for president than a candidate for retirement. As I tried, intently, to steer the conversation toward the avalanche of Republicans guaranteed to seek the White House if Trump sits out, he kept resisting, steering it right back to himself and the likelihood that he was headed toward a rematch with Biden—if, you know, he wasn't already president by then, anyway.

"I'm going to make an announcement at the appropriate time," Trump said, suggesting that the GOP's immediate future lay stuck in its immediate past. "I'm looking at it very seriously. I love our country and I'm going to do what's right for our country."

The former president seemed more than a bit bewildered that the betting line on will-he-or-won't-he tilted won't. Although Trump filed papers to run for reelection in 2020 within hours of his inauguration in 2017, there are strong incentives to delay that, in retrospect, he has come to appreciate. Holding off preserves his ability to raise vast sums of money for his political organizations without having to stick to constraining federal fund-raising limits or file those pesky quarterly reports with the Federal Election Commission. Yet even inside Trump World, there are doubters galore—political operatives who would thrill at another campaign but anticipate that over time the former president's thinking on the matter will evolve.

"I can tell you, unequivocally, he has told me he is running again in 2024," a Republican close to Trump said. "He's definitely wanting to run, to avenge his ego, and to prove that he really can win this if everything is fair and square."

Give it some time, this Republican operative said, predicting that eventually Trump would conclude "the trappings" of the ex-presidency are more attractive than the trappings of the actual presidency. That being regaled is better than being responsible.

Crowd size is everything to Trump. It's how he judges himself and how he compares himself to political rivals. So as the forty-fifth president assesses the field of Republicans vying to succeed him atop the party— and I can assure you, he is assessing the field—I thought it revealing to find out if he believes any have the juice to put fans in the seats. "No," Trump said, practically cutting me off before I could get the question out. "This isn't being disrespectful, but the answer is no."

But is it at all relevant? Biden booted his predecessor from the White House after running what Trump and his fellow Republicans somewhat accurately describe as a "basement" campaign that was hamstrung by health precautions necessitated by the coronavirus.

"It's a very interesting…" The former president sidestepped the question. It was as if he was aware his campaign rallies, and the effort he devoted to them, might matter less than he was willing to accept. In any event, Trump was not through making his point about 2024, and crowds, if he doesn't run.

"I know it can't happen with the Republicans, and I know it can't happen with the Democrats." Oh, but there was more. "And I know it can't happen for any candidate anywhere in the world, because what happened [in 2016 and 2020] has never happened before worldwide."

A campaign without Trump, Trump finally conceded, "will be more of a normal campaign."

It's impossible to game out, in the unpredictable roller coaster of twenty-first-century American politics, exactly what Trump's endorsement might be worth in late 2023 or early 2024. Or if he'll grant one. In crowded congressional primaries, where Republicans are climbing all over themselves to win his approval, he is often content to sit back and endorse the winner, the better to prevent squandering his influence by backing the losing candidate. Still, I figured Trump has to be looking for something substantial in the Republican who will carry the burden of his legacy into the next presidential election, whether willingly or unwillingly. Maybe the forty-fifth president is looking for a MAGA loyalist—a Republican who will perpetuate his protectionist trade policy and/or his inward-looking, noninterventionist foreign policy? Maybe he is looking for an authentic conservative populist who will embrace cultural combat and do their best impression of Trump the (formerly) tweeting pugilist. Maybe he wants a political outsider? A good leader?

"First of all, to me—and call this a human failure, but I'd want somebody that I like," Trump told me. "I guess you could say that shouldn't bear on it, but it does. And most of the people that we're talking about, I like."

And by "most of the people," Trump means not all of them. First, I wanted to ask him about a 2024 contender he is clearly on the fence about but shouldn't be: Mike Pence. The former vice president was about as loyal a soldier as you'll find in politics—especially considering everything he had to put up with, with Trump. And yet on January 6, 2021, when Pence refused to play dictator and erase Biden's victory, overturning the verdict rendered by the voters, Trump essentially called his vice president a coward. I confronted Trump about this. Did his running mate deserve to be treated so poorly after such loyal service? Why not just declare Pence wrong on his reading of the Constitution while embracing his vice president for all he helped him accomplish? It was one of the few questions I asked during our 102-minute conversation that elicited the visible trace of a dirty look on the face of the former president.

"I like him a lot. I spoke to him yesterday. I mean, I like Mike a lot. He's a good person," Trump gushed, trying to prove the premise of my question wrong. "He just should have sent the corrupt [Electoral College] votes back to the legislature. He had every right to do it."

He didn't stop there, however. True to form, the stubborn forty-fifth president ended up back where he started. "I think he was given bad advice, very bad advice, and he should have had the *courage* to override that advice."

Nikki Haley is a 2024 contender Trump used to gush about. Until the woman he appointed US ambassador to the United Nations publicly torched the forty-fifth president over his handling of the postelection period. The blowback against Haley from grassroots Republicans and Trump loyalists all around was swift and brutal.

Trump himself didn't seem angry; he seemed amused. "I'm not that surprised with her…Because just, her reputation," Trump said. "She was just eviscerated by the base."

The former ambassador was struggling to reestablish a delicate balance with Trump that had set her apart from the pack in which she neither alienated him nor debased herself to win a pat on the back. It wasn't going well, and Trump, recalling Haley's request for a one-on-one with him at Mar-a-Lago so the two of them could mend fences, enjoyed watching her squirm.

"She wanted to come and get together," he said. "I turned it down."

Trump's nice list is relatively predictable. Mike Pompeo, whom he appointed director of central intelligence and secretary of state? "He's a terrific person," the former president said. "He's very loyal. He's very respectful."

Tom Cotton? "Excellent guy, always been with me," Trump said, seemingly unaware that the Arkansas senator led the charge to block his effort to overturn the 2020 election. Or maybe he's just forgiven Cotton for the indiscretion. "I think he's a really good guy—and smart."

Speaking of forgiveness, what about Ted Cruz? It was clear Trump still takes pride in having, to borrow a word from earlier, eviscerated the Texas senator when they faced off in 2016. "Lyin' Ted," he said, recalling the nickname he used to fatally brand Cruz during that campaign. But do you still think of Cruz as "Lyin' Ted"? I asked.

"No," Trump answered quickly.

According to the former president, he and Cruz have legitimately made amends. Trump credits the development to Cruz reaching out to him after their blowup at the 2016 Republican convention in Cleveland and, ever since, showing him the proper deference.

"We only had one bad time," Trump said.

And "Lil' Marco"? He's been forgiven his trespasses, too. Not surprisingly, it had nothing to do with the Florida senator's post-2016 conversion from Reaganism to populism. Nor did Rubio get out of Trump's doghouse because he concocted a new, nationalist economic philosophy—"common good capitalism"—inspired by the forty-fifth president.

"Marco did something really good," Trump declared. "Marco made a statement that President Trump had absolutely nothing to do with Russia. He went up, in my estimation, so much," Trump said. "I endorsed him, recently, for this—but I thought it was very nice what he did."

———

When Republican pollsters test Trump's adult children in presidential primary surveys, **Donald Trump Jr.** is always a shining star. Midway through the Trump administration, a Republican operative keeping tabs on the hypothetical 2024 field found the forty-fifth president's eldest son polling in the top three among potential contenders in key early primary states. In some of these surveys, Don Jr. finished in first, with Pence, the sitting vice president, trailing substantially in second. At the beginning of the Biden administration, Don Jr. landed in third in the CPAC straw poll, which over the years has functioned as a fairly reliable compass for locating the center of gravity in the GOP base. The 2021 straw poll, gauging interest in prominent Republicans if Trump does not run again, found Don Jr. trailing only Florida governor Ron DeSantis and South Dakota governor Kristi Noem.

That support, plus Don Jr.'s ubiquitous presence on the campaign trail for his father and other Republicans running down ballot and his antagonistic social media persona, has sparked speculation he might run for president—as early as 2024. However. Ask Trump about where, and how, his children fit into his political legacy, and he immediately jumps to eldest daughter **Ivanka Trump**, born forty-six months after his first child. Trump expressed pride in all his children; but she is clearly a favorite.

More than once, I tried to shift the discussion to Don Jr. The former president initially resisted, returning again and again to Ivanka.

"I think if Ivanka ran for office, she'd win almost any office, I really do," the former president told me. "I was thinking of putting her at the United Nations instead of Nikki."

Trump said the only reason his daughter didn't end up as a high-ranking US ambassador is because she didn't want the gig.

"I said, 'Would you like to go?' I could have gotten that approved," he said. "I think she would have been phenomenal. She didn't want to do it."

The issue of the Trump clan and its impact on the future of the Republican Party is not insignificant. Five months after leaving the White House, the patriarch turned seventy-five years old. However vigorous and vital, Trump simply has fewer years left in him than his three politically active adult children, plus a son-in-law and a daughter-in-law, who at the outset of his postpresidency ranged in age from thirty-seven to forty-three. But gerontology is not even the half of it. In the modern era, running for president is a family affair—by default and necessity. By default because the intense scrutiny on White House hopefuls is inevitably directed toward the personal and professional lives of immediate family members. By necessity because there is no more efficacious political asset in a presidential campaign than the public expression of love and support from spouses and children.

But the Trump children were unusually central figures in Trump's political operation and in his administration. Ivanka Trump, thirty-nine, served as a senior White House adviser and had her father's ear. Her husband, **Jared Kushner**, forty, also a senior White House aide, was Trump's jack-of-all-trades with purview over Trump's reelection campaign and, although he never held the formal title, essentially the forty-fifth president's chief of staff in the West Wing. Don Jr., forty-three, was a top Trump campaign spokesman and surrogate, and over time filled the role of Trump emissary to the preexisting Republican establishment in Washington. **Eric Trump**, thirty-seven, was a regular fixture on Fox News and in other conservative media outlets speaking for his father, while his wife, **Lara Trump**, thirty-eight, played a key role in Trump's reelection campaign reaching out to female voters, with an emphasis on suburban women.

Lara Trump developed into such an effective communicator, and was so at ease on the trail, that her name was floated for the US Senate in North Carolina. Trump and I spoke prior to his daughter-in-law declaring she would not run for the US Senate in 2022. "I think she'd like to do it," Trump told me, when I asked him if he warned Mark Walker about her.

Trump ended up endorsing Representative Ted Budd over Mark Walker for the open North Carolina Senate seat after Lara Trump opted out. But if she ever changes her mind, her candidacy could answer questions about the family's staying power in Republican politics and deliver the first true test of the Trump brand in the aftermath of the forty-fifth president's ouster and reveal whether it extends to his children.

"If Lara Trump runs—and then runs and wins or runs and loses— that could have huge impact," said Doug Heye, a veteran Republican strategist in Washington. Heye, who hails from North Carolina and once worked for Richard Burr in the US Senate, is often critical of Trump. The Trump aura over the Republican Party could well dissipate the further his presidency recedes into the past. Yet grassroots Republicans have embraced the entirety of the Trump clan as political royalty in a way they never did the Bush family dynasty. The Bushes proliferated in GOP politics despite underlying suspicion of second-generation family patriarch George H. W. Bush by the party's conservative base and the traditional distance his children, among them two governors, one later elected president, observed during his single-term presidency.

Maybe Trump isn't in a hurry to cede the spotlight to his next generation; maybe he is just realistic about the rigors of national politics, but the former president seemed content with the possibility that none of his children would follow in his political footsteps.

"I mean, you've got to want to do this," he said wistfully. "I think they would have a great future if they wanted it. I'm not sure they want it. If you don't want it, it's going to be very tough."

Of all his kids, Trump sounded convinced that Eric was the least likely to subject himself to the rigors of political life beyond advocating for his father.

"He gets treated terribly, just terribly," the former president said. "I think he would like to have a normal life."

Trump harbors the same doubts about Ivanka. But he is captivated by the possibility of his daughter as the next-generation elected Trump in a manner unequal to that of the rest of his brood. They discussed the possibility of Ivanka running for the US Senate in Florida in 2022, he tells me. Ivanka and Kushner relocated to Florida from New York City after Trump left office, and she gave some loose consideration to mounting a bid in her new home state. Or, as some Republican insiders told me, she enjoyed stoking the speculation despite in no way ever intending to run.

"She's happy with her life," Trump said with a twinge of disappointment.

Rubio lucked out.

Over time, Trump has clung ever tighter to the unsupported claim that Biden and the Democrats absconded with the 2020 election that made him a one-term (for now, at least) president. That is, if it is even possible for Trump to cling any tighter to his through-the-looking-glass view of the November 3 vote than he has since that day.

Trump is fond of telling anyone who will listen, as he relayed to me, that none other than Republican guru Karl Rove called him on Election Night, around ten o'clock, to congratulate him for winning a second term. "Congratulations, Mr. President. The election has been won by you. Great job," Trump said, detailing Rove's comments, before adding: "Then, all of a sudden, you look at those ballot dumps and other things. This was a rigged election."

Except that's not what happened. I'm told that Rove, the last Republican strategist to help steer an incumbent GOP president to victory *and* first place in the national popular vote, did not call Trump until around four o'clock the next morning, as he was leaving the Fox News studio where he had been providing election analysis. He did so at the request of an unnamed individual because word was getting around in Republican circles that the forty-fifth president was "melting down" as mail-in ballots were counted and the election was swinging toward Biden. Rove was too mentally exhausted to explain "Elections 101" to Trump: that as different counties finish counting and report their tallies, there are so-called "spikes" that are not spikes at all, simply different ballots already cast being counted at different times. It's completely normal. So Rove kept it short, telling Trump he was still in the game and to not be overly concerned.

Conversely, Trump's embrace of the January 6 conspiracies that have proliferated in some quarters on the right has been gradual. And more recent.

I interviewed the former president nearly four months to the day after his grassroots supporters breached the US Capitol in an effort to halt congressional certification of Biden's victory. The day we spoke, Trump said nothing particularly complimentary about the rioters and suggested he was surprised by what happened, given his view that Americans who voted for him are supportive of law enforcement and would not disobey police officers or commit acts of violence against them, as has been alleged. Trump emphasized that he had recommended to the secretary of defense that the National Guard be deployed in Washington to help with security related to the big "#StopTheSteal" rally he was headlining that day. And he certainly did not say anything about Ashli Babbitt, who was killed by a plainclothes Capitol Police officer when she tried to force her way into the lobby outside the floor of the House of Representatives, where members of Congress had barricaded themselves for protection against the mob.

Were you caught off guard by what happened? I asked Trump. "I was not surprised that they went down to the Capitol to cheer. But I was surprised that they went [into] the Capitol," he said. "And the relationship between the police and these people, the Capitol police and these people, was very good." But it happened. Shouldn't you have denounced it quickly, forcefully? Any regrets? Trump never answered directly. But he told me the protest outside the Capitol might never have gotten out of hand, and the mayhem inside averted, had the Secret Service greenlit his plan to join his grassroots supporters on Capitol Hill. "I wanted to go down with the crowd. I said I was going to go down with the crowd. But they wouldn't let me," Trump said. "I think if I did go down there, I would have stopped the people from doing anything bad." He added: "I also had heard that Mike Pence was not in trouble...because certainly I wouldn't want anything to happen to him." When I interviewed him in May, the only hint of conspiracy in Trump's remarks about January 6 was that "some" of the rioters were Black Lives Matter protesters and ANTIFA anarchists.

One week after July Fourth, Trump was singing from an oddly different hymnal.

In an interview with Fox Business Network's Maria Bartiromo, the former president downplayed the storming of the Capitol, saying "no guns were seized" and that the violence paled in comparison to the civil unrest that struck Portland, Seattle, Minneapolis, and other urban centers since the summer of 2020. Meanwhile, Trump demanded to know "who shot Ashli Babbitt? Why are they keeping that secret? Who is the [person] that shot an innocent, wonderful, incredible woman—a military woman—right in the head, and there's no repercussions?" he said. "Who shot Ashli Babbitt; and why?" Asked by Bartiromo if he had any insight into what happened, Trump took the fanciful speculation a bit further. "They know who shot Ashli Babbitt, they're protecting that person. I've heard also that it was the head of security for a certain high official, a Democrat."

There was more. "What's happening currently to people that are incarcerated?" he asked, suggesting suspects facing criminal charges for allegedly participating in the January 6 insurrection are being politically persecuted by the government. "You have people with no guns, that walked down, and frankly the doors were open and the police in many cases, you know, they have hundreds of hours of tape and they're not releasing the tape.... There was also a lovefest between the police, the Capitol police, and the people that walked down to the Capitol."

―――――

If the only thing you know about Don Jr. are his tweets, you might think he's a moron, or a poor imitation of his father, or an over-the-hill wannabe social media influencer. You'd be wrong.

Donald Trump's oldest son was a thirty-eight-year-old political neophyte in mid-June 2015 when his boss at the Trump Organization announced for the White House. The construction and hospitality firm specialized in hotels, golf courses, high-end office and apartment buildings, and other commercial and residential real estate projects. Don Jr. headed up the company's overseas deals. In fact, he derived a significant portion of his income from traveling the globe to deliver paid speeches on international business development—lucrative work he reluctantly gave up some months into his father's presidency because of the ethical minefield it presented and problematic media coverage it garnered. Whatever the hit to his pocketbook, and however much time his father's presidency opened up in his day planner, Don Jr. discovered something new about himself: He enjoyed politics.

And, as it turned out, he was good at it. Don Jr. also stood out from his siblings because among them, he was perhaps the only real Republican, at least in the beginning of his father's first campaign. The upper-crust child of Manhattan privilege was an experienced hunter and avid outdoorsman. During the 2016 campaign, Don Jr. advised his father on the Second Amendment, helping him build trust with the Republican base on gun rights, a crucial issue in GOP primaries. As an ardent defender of his father, no matter the charge against him or subject matter, Don Jr. quickly developed a reputation for being antagonistic and combative, using Twitter like a bludgeon to hammer critics and opponents and letting attacks and counterattacks fly, at first blush without reservation. Detractors inside and outside the Republican Party thought Don Jr. crude and juvenile. Grassroots Republicans saw a fighter and a showman, just like his father. They loved it. When he was campaigning with his father in February 2020 in the key early primary state of New Hampshire, the rally erupted into cheers of "Forty-six," signifying support for the prospect of Don Jr. as the next president of the United States. That is just one of many such examples.

"He's someone who, in a lot of ways, embodied MAGA even before there was a MAGA—someone who was a bomb thrower even before it became cool," a member of Trump's inner circle told me eight months before Trump's defeat. "He's a true believer...He's someone who's a spiritual successor to the head of the MAGA movement."

Underneath, Don Jr. was becoming much more than fan or foe was able to detect from his very simplistic public persona. By the time the forty-fifth president exited the White House in January 2021, a forty-three-year-old Don Jr. had evolved into a sagacious political operator with possibly more substantial relationships across the party than his father, and a foundation, keenly laid, for a future of his own.

And Don Jr. isn't as prickly as the former president, or as prone to outrage over the unflattering press coverage that comes with the territory of being a prominent (Republican) political figure.

"Don is smart. He knows what he knows, and he knows what he doesn't know, and he does ask questions," said a Republican operative who worked closely with the Trumps on political matters during the administration.

Don Jr. is setting himself up to be a very different political figure than his father. The former president arrived in Washington at age seventy with few allies, fewer friends, and a lack of understanding of how the town worked—a quality Republican voters appreciated but that handicapped major components of his agenda. Don Jr. is filling in his father's gaps, and at a relatively young age. "Project [out] ten years from now," this GOP insider emphasized. "It's like training to be a prizefighter."

In interviews, the same Republican insiders who would complain about Trump and how his peculiarities put the party at risk pointedly did not offer similar misgivings about his oldest son. And where they pointed out that Eric and Ivanka were not particularly involved in efforts to grow the party down ballot—or save the party, as it were—they emphasized that "Don Jr.," which is how almost everyone in Republican circles refers to him, almost always answered the call to help.

And Don Jr. didn't just phone it in; he worked it, hard. In the 2018 election cycle, during a six-month period from May until Election Day, Don Jr. traveled virtually nonstop to headline more than eighty fundraisers and other campaign events for Republicans running for the House of Representatives and the US Senate. During a grueling swing through Texas to stump for Cruz, whose reelection was in doubt, Don Jr. piled into a small plane with girlfriend Kimberly Guilfoyle, political adviser Andrew Surabian, and the senator and his chief political adviser, Jeff Roe, hitting six events around the state in a single day. The Republicans were swept from power in the House in a forty-seat shellacking that year but actually gained two seats in the US Senate. In 2020, with his old man on the ballot, Don Jr. hit the trail again. From September 4 through November 1, he headlined or participated in more than one hundred events for the president's reelection, the party's congressional candidates, or party campaign committees.

And Don Jr. was versatile. He raised money on the stodgy rubber chicken circuit, joined business-themed roundtables, ginned up the grass roots at MAGA rallies and mini-MAGA meetups, and was the guest of honor at pigeon shoots. He often hit several events per day in multiple states.

Don Jr. made friends along the way, good friends. The relationships he cultivated had an influence on his father, who is in a perpetual hot peace with the Republicans who once slighted him. Remember Dean Heller, whom Trump claims he reluctantly endorsed for reelection in 2018 after the Nevada Republican supposedly "kissed [his] ass"? Trump's endorsement was the product of behind-the-scenes encouragement by Don Jr. Heller endorsed Jeb Bush, the former Florida governor, in the 2016 Republican primary, rejecting Trump as dangerous to the party.

"We're digging a deep hole," Heller told me in December 2015, during a joint interview with then-governor Brian Sandoval, a Republican, for the *Washington Examiner* in Las Vegas, just ahead of a GOP presidential debate. The senator, defeated by a Democrat less than three years later, was, like many Republicans at the time, dismayed by Trump's rhetoric, which he basically described as sexist and racist—"against the disability community…against women…against a particular race." Trump, naturally, never forgot and never really forgave.

Don Jr. didn't forget, either. But he is pragmatic, and slightly conventional. He understood that the best chance Republicans had to hold a Nevada Senate seat on the rocks was for Heller to be in good shape with the president's loyal, MAGA voting base. But there was more to it than that.

"Junior and I had one thing in common and I think that's what kept us together," Heller told me in a subsequent interview in September 2020. "We both loved to hunt."

Their bond blossomed into a political lifeline that gave Heller a fighting chance to win reelection and a legitimate friendship that Don Jr. has nurtured ever since, despite the Democratic sweep in Nevada that year.

"We have a very good relationship since my race," Heller said. "We've texted back and forth a little bit and kind of talked about whatever our activities were hunting-wise, but nothing too political."

In a more direct way, Don Jr. regularly put his good relations with the Republican establishment to work for his father. After Trump nominated Richard Grenell for US ambassador to Germany, Don Jr. lobbied Republican senators to support his confirmation. It was no small thing. Grenell, who served as acting director of national intelligence after leaving Berlin, is a capable foreign policy professional with impeccable credentials in his field. But in the administration of George W. Bush, he was passed over for a top assignment, and later jettisoned from advisory roles in Mitt Romney's presidential campaign, because he is gay. That didn't matter to Don Jr., who became fast friends with Grenell during the 2016 campaign. Nor did it matter, as it turns out, to his father.

In the first months after his father's defeat, Don Jr. was mum on exactly what sort of political future he envisioned for himself. With five young children to educate and put through college, and unsure if he has any interest in the frustrating work of governing, at any level, a 2024 presidential bid was off the table. Recommendations that he pull a Hillary Clinton and move to a state where the Republican base and general election voters were practically one and the same, and run for governor or for the US Senate, also appeared less than desirable.

Some Trump World insiders with high hopes for the forty-fifth president's oldest son saw the potential for him to play an outsize role in influencing the outcome of key Republican primaries in 2022. They believe he could fuel GOP enthusiasm that would help the party take back Congress in the general elections, functioning like a more sophisticated version of Sarah Palin in the 2010 election cycle. Don Jr., to them, is strategic, and without the diva drama that followed Palin around, lending itself to the acquisition of broader political appeal and long-term staying power.

Don Jr. was moving deliberately to avoid any suggestion of supplanting his father as CEO of the newest family business—of inaugurating the next generation of Trump—when the current generation showed no signs of shrinking from the ring. Many of the moves he made as a political operator over the past almost half dozen years were governed by that sort of deferential thinking.

On occasion, there have been faint hints of separation. Don Jr. would never contradict his father's claim that the 2020 election was stolen. Publicly, he was equivocally supportive. On January 6, 2021, Don Jr. appeared at a rally in Washington, echoing his father's threats of political retribution against Republicans who voted to certify the election results—comments that Democrats and quite a few Republicans say incited the storming of the US Capitol. But on balance, Don Jr. was less vocal about whatever doubts he *might* have harbored about the 2020 election. In the weeks that followed, he devoted more energy, and rhetoric, to GOP efforts to win a pair of runoff elections in Georgia and salvage control of the US Senate than did his father, who was plainly fixated on the mechanics of his loss.

Subtle, hard to notice, not accidental. Don Jr. was preparing for political life after his father. As Trump's presidency progressed, Don Jr. was in demand: to headline campaign events, sign email fund-raising appeals, and serve as the marquee for gatherings with wealthy Republican donors that commanded up to $500,000 in one sitting, on par with what top elected officials could attract from party financiers. Eventually, Don Jr. started requiring the candidates, campaigns, and party committees he raised money for to sign data-sharing agreements. Trump is now sitting on a treasure trove of donor data, information on big-check writers and a healthy email list of grassroots conservatives who give in small amounts and are responsible, collectively, for hundreds of millions in contributions to GOP campaigns every election cycle. Maybe one day, a "Don Jr." campaign.

"I would help him," Trump told me. "There are certain places where he couldn't be beaten."

————

As my interview with Trump concluded, he asked me if I was returning to Washington. When I told him that I was spending another night in Palm Beach, he invited me to stay for dinner at Mar-a-Lago and asked his staff to work it out. In other words, the former president requested that they find me a table on the coveted patio despite the venue being near completely booked for the evening. I thanked Trump for the hospitality and we dispensed with the fist bump and shook hands, deciding that, both of us having been vaccinated, it was acceptable.

"If not, we have a story, right?" he said. "You go out and enjoy; have fun."

With that, he exited the room for another meeting. I turned to Margo and told her I'd love to stick around for dinner, but that I couldn't let Trump pay for me—could they arrange it so that I could cover the bill? During dinner-service prep, I had heard the manager remind the wait staff that some of that evening's guests were not Mar-a-Lago members, and they would be paying for their meal like they would at any normal restaurant. I felt a little guilty putting this extra pressure on Margo after she had spent the last hour and forty minutes listening to me interrogate Trump, but I was eager to observe the club pageantry and planned to stick around, as long as I could pay my way. After being assured it wasn't a problem, I was escorted down the center aisle of the square Mar-a-Lago patio and over to a high-top near the bar. Outdoor tables, my preference, were full. I ordered a bourbon and got comfortable. Maybe ten minutes went by before the manager showed up and told me a table on the patio had opened up and asked if I'd like to move. I gathered my briefcase and my bourbon and grabbed it, a corner four-top that looked out onto the patio, from where I could watch the evening unfold. And from where I ordered another bourbon and enjoyed a sampling from almost every station of the buffet.

When I finally decided to call it a night, I asked my server for the bill, and that was when I ran into trouble. He very politely told me that the boss, meaning Trump, had made clear that my meal was to be comped. My blood pressure might have started racing if not for the drinks. I was imagining a future Save America PAC statement from the forty-fifth president after reading parts, maybe all, of the book he didn't like: "Fake news, and I bought him dinner, too..." I demanded the manager, who showed up quickly. I told him my predicament. I'm a journalist, I'm writing about the owner of the club, I cannot allow him to pay for my dinner. He seemed sympathetic but told me he was under strict orders from his boss not to take my credit card.

"I would get fired," he pleaded with me.

Who knows, maybe he would have been. I slumped back in my chair. Resistance, apparently, was futile. I devised a solution. In lieu of paying for dinner, I estimated the market cost of the sumptuous Mar-a-Lago buffet, and my drinks, thought about what I would have tipped, and made a $350 donation to a Palm Beach County charity: the Promise Fund of Florida, which focuses on providing access to quality health care for those in need.

As the kids say, I have the receipts.

Acknowledgments

It didn't exactly take a village. But almost.

Journalism is my second career, which means I was old enough, and wise enough, to know better by the time I decided to make political reporting and storytelling my life's vocation. Over the years I learned the tricks of the trade. The art of the punchy, hard-hitting newspaper article and the rhythm of the longform, meandering. but revealing magazine story became ingrained in my psyche like the muscle memory of knocking down twenty-foot jumpers on the hardwood, one after the other, without a second thought. But in more than twenty years of writing professionally, I had never come close to attempting anything resembling the writing of a book. And so I had no idea what I was getting into, nor was I in much better shape when it came to knowing where to start. In that regard, several people, without whom *In Trump's Shadow* would never have come to fruition, deserve, and have, my heartfelt and eternal gratitude.

This book never would have hit the shelves (or the digital shopping cart) without my agents at Javelin, Keith Urbahn and Matthew Latimer. Urbahn taught me over a couple of years, and a half dozen pitches that he rejected, what made for an intriguing idea that people would want to read. Once I figured out how to do that and came to them with a solid pitch, Latimer helped breathe thematic volume, and broader narrative, into my initial idea. Both of them worked with me on a write-up to present to prospective publishers. It's no exaggeration to say that I did not know how to structure one until they taught me. Urbahn told me early on in our relationship that he could sell any book somewhere but that he believed in placing promising projects with top-tier publishing houses. He and Latimer delivered when they paired me with Twelve Books.

At Twelve, editor Sean Desmond was an invaluable partner. Like a great athletics coach who teaches the fundamentals, he showed me how to assemble my reporting so that I could make sense of it all. Then he offered tips on how to structure my story so that it read like a story rather than a collection of factoids and tidbits. *Then*, when I was finished, he cut the fat, helping me tie it all together that much more seamlessly. Through it all, Desmond helped me tell the story I wanted to tell, as my reporting and analysis presented themselves to me, rather than tell some different story that he might have told if he had been the author, rather than the editor.

I need to thank the *Washington Examiner*, my employer, for providing me an amazing platform from which to cover the Republican Party and national politics. It's the reporting I did for the *Washington Examiner* that first gave me the germ of the idea that became *In Trump's Shadow*. Special thank-yous are in order for my colleague Salena Zito, who offered daily encouragement and a safe space in which to mull ideas out loud; my direct editors (and published authors) David Mark and Keith Koffler, who granted me the vacation time I requested to work on the book; and Editor in Chief Hugo Gurdon. I'd also like to thank Alex Rosenwald, the *Washington Examiner*'s head of all things public relations and brand promotion, for taking an interest in my project. Finally, I would be remiss if I did not express my appreciation to Philip Anschutz, the generous owner of our parent company, Clarity Media Group; and Ryan McKibben, Clarity's supportive chairman. It's Anschutz's commitment to the work we do at the *Washington Examiner* that has made so much of what I have done over the last several years possible—a commitment that included no layoffs and no pay cuts during a coronavirus pandemic that devastated advertising revenue.

To the extent that I fashion myself any good at my job, I need to credit the superb on-the-job training (OJT, as my late father was fond of saying) I received from the editors who hired me and tutored me in the basics and not-so-basics of political reporting, analysis, and writing earlier in my career. In chronological order: Frank Pine and Steve O'Sullivan at the *Inland Valley Daily Bulletin*; Tim Curran and Josh Kurtz at *Roll Call*; and

Stephen G. Smith at the *Washington Examiner*. I've also worked with some extraordinary editors at *Vanity Fair*'s the Hive, where I've been given an amazing opportunity to spread my wings and deliver pieces with depth and impact. Past and present, they include Jon Kelly, Benjamin Landy, and Claire Landsbaum.

Have you ever noticed that televised awards programs save the most consequential honors for last? So it goes here. None of this—my career, *In Trump's Shadow*—would have been possible without the love and confidence of my family: My parents, Ronald and Sari Drucker, taught me to dream big and work hard and never accept second best. My sister, Pamela Drucker Mann, believed I could write for a living before I did. Without her insistence on giving it a shot, it probably never would have happened. But above all, I need to try and find adequate words to express how much the love and support of my wife, Jenny, and my two sons, Jacob and Ronald, mean to me. People in the business of news and politics are half-lunatic— never really off, never really at ease, lots of travel and working odd hours. Through it all, my family has put up with me and been my ballast. During the year-plus long process of reporting and writing *In Trump's Shadow*, my wife spent most weekends, vacations, weekdays, evenings, and mornings cheerfully parenting two very understanding boys alone while I buried myself in this project.

I could not have delivered it without her.

Index

About the Author

David M. Drucker is a senior correspondent for the *Washington Examiner*, focusing on Congress, campaigns, and national political trends. Prior to joining the *Washington Examiner*, he was a reporter for *Roll Call* in Washington, DC, and covered California politics and Governor Arnold Schwarzenegger from the Sacramento bureau of the *Los Angeles Daily News*. Drucker graduated from UCLA with a BA in history and spent eight years managing a family-run manufacturing business in Southern California, giving him a unique perspective on how what happens inside the Beltway impacts the rest of the country. Drucker is a *Vanity Fair* contributing writer and appears regularly on cable news and nationally syndicated radio programs. He resides on Capitol Hill with his wife and two sons.